OPERATIONS
AUDITING

OPERATIONS AUDITING

Roy A. Lindberg
Theodore Cohn

American Management Association, Inc.

© 1972 AMACOM
A division of American Management Association, Inc.
New York
All rights reserved. Printed in the United States
of America.

International standard book number: 0-8144-5258-2
Library of Congress catalog card number: 70-188843

Fourth Printing

This book is dedicated to the proposition that no company can fail to benefit greatly from acting upon the findings of honest and timely review of what and how it is doing.

Preface

Two needs occasion this book. The first is the need for more information and discussion about operations auditing (which most people call operational auditing) so that its general nature, benefits, and limitations can be better understood. The second is the need for more and better ways to evaluate management performance. Both needs are, in view of the rapidly expanding responsibilities and changing content of management, significant and pressing.

Auditing in many companies has moved beyond asset attestation to include the measurement of resource utilization and progress toward corporate goals. As with many other developments in the field of business management, the movement has progressed considerably faster than its supporting technology. Our intent is to help close the gap.

The volume is also intended to be a workbook; it contains some of the knowledge and techniques needed to perform operations audits. It is primarily addressed to those who are inexperienced in operations auditing, and it is intended to be helpful to them in performing their first operations auditing assignments. It is not expected to be of much help to those with formed views of the nature and content of OA.

Two facts about OA must be comprehended immediately if this book is to hold value for the reader: the art is young, and it is still uncertain of direction. Those facts occasion two qualities of this book—it has a point of view, as any work in a field in flux must have, and it says some things about OA that will, in time, undoubtedly be untrue. The reader will do well to keep those points in mind and couple with their recognition a degree of tolerance for the shortcomings he finds.

As to viewpoints, there is no escape from holding them. To say there are differences of opinion about the nature and role of operations auditing is to treat the opposition of views on the subject with excessive delicacy. Operations auditing is quite new, and it might be expected that opinion about its nature and role would take some time to solidify. Quite to the contrary, opinion not only has solidified but has polarized with amazing swiftness. The result is that the technique is being contorted first by one interpretation of OA and then by another. Between the extreme interpretations there is currently an unbridged void.

The void occasions our selection of the name "operations auditing" for the practices we describe. The process we advance here is sufficiently different from the auditing forms that are called operational and management auditing to deserve a distinctive name. It is not auditing that is operational in nature, nor does it apply exclusively to management. It is auditing of *operations,* hence the name we give it.

The two major opposing views of OA are these: (1) It is only a fact-gathering tool that will help management appraise performance and identify areas in which additional investigations may yield improvements. (2) In addition to the foregoing, OA should be directly involved in recommending specific changes intended to correct the shortcomings it has revealed. We hold the first view—distinctly a minority view—for reasons that we will make clear in the text. However, the issue is not inimical to the theme of the book, which is that every company will gain material benefit from an intelligent appraisal of its performance. The subject is really corporate improvement maintenance—activities far too important to be left to chance. Whatever else operations auditing may mean, it does mean systematized appraisal of performance.

As will soon be seen, OA is not a precision instrument. In its present state of development, it is a crude tool, and so it may remain. At present it is not possible to lay down universal or even consistent rules of applicaton, and so the material offered has, in application to a specific audit assignment, obvious shortcomings. No company is completely like another, and the task of trying to anticipate all operations auditing needs is beyond execution. Accordingly, the user of this book has a sizable task on his hands in bending it to his purposes.

In the following pages we describe some of the measures we consider suitable for use in evaluating performance in key business areas. They are not the only measures that can be applied, nor are they necessarily the right ones in all instances; to ask otherwise is to ask the impossible. However, that unequivocal or universal measures do not exist does not lessen the value of those that are offered here. Each has at least some worth as an indicator, if not a direct measure, of corporate effectiveness.

The qualification "in key business areas" appears in the preceding paragraph because (1) there are areas that lie beyond the evaluative capacities of the operations auditor and (2) the object field of operations auditing, in our view, is business *operations,* and nothing more. As to point 1, some auditors think that, for example, individual performance should be appraised during operations auditing. Ours is a much more limited view: we hold that any area that lies beyond the reach of standards is beyond the reach of operations auditing.

As to point 2, operations audits can be applied to a wide variety of enterprises, but we have written with the commercial enterprise primarily in mind. Indeed, throughout this book it is assumed that the unit of organization to be audited is a company, and so "company" is used as a unit name. The reader will have no trouble in changing "company" to "division" or "department" as necessary.

In the second and third parts of the book and the Appendix are general descriptions of the areas to be covered and questionnaires to be used in the investigatory phase of the audit. Both are important to the performance of effective audits, particularly those by in-house staffs on a continuing basis. The general descriptions are not conventional, nor are they exhaustive of their subject; they primarily serve to bring the auditor abreast of developments and create awareness of auditable aspects. The questionnaires are examples of working documents. They are useful in directing inquiry, assuring completeness in field work, and providing comparability between successive audits.

Parts 2 and 3 are primarily applicable to medium-size organizations or functions of typical size. The questionnaires of Part 3 are therefore best suited for use in organizations between $50 and $250 million in size, although they can be quite easily adapted to any but the smallest units or functions.

The reader of this book will encounter several dichotomies that can tear his understanding apart unless certain ideas are given precedence. For example, although a business forms a unity, its effectiveness can be measured only through incremental analysis; that is, by taking measurements in specific areas and occasionally through time as well. Accordingly, it has been necessary to talk about parts or functions within what is really a unity, but the division is not intended to be rigorous. In dividing any unity into constituent parts, there is always some arbitrariness and impurity of definition; in talking about a given functon or activity, something of other functions or activities is always included. In talking about manpower, for example, there is always something of organization included, and in talking about organization, planning cannot be left out. Therefore, the subjects presented in Parts 2 and 3 constitute little more than a kind of scaffold for the construction of understanding. Once the understanding has been built, the scaffold can be taken down.

As to the order of presentation of the subjects in Parts 2 and 3, we have elected to present them as they fit on a scale ranging from generality to particularity. We think the typical reader will move through the book chapter by chapter, even though he may not read every page completely, and there will be benefit to him in covering the general functions before the specific ones.

Finally, it must be said that, although quite strong convictions underlie its writing, the book doesn't presume to be right—it presumes only to offer an alternative model and guides to a practice that has been affected by a good deal of contention and lack of understanding. If it helps on the one hand to firm up a practitioner's convictions or on the other hand to resolve some uncertainties, the authors will be well satisfied.

Many sources have provided material for the book. Some of it has been taken from J. H. Cohn & Company's newsletter, *Time and Tide,* and many business associates and friends contributed ideas and material. We are especially indebted to our colleagues Morris Kadin, Robert Green, Frederick Olsen, and Sylvan Shuster and to Norbert Stahl of Union Carbide Corporation, Augustus R. White of The Emerson Consultants, Inc., Frank Thacker of Davidson County Community College, Richard C. Schultz of Shell Oil Company, J. Justin Rothschild of National Credit Office, Dun & Bradstreet, Ira Shaw of New Jersey Bank, Herbert Sinofsky of Rentex Corporation, and Edward Stulpin of P. N. Thorpe Company for their assistance and valuable contributions and criticism. Among companies that helped are IBM, Glen Alden Corporation, Honeywell, Inc., American Cyanamid Company, and Questor Corporation.

Roy A. Lindberg and Theodore Cohn

Contents

Contents

1

THE OPERATIONS AUDITING FUNCTION

1

NATURE AND ROLE
OF OPERATIONS AUDITING

Auditing is almost as old as civilization. It was used in ancient Egypt, the Roman Empire, and, of course, the great mercantile establishments of the Middle Ages. The common areas of audit action throughout its history have been examining, verifying, and reporting. Auditing has become a key factor in controlling every kind of organization with financial and economic aspects.

Although auditing has for most of its existence focused on the correctness of accounting records and the propriety of activities reflected in those records, its subject matter has been changing in recent years. It is now responding to a demand for more useful information about results than can be found solely in financial statements. In the late 1940s, for example, financial analysts and bankers showed a sharp rise in their desire for information suitable to management appraisal. Many other groups, such as investors and governmental bodies, have increasingly sought information by which the quality of management can be judged. As a result, the techniques of financial auditing are being applied more and more to the nonfinancial aspects of business operations and growing numbers of people are involved in operations auditing.

VARIETIES OF AUDITING
It is necessary to refer to varieties of auditing because most practitioners adopt a specific approach without a clear idea of what operations auditing is and without considering the ramifications of the auditing course they choose to follow. Operations auditing (OA) is a significant corporate activity, and the way it is performed can have powerful effects. Accordingly, it is of paramount importance to select with care and intelligence the premises supporting and entering into the implementation of an OA function. Among other considerations, that requires attention to similarities and differences among the principal forms of auditing.

There are three main types of auditing: (1) attest or financial auditing,

3

(2) internal auditing, and (3) operations auditing and the similar operational and management auditing. These types have a number of characteristics in common:

1. All auditing measures against predetermined and relevant standards.

2. All three types are deductive in character and are therefore disciplines in which judgment is required.

3. Although the process of judgment formulation involved is similar in methodology to that of science, the conclusions reached in auditing are based on smaller samples.

4. Independence is imperative in all branches of auditing; and the auditor, though he may be skilled in the activity he is auditing, must be able to arrive at his conclusions as if possessed of nothing more than the ability to follow a set program faithfully.

There are, however, sufficient real or assumed differences in the three types of audit to warrant an effort to define them.

Financial auditing. The earliest of the three types, financial auditing, can be defined as an exploratory, critical review by an independent public accountant of the underlying controls and accounting records of a business enterprise that leads to an opinion of the propriety of the financial statements of the enterprise.

Internal auditing. The second type, internal auditing, descended from financial auditing. According to the Institute of Internal Auditors in 1947:[1]

> Internal auditing is an independent appraisal activity within an organization for the review of the accounting, financial, and other operations as a basis for protective and constructive service to management. It is a type of control which functions by measuring and evaluating the effectiveness of other types of control. It deals primarily with accounting and financial matters, but it may also deal properly with matters of an operating nature.

This definition reflects some loosening of the traditional constraints on financial auditing.

In 1957 the preceding statement of responsibilities was revised to move internal auditing further toward operations auditing by lifting the restriction that it "deals primarily with accounting and financial matters." The overall objectives of internal auditing were then described as assistance to all levels of management, whether financial or operating, and as assistance with any phase of business activity. That view is reflected in current internal auditing, which is largely construed as a broad business function. The following statement reveals something of that fact:[2]

> The concept of internal auditing . . . to an increasing degree . . . is reviewed as an arm of management. This development is a product of the modern business environment. The larger and more complex the business organization, the greater is the gap between administrator or executive and the individual operator. Consequently, a sort of liaison is necessary . . . reviews are necessary to keep the business machine functioning smoothly. It is in this area or void that the internal audit is proving to be of value.

Operations auditing. Some writers look upon internal and operations auditing as being virtually the same. Carl Heyel, for example, thinks the terms should be considered synonymous; he says:[3] "The operational controls which are reviewed and analyzed by the internal auditor include (1) organization structure, (2) procedures, (3) accounting and other records, (4) reports, and (5) standards of performance (such as budgets and standard costs)." Most internal auditors agree with Mr. Heyel. The following statement is typical:[4]

> Operational auditing should be considered as an attitude—a manner of approach, analysis and thought—not as a distinct and separate type of auditing which is characterized by special programs and techniques. A rather common misconception on the part of some internal auditors is that there is a clear-cut distinction between operational auditing and traditional financing auditing. Auditors look for special manuals which will tell them how to make operational audits—when all that is really necessary is a change in their own manner of approach and analysis.

However, not all persons engaged in one form of auditing or another see an identity between internal and operations auditing. One writer, in a report on professional accountants' views of OA, said that practitioners differ on how to approach an operational audit. In one view it is only an extension or modification of the traditional audit; in another it is a special type. In still others the operational audit currently is incompatible in scope with either the audit function or the management services function.[5]

The divergence in views is not to be wondered at. In recent years, conditions have become such that it was perfectly natural to ask internal auditors to serve in an increasing variety of ways. The economy has been growing at an accelerated rate, and companies have been forced to grow larger and/or become more differentiated. Companies growing larger have been forced to become organizationally viable by decentralizing, delegating more authority, and developing more sophisticated systems. In the proccess it was inevitable that internal auditors be asked to take a hand in making the changes. It is therefore not to be wondered that internal auditors now generally view their prime role to be synonymous with that of operations auditors.

We, however, view operations auditing as a practice distinct from both financial and internal auditing. We agree that almost all modern internal auditors practice some form of operations auditing, but we also think that operations auditing must be practiced as a distinct activity with its own purposes and techniques. And despite many allusions in the literature to the contrary, we do *not* regard the separation of OA from other forms of auditing to be invalid or undesirable either in principle or in practice. On the other hand, we do see several disadvantages (unjustifiable risks) issuing from a joining of internal and operations auditing.

Definitions of operations auditing are hard to find, and an explicit definition with widespread acceptance among practitioners apparently does not exist. Most efforts to define OA are discursive, as exemplified by this one taken from a company's procedural manual:

> The operational audit evolves somewhat naturally as an extension of the financial audit, going beyond that generally considered the accounting

function; it deals with nonfinancial activities that sooner or later are quantitatively expressed in the financial records of the company. A few illustrations of an operational audit are shown below.

Appraising compliance with policies and procedures.

Reviewing purchasing practices.

Reviewing general housekeeping conditions and plant safety standards.

Reviewing production and scrap reporting processes.

In essence, operational audits approach how and why things are done, and attempt to measure that which is actually happening against performance standards.

This takes into focus a much broader plane than financial auditing and becomes a great deal more complex, requiring considerable cooperation among the individuals involved.

If we had a definition of OA, this statement might be illuminating; as it is, it does not help much. The next move, then, should be to arrive at a definition, and we will do so by examining the need OA fills and the key features of OA.

THE NEED FILLED BY OPERATIONS AUDITING

The first thing to do in clarifying the nature and value of a management tool is to ask whether there is need for the tool at all. If there is none, the existence of the tool cannot be justified. On this score there need be no doubt; operations auditing clearly fills a need. It came into being, in the opinion of the authors, because traditional sources of information do not fully meet the requirements of managers in many current forms of organization. Specifically, operations auditing arose from the needs of managers responsible for areas beyond their direct observation to be fully, objectively, and currently informed about conditions in the units under their control.

Central to the whole concept of operations auditing is the idea that, if they are to operate incisively and creatively, managers need some kind of early warning system for the detection of potentially destructive problems and opportunities for improvement. That is, modern business has had to develop ways to anticipate and cope with the heightened risks and more sophisticated resources involved in reaching its objectives. Operations auditing is one of those ways. By means of it, management can maintain effectiveness even though time scales, financial commitments, organizational complexity, and communication network sizes have greatly increased.

KEY FEATURES OF OPERATIONS AUDITING

When it is understood that operations auditing is a specialized *management information tool*, it is apparent that a principal source of the problems that plague the practice today is the tendency to confuse it with traditional management tools and use it accordingly. When this occurs something other than operations auditing is being done and the benefits of OA are being lost. Either OA has a unique work content or there is no justification for the name. If OA is a distinctive technique, there is no justification for performing other work in its name.

Failure to establish a separate role for it subjects operations auditing to loss of confidence and ultimately threatens to disenfranchise it. When OA is made into a dolled-up version of well-established managerial information sources, it accrues the same deficiencies as the traditional sources and fails in its basic mission, which is to create confidence that things are going well or to discover problems or opportunities for improvement on the basis of efficient and nondisruptive investigation.

To see how OA differs from other information sources, consider the traditional sources of managerial intelligence. Until recently, they were the unit's manager, staff assistants or assistants to the manager, regular performance reports, the operating of controls, and studies and surveys. Even when these sources are used to the limits of their capabilities, they fail to provide information for the best direction of units all of whose activities do not come under direct observation of their managers. The shortcomings of these information sources are more or less as follows.

1.   In a large-scale enterprise the executive usually has too many responsibilities and too little time to act as information gatherer and problem finder. On their part, managers are limited in and by their experience and are usually too engrossed in implementation to take adequate readings of positions and directions.

2.   Extensions of the manager—staff assistants and assistant-to—are normally used more for transmitting information than for generating and analyzing it. Even where they are qualified to act as knowledge centers (a rare circumstance), they usually have or represent vested interests that prevent them from being fully objective.

3.   Performance reports in the shape of regularly issued accounting statements and audit reports are historical in nature. Even when they are combined into extrapolations, such as extensions of trends, they fail to provide insight into particular problems that may be growing somewhere in the unit.

4.   Controls, when they operate, do give notice of a failure or irregularity, but they are so specific in activity coverage that they fail completely as barometers of environmental conditions.

5.   Studies and surveys are excellent sources of information upon which the manager can act, but the analyses on which they are based usually take a great deal of time, require specialized talent, cost a lot of money, disrupt work, and cannot be performed frequently enough to serve the needs of ongoing control. Assignments to investigate are usually focalized, intensive, and disruptive. When internal specialists perform the studies, they usually treat units served as clients and spend more time creating acceptance than improvement. External consultants are usually not called in until a unit is already deeply in trouble because of *past* problems, and then they must spend a great deal of time in becoming informed about the state of *current* affairs. Temporary units in the form of committees, task forces, and project groups often tie up manpower resources badly needed elsewhere.

These five shortcomings add up to deficiencies in convenience, timeliness, and cost that are severe handicaps to managers being informed. Therefore, none of the sources of information listed provides managers with the means whereby they can obtain fresh, inexpensive, and quietly gathered knowledge that things are proceeding according to plan and accepted standards or that they are going wrong and what, where, and how. Operations auditing has come into being to provide such knowledge and to fill the gap created by modern business conditions in the traditional range of information-supplying devices.

OTHER FEATURES OF OPERATIONS AUDITING

Another characteristic of OA, from the authors' and many accountants' point of view, is that it is strictly a verification and problem-finding tool. It *relates* to the process of solving problems and securing improvement, but it should not, in the opinion of some, be part of that process. In other words, operations auditing, as the authors conceive it, is a means of discovering company deficiencies without offering suggestions on how to rectify those deficiencies. Contrariwise, most internal auditors accept the responsibility for both identifying deficiencies and making recommendations for their correction. In support of their view is the fact that, although they are hardly ever asked to implement improvements, they are often charged with offering corrective suggestions. Nonetheless, the authors take issue with that view and consider the job of operations auditing to have ended when the significant problems have been located, identified, and accurately defined. That leaves no room for developing solutions.

Plainly, what is needed is better use of and improvement of the problem-solving tools already at hand, and not extension of operations auditing into activities almost certain to destroy its special value as a management tool. Solving an identified problem through intensive application of deep knowledge is *not* new; routine, systematic search for problems and opportunities for improvement *is* new. More on this subject will be said in the subsection "Limitations of Operations Auditing."

Another key feature of OA is that it is based on evidence; an appraisal based on personal opinion, unsupported by factual evidence, is not operations auditing. What distinguishes OA from other forms of auditing more than anything else is the extent to which it will go and the variety of tools it will use to obtain the evidence needed to fulfill its objectives and define the problems it uncovers. As in all appraisal work the best results are obtained by using an external frame of reference. Admittedly, judgment is an inevitable part of the final results. But judgment becomes valuable only after the operations auditor has gathered essential facts and compared the evidence with standards.

A further characteristic of OA, then, is that it measures against standards, which are the only acceptable basis for a comparison of units and periods of time. Without standards an audit can be nothing more than a collection of opinions that vary with each examiner. That kind of evaluation is, in fact, now being made by some operations auditors; it is susceptible to criticism and is totally inadequate.

Despite the opinions of some authorities, adequate standards for effective operations auditing *are* available—if for no other reason than that the goals of enterprise are primarily economic. Further, since the primary mission of most organizations is the effective use of physical and human resources, the controlling interests in the organization will almost certainly have set standards of some kind based upon economic criteria. Further, it is virtually inevitable that social, legal, and ethical standards will be imposed by the company's environment.

Standards of greatest value in operations audits come mainly from two sources: the company and the industry of which the company is a part. For the discovery of company standards, OA relies heavily upon documentation of the unit being audited. Performance yardsticks can be found in (1) objectives, goals, and plans, (2) budgets, (3) records of past performance, and (4) policies, procedures, directives, and so forth. For industry standards, OA relies on the common body of knowledge of sound business practices and industry statistics provided by professional association and government sources.

There are two types of standards: those that apply to objects and those that apply to activities. Standards of the first type tend to be precise and well defined because they generally deal with the qualities of things; the others tend to be imprecise and amorphous because they generally deal with the actions of people. Hence, the standards by which corporate activities are evaluated necessarily entail considerable relativity and practical experience. They are nonetheless necessary; they are basic to the auditing function. To audit is to evaluate, and only an evaluation against a standard can be objective and dependable.

Preparation of standards is therefore a significant activity; it is among the OA manager's most important responsibilities. Developing a body of standards is a time-consuming, painstaking task, but there is no more important factor in the success of an operations audit.

SPECIFIC DEFINITION

Before we attempt a clear definition of operations auditing, two things about OA must be recalled: (1) OA is new and (2) managers must have a means whereby they can readily and conveniently have assurance that things are going well or know what the existing or coming problems are. The tools that predate OA reveal too little, and that little too late, to meet the needs of the modern manager. They do not help him see problems while they are still in their infancy. The old-time tools have not, of course, lost their original advantages, but for the purposes of the burdened manager they are often unilluminating, ponderous, and costly. Operations auditing, on the other hand, is responsive to the need for a performance-gauging tool that costs relatively little, is nondisruptive, and identifies problems before they mature and get out of hand.

In its most general definition, operations auditing is a formal procedure for systematically analyzing, evaluating, and describing company, unit, or functional performance. That, however, is true of all appraisal instruments, and so the authors have developed the following, more restrictive, definition: Operations auditing is a technique for regularly and systematically appraising unit or function effectiveness against corporate and industry standards by utilizing personnel who are not specialists in the area of study with the objectives of assuring a given management that its aims are being carried out and/or identifying conditions capable of being improved.

The phrase "regularly and systematically" points to a feature of OA not yet touched upon, namely, that it is a formalized activity. It is commonly held that effective managers perform, in their own way, the equivalent of OA. The idea is attractive but unsound. True, every good manager does instinctively measure the effectiveness of the units he is in contact with but to say that OA is just another version of that informal measuring is to grossly underrate the tool. It is precisely because the manager requires something more dependable than his own informal appraisal that OA arose. Operations auditing differs by being consciously and systematically performed against acceptable standards. In other words, it is a formal activity with a distinctive work content.

LIMITATIONS OF OPERATIONS AUDITING

Like any tool, operations auditing must be used properly if results are to be satisfactory. If it is to be used properly, its constraints as well as its capabilities must be understood and heeded. The principal constraints are time, knowledge, and cost. Time is a limitation because a manager must be advised about the state of affairs in his area of responsibility promptly enough that he can act effectively. Therefore, audits must be performed regularly and often enough that problems can be caught before they become big or entrenched. On the other hand, audit engagements must not disrupt either productivity or morale. If they are to be performed with regularity, timeliness, and convenience, operations audits cannot be lengthy, drawn-out affairs.

Knowledge is a constraint because, obviously, no man is expert in all business fields, nor can a company afford to have on its staff a specialist on every aspect of the business that is to be audited. Necessarily, then, operations audits must be performed by men who are trained more fully in auditing than in what is being audited. Among other things, that means that OA cannot be used as a vacuum cleaner; realistically, it can be used only to search for major deficiencies and opportunities for improvement. Of course, the operations auditor will not turn away from the small problems and opportunities he comes across, but discovering them will be a byproduct of his major effort. In any event, he will detail and seek to prove only the deficiencies and opportunities for improvement that are significant in terms of dollars or effectiveness.

Together, time and knowledge as constraints produce the third limitation, cost. The statement lacks precision, but it must be said that an essential characteristic of OA is that it is a low-cost appraisal tool (no dollar standards are available). When the cost of a single operations audit rises above, say, $5,000 or $6,000, it is likely that a good deal more than the discovery and delineation of problems or opportunities for improvement has been undertaken. As a result, auditors are often thrust into the manager's or specialist's province and, despite the greatest precautions, hostility is often stimulated.

A recently issued brochure promoting an OA course gave one indication of this practice: "Suggesting solutions is exactly what operational auditing is designed for." From the point of view of this book, "suggesting solutions" (that is, developing programs of remedial action) is exactly what operations auditing is *not* suitable for.

Following is a statement that typifies the urge to make OA into an instrument of execution:[6]

> Operational auditing is a review and appraisal of the efficiency and effectiveness of operations and operating procedures. It carries with it the responsibility to discover and inform top management of operating problems, but its chief purpose is assisting management to solve problems by recommending realistic courses of action.

From the authors' point of view the operations auditor cannot be in a position where he can contribute dependable recommendations.

The reasons for this are not difficult to see. To begin with, the operations auditor does not do an intensive study. He engages, substantially, in sampling activities. In the second place, when the survey phase of the audit is over, he must spend the time left to define the problems he discovered in the most precise, meaningful terms possible so that management can decide what priority the problems should be given in using the resources of the enterprise. In the third place, he does not (if he is a typical auditor) have the knowledge needed to provide solutions management can trust. After all, the process of finding the best solution to any problem worth solving is a complex, time-consuming one involving, among other things, developing alternatives, testing them, and selecting the one with the most favorable trade-offs. It is not an activity the operations auditor has either the time or, in most cases, the best qualifications for.

It is often said that the prime job of the manager is to find problems, not to solve them. If this is true, then according to one writer on the subject the main objective of OA is to serve as an instrument of management intelligence, not problem solving.[7] Such a view does not "flatten" OA into a thin, narrowly useful instrument. Finding, identifying precisely, and describing a real business problem accurately is no mean task. When it is done, finding the solution is comparatively simple.

A view common to personnel in units or functions subject to audit is that operations auditing is critical in nature. Because audits are performed by persons outside the unit or function being audited, and audits usually lead to the discovery of problems, a tendency exists to involve the auditor in the design and execution of change. The view stems from the defensive position, "OK, if you're so good at finding problems you ought to be good enough to tell us what the solutions are."

This position is based on a serious misunderstanding of the purpose of OA and leads to gross misuse of the technique. Many authorities warn against OA becoming an instrument of change and suggest that the auditor who recommends or takes part in making changes that stem from his work impairs his future usefulness to his firm since he cannot very well audit his own work objectively. The Institute of Internal Auditors seems to take this position in saying, "Internal auditors must take an objective attitude and, therefore, should not take a hand in developing or installing procedures that will be subject to later internal audit review and appraisal."[8] Framing a recommendation for change later enacted does not leave the auditor in an independent position even though he took no hand in implementation.

The Operations Auditing Function

It is no accident of circumstance that the word "auditing" has come to be pinned to the tool. Attest auditing arose in response to the need for a convenient, efficient means of verifying that the equity of an enterprise had not been tampered with and that the chips were where they were claimed to be. In the furthest stretch of an attest audit assignment, a collateral statement may be issued that assets are not being used to the best advantage. But direct suggestions of how to use assets more productively (for example, recommending by name institutions in which to invest funds) are definitely irregular and out of keeping with the audit assignment.

The operations audit has similar characteristics. In the opinion of the authors, its prime job is to ascertain, verify, and report—not to recommend or implement solutions. These qualities alone favor applying the term "auditing" to the operational as well as custodial functions.

It is not always possible for the auditor to avoid becoming involved in change. The level of independence of internal auditors varies, of course, and the internal auditor is never completely independent of the wishes of his employer. It is to be expected, therefore, that he will occasionally be ordered to prepare specific recommendations or plans for change. When the role of the operations auditor is not clearly seen or when it is mixed in with specializations such as systems and procedures, this is very likely to happen. On the other hand, where the role is clearly seen, the auditor is not expected to make recommendations unless specifically instructed to do so. "Unless the auditor is assigned this project as a special study, he is not in a position to make definite recommendation as to change. His primary responsibility is fulfilled when he has brought the results of the policy to attention through his report—which should present the facts in such manner that the situation may not be overlooked or dismissed without adequate review at an appropriate management level."[9] The following statement lends support to the authors' view: "The findings of operational audits are similar to those which are generally reported in the management letter of the traditional audit."[10] It is rare for a management letter to contain specific recommendations for change unless the description of the problem provides a self-evident solution.

Whether the reader accepts the authors' view or not it cannot be doubted that the operations auditor must be very careful about making recommendations. Nothing holds greater danger to the work of OA or the welfare of the corporation than a carelessly made recommendation. The following comments show this.[11]

> The auditor will encounter many situations in which no definite recommendation may be possible—either because his experience does not qualify him to give a definite opinion, or the facts of a situation may not permit a specific recommendation. Here evaluation is confined to determining whether the established controls revealed a questionable situation to management; if they did—and were recognized by management—no specific action or recommendation may be feasible for the auditor.

In the authors' view operations auditing people must positively resist carrying their OA assignments beyond the appraisal level. This view is upheld by a practicing minority who regard the tendency to get into recommending and even implementing changes as deadly to the spirit and purpose of OA. The tendency destroys independence and implies a virtuosity and expertise at odds with the economics of the operatons auditing function.

Every firm large enough to need OA has resources in the form of managerial, specialist, and consulting personnel—often among the most expensive of all personnel. The company needs these experts to survive, but it cannot be very profitable if it does not use them effectively. What is needed is a device for efficiently locating problems that the specialist forces can work on, and this is one of the important services OA can perform (a pathfinder function, so to speak). The trouble is that in their normal desire to enhance their unit's value and prestige many operations audit managers feel that OA should provide answers. Our position is that, although this is the common view, it tends to weaken OA's unique role.

The tendency of some auditors to assume responsibilities beyond operations appraisal, of course, is not completely ill founded. Operations auditors feel impelled by moral and knowledge factors to contribute to the maintenance of the enterprise of which they are a part. This is all to the good; every employee should help his company in every way he can, but this does not include adding limitations to those natural to any specific work assignment. Therefore, OA should do nothing that impairs its usefulness. It can appraise the effectiveness with which goals are met or work is done, but it cannot be sure of finding the best solutions; it can report problems accurately, but is in no position to say that the time is ripe for dealing with them. When it becomes necessary to point the way to a possibly useful change (because no one else seems aware of the direction to take or because the auditor alone has the requisite knowledge) the operations auditor should clearly be disassociated from his operations auditing role—be loaned out as a specialist, a project worker. To do otherwise makes the OA function party to that which it eventually may be asked to audit.

Additional limitations are often imposed on operations auditing by a lack of standards on which to base an evaluation of important functions and the traditional reluctance of managers to provide information about actions taken. If he fails to consider those limitations, the operations auditor gets into areas he should avoid, such as appraising employees, evaluating unique and highly specialized projects, and measuring performance without benchmarks.

Operations auditing is not a normative discipline. It cannot prescribe performance standards; it can only utilize standards that possess established degrees of objectivity and acceptance in reaching conclusions relevant to the formation of judgments about performance. Accordingly, OA can be practiced only in situations within view of reference points in some manner exterior to and independent of that which is being evaluated. These take many forms—as will be seen in the section on OA standards—but they are not available in every situation. The appraisal of individual competence is one such situation.

An auditor can, on the basis of sound evidence, conclude that a given job is not being performed effectively, but he is not qualified to conclude that John Doe either is unfit to perform it well or is not performing it well for purely personal reasons. There can be many explanations of why job performance does not meet the needs or intentions of the company. It may be that the incumbent is not being allowed to do the job; the job may be organizationally ill situated; or the job may not be performable in the first place. The auditor can comment on any or all of these or similar reasons, but, we repeat, he is certainly not qualified to appraise personnel performance.

The bulk of CPA practitioners adhere to this view, as attested to by the finding of one study:[12]

> A large majority of accountants interviewed said that their firms either made no recommendations on the competence of personnel or they did not commit such evaluations to paper. There was a strong feeling that a lack of management competence could best be pointed out indirectly.

The preceding considerations make it apparent that OA is not a useful tool in all situations. It is not so much a big-business or sophisticated tool as it is one the usefulness of which is related to organizational and managerial circumstances. It is, in short, a situation-oriented tool.

Selectivity. Since OA is a tool of managers who, because they operate in highly differentiated organizations need to be informed about areas out of their sight, it follows that OA is a complex situation tool. That may be somewhat of an oversimplification, depending on the construction placed on "complex," but managers who can keep an eye on most activities have less need for OA. This is not to say that smaller or less differentiated companies or organizational units cannot benefit from OA. An audit carried out by an external agency may produce benefits, such as confirmation of internally held views of performance or the discovery of problems unseen because of familiarity. In the last analysis, however, the ability of OA to contribute varies directly with the scale and complexity of the affairs it audits.

Taking this position does not place restrictions on the range of operations auditing *investigations;* OA can and should be used in any area of corporate activity within reach of standards. However, the position does make it plain that OA must be used selectively. There are, quite definitely, some tasks OA should not be used for. For example, OA should not be employed as an arm of corporate development.

Every company must have renewal activities, of course, and such activities require input from every source and level. The process of organizing, systematizing, and running a business is not something that has a beginning and an end. Every enterprise tends toward anarchy the moment the process falters or ceases; once established, a business sytem (like everything else in life) tends to return to a random, chaotic state. To prevent this from happening, a company must have renewal resources.

Herein lies another danger to the OA function. Because it is a rich source of ideas for restoring and improving functions, there is a tendency to utilize OA in corporate development activities. That is a mistake because corporate development is a nonlinear function that treats the opportunities for employing the company's resources as in some manner unique to the firm. Corporate development can be audited as a function; for there are certainly standards that are applicable to the task of measuring how well a company identifies its opportunities and commits its resources. But operations auditing is a poor tool for helping form the decisions entering into such commitments.

The significant differences between the various audit forms and management consulting as seen by the authors are presented in Table 1.

SIDE BENEFITS

OA has many benefits to offer besides those relating directly to management control. They should be looked into and be kept in mind by persons concerned with selling the value of, or thinking about setting up, an OA function.

Operations auditing is valuable training for potential managers. The work offers rich opportunities to obtain bird's-eye views of a corporation and the administrative process that are especially beneficial to operating personnel. A man with mostly hands-on experience with new problems and situations is forced by some exposure to operations auditing to make fuller use of his judgment and imagination, and so the company's manpower resource is enriched.

Much the same is true of such specialists as the financial auditor, who can contribute more significantly to the effectiveness of a business by working in operations than he normally can by working only in the financial area. In the process he too increases the company's human resources.

Some companies make planned use of OA for personnel development. They usually have a permanent OA manager and a nucleus of key personnel. The rest of the staff consists of people who are likely candidates for future reassignment. Staff members assigned to OA groups primarily to give them the exposure resulting from working in many phases of the company are moved to positions elsewhere in the company as the need arises.

Even public accounting firms see developmental value in OA work and expand the competence of their professionals by rotating assignments. One year the auditor is given EDP units to audit; next year, production units; the year after, purchasing; and so forth.

Whether deliberately used as a training ground or not, operations auditing is a great source of personnel for reassignment. A man who does a good job of OA is prized for the qualities that make him competent in the field and is regarded as promotable. Since the average compensation of operations auditors is usually well below that of managers and some staff specialists, the operations auditing group becomes a good source of promotable personnel. As a result, tenure in OA work tends to be on the short side.

SOURCE OF AUDIT

Though most companies with $5 million and above in volume can benefit from having their operations audited, not many can afford to maintain full-time OA staffs. The company that cannot employ an OA staff on a continuous basis will find it cheaper and better to have the work done by outside agencies. Full-time OA staffs are maintained by several types of service organizations.

In direct response to a need for more information about nonfinancial activities, many public accounting firms, and particularly the larger ones, have gone into OA work. Most firms with management services departments engage in operations auditing, which they consider essential to full-service auditing.

A few management consulting firms offer OA, but the great majority do not. They regard it as a not thorough enough basis for problem solving, which, after all, is the bread-and-butter part of their business. Their view

Table 1 Characteristics of the three varieties of auditing and management consultation.

	OPERATIONS AUDITING	INDEPENDENT (CPA) AUDITING	INTERNAL AUDITING	MANAGEMENT CONSULTANCY
Main objective	To verify fulfillment of plans and *sound* business requirements; to notify of rising problems or opportunities for improvement	To evaluate the integrity of accounting information	To measure and evaluate the effectiveness of controls	To produce results as directed
Requires judgment	Yes	Yes	Yes	Yes
Measures against standards	Yes	Yes	Primarily	Not always; frequently initiates new methods
Measures employed	Standards of firm or industry	Generally accepted accounting principles	Corporate policies and goals; control technology	Needs specific to each problem
Based on evidence rather than opinion	Completely	Mostly	Mostly	Mostly
Utilizes sampling	Frequently	Heavily	Frequently	Occasionally
Independence	Yes; OA does not solve problems nor implement solutions	Yes; audit independence is essential to CPA	Partial; often results in recommendations and auditor often encounters his own work	Yes, as to new problems; no, as to problems arising from implementation of recommendations made
Opinion for outsiders and management	No	Yes	No	No, except in special situations
Protective, constructive service, evaluation of controls	Primarily	Heavily	Primarily	Not always prime object
Deals with:	All measurable aspects of business	Physical and financial assets primarily	Most levels and operations of a business	Generally specific areas and problems
Defines problems and opportunities for improvement	Exclusively	No	Among other things	Among other things
Searches for alternatives; tests alternatives; chooses best solution	No	No	Often	Almost always
Involved in solving problems	No; insufficient time; personnel not expert	No; not part of responsibility	Yes, when asked to	Yes; main service

Size of organization	Useful only in companies large enough that management cannot directly oversee all operations	Performed in every size company except the smallest	Rare in companies under 500 employees	Employment not markedly related to company size
Time required	Short; generally from 2 to 8 man-weeks	Generally short; annual audit by CPA's in most situations does not take a long period	Fair amount of time; more time is required than for an OA procedure when problem solving is expected	Usually extensive; except for advisory services the background information required by projects involving solution finding and implementation is extensive
Function performed regularly	Yes	Yes	Not always	Hardly ever
Periodicity	Once every 6 to 24 months	At least annually	According to schedules established	Follow-up assignments rare
Expertise required	Minimal in object of audit; primary skill is in systematic information gathering, analysis, and interpretation	Yes; professional standards established by states and professional regulatory organizations	Yes; audit skills are comparable with those of CPA; contributing to problem solving requires broad experience	At its best high skills are involved; professional standards are loosely applied
Disruption of work	Least of all; uses mostly available data	Considerable; needs of special auditors and questions must be quickly answered	Fair amount; greatest when changes are suggested	Fair amount to greatest, depending on nature of assignment
Evaluating nonlinear functions (one-time projects that have no standards)	No	Rarely	Yes	Yes
Tests effectiveness of controls	Among other responsibilities	Comments mainly on effectiveness of internal controls only	Focuses on appraising controls	Only on occasion; consultants called in most often to deal with the consequences of failure
Directly evaluates personnel	Never	Never	According to assignment	Often
Corporate development	Indirectly; OA may identify but does not tell how to exploit opportunities for improvement	No; goal is limited to performing audit to give opinion on financial statements	Yes; where problem finding and problem solving are considered part of function	Yes; identification and exploitation of opportunities for improvement are a specialty of outside consultants

is correct so far as problem solving is concerned, but it does not in the least void the argument that OA holds immense value for the company that wishes to *know* on an objective, verified basis where it is and how it is doing.

REFERENCES

1. Statement of the Responsibilities of the Internal Auditor (New York: The Institute of Internal Auditors, Inc., 1947).
2. J. Brooks Heckert and James D. Willson, *Controllership* (New York: The Ronald Press Company, 1963), p. 671.
3. Carl Heyel, *Encyclopedia of Management* (New York: Reinhold Book Corporation, 1963), p. 369.
4. Bradford Cadmus, *Operational Auditing Handbook* (New York: The Institute of Internal Auditors, Inc., 1969), p. 9.
5. Corine T. Norgaard, "The Professional Accountant's View of Operations Auditing," *The Journal of Accountancy*, December 1969, p. 46.
6. Peter A. Pyhrr, "Operational Auditing: A Run for Daylight," *Financial Executive*, May 1969, p. 19.
7. Norgaard, loc. cit.
8. "Statement of Responsibilities of the Internal Auditor," booklet issued by The Institute of Internal Auditors, Inc., New York, 1947.
9. Cadmus, op. cit., p. 14.
10. Norgaard, loc. cit.
11. Cadmus, op. cit., p. 31.
12. Norgaard, op. cit., p. 47.

2

MANAGING
THE FUNCTION

Administration of the operations auditing department differs with the company. Some differences are caused by variations in ideas among the individuals who head the function, but most are probably caused by variations in what management wants. Therefore, a description of how an internal auditing department ought to be run is not really possible. Nevertheless several elements are common to the functioning of all successful OA activities. The minimum requirements for effective internal auditing are:

1. A clear, liberal delegation of authority from management.
2. Effective, continuing management support.
3. A body of guidelines in the form of objectives, policies, and standards.
4. Established machinery for planning, scheduling, and control.
5. A staff chosen for the ability to think in management terms, research and analyze competently, and deal effectively with people.

To be effective, operations auditing requires each of these elements. As to point 1, little purpose is served if a company that goes into OA so restricts the audit manager that he cannot use his resources for what he thinks is to the best advantage to the business. That argues that the OA function must be regarded as having significant effects on the profitability of the company and the position of operations audit manager must be regarded as deserving of significant authority.

As to point 2, it is futile to expect good results of OA if management is not solidly behind it. The results turned out must receive adequate attention, and any confusion about the authority or objectives of the OA unit must be dealt with decisively. That kind of clout can seldom be achieved without high organizational connections.

In respect to point 3, the operations auditor needs all the guides to the execution of work it is possible to give him. Larger OA departments usually have audit manuals that contain procedural recommendations, notes on information sources, and programs for regularly performed audits. The manual can be quite specific and detailed, like the one of a large mining and metals-producing company on plant maintenance only, or so loosely structured that it consists mainly of the bulletins issued over a period of time to the audit staff.

The fourth point touches upon the necessity for OA to be more than the amorphous, loose-jointed operation it too often is. Many analysis-oriented organizations manage themselves poorly even though they are in the business of helping others manage better. Assignment planning is often thin or unrealistic, and the system of controls is often loose and patchy. When the OA department is so managed, audit performance tends to lack uniformity and the results obtained tend to lack acceptance. If the OA administrator is to check on the activities and progress of his department and plan the best utilization of his audit resources, he needs a well-designed and -run control unit.

The last point requires little comment. Operations auditing will be of scant benefit to the business if the audit staff is incapable of doing the work assigned to it. The problems of recruiting and training personnel are discussed later in this chapter.

PLANNING

The process of establishing aims, committing resources, and scheduling and sequencing events is as important to operations auditing as to any other business function. Effective auditing begins with an annual schedule prepared before the beginning of the fiscal year, and that requires an adequate administrative apparatus. The schedule will, of course, relate to its associated budget and the amount of slack that has been built into it. Some unscheduled mandays allowance is usually required in every schedule, especially in the early years of the unit. Final arrangement of the schedule will ultimately depend on the size of the company and the scope of auditing practiced.

Because audit work can seldom remain faithful to it, the schedule should be looked upon as subject to adjustment. It should be reviewed and brought up to date periodically. That, if it is to be done right, requires administrative machinery of some sort.

An information and control system based on these or similar elements will be helpful:

Standard project descriptions.
Project board.
Employee activity charts.
Performance evaluation reports.
Time reports.
Manpower utilization summaries.
Monthly reports.

A standard project description, always in the same format, is a statement of what the audit will include. It is distributed to top management of the unit to be audited and any others who exercise approval rights. Essentially,

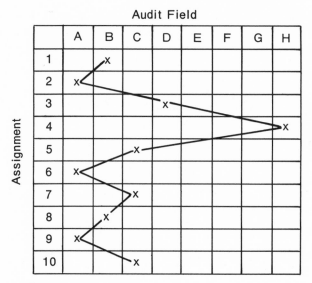

Figure 1 **Employee activity chart.**

it serves to answer the what, why, how, and so on of the study. Once approved, it becomes the guideline for the conduct of the audit.

A project board is so posted that everyone concerned can quickly see the status of current projects. It should show a project's code number indicating job number, man-days involved, and schedule dates. Nine digits should be sufficient. It is difficult to imagine a company so large that it will perform more than a thousand audits per year, so three places are enough for job number. No audit should run much more than 60 man-days, and so two places shoud be enough fot audit duration. The last four places are for the month and year of the audit. An example is 093440872.

Some kind of employee activity chart is a useful device for so representing the assignments of a given staff member that excessive concentration in one audit field can quickly be detected. A simple example is shown in Figure 1. Many variations are possible; for example, the number of weeks on each assignment can be included. Whatever form the device takes, it is bound to be helpful in many ways, as by helping to make sure that auditor development goes according to plan.

Performance appraisal is, of course, as important in the operations auditing field as in other areas of the business. A written report should be prepared on each auditor either at the end of a major project or every six months. In addition to describing his duties and accomplishments, the report should rate the auditor in such specific categories as cooperativeness, acceptance of responsibility, initiative, knowledge, ability to meet deadlines, and gaining of personal acceptance. Outstanding or unsatisfactory ratings should be elaborated. The report is invaluable in assigning work, ascertaining training and development needs, and deciding promotion and compensation questions.

A special time report for the audit staff will be of help in administering OA activities. Time can be recorded in the sheet against the main activities—

training, preparation for an audit, performing audit field work, writing the final report, and meetings related to presentation and explanation of the findings. The time sheet lends itself to the preparation of manpower utilization summaries, an analysis of which allows management to see how staff time is being spent, to estimate audit engagements, and to adjust resources in planning for anticipated work loads. Analysis will also help in the determination of audit standards and cost budgets.

Last, audit activities should be reported on a monthly basis. The purpose of the report should be to inform top management, staff members, and selected individuals about the accomplishments of the audit staff. The report should describe the projects under way, progress and problems to date, and significant developments in the other activities and responsibilities of the audit office.

To return to the matter of organization, few companies maintain independent operations auditing activities. In most cases, OA is part of the internal audit department (although there is a discernible move under way to separate the two); in a few cases, it is part of an administration or a procedures unit. Large companies that have significant activities in more than one geographical area may have local branches to provide area auditing services. Those offices are nevertheless under the direct control of the chief operations or internal auditor at headquarters.

CREATING UNDERSTANDING AND ACCEPTANCE
Operations auditing cannot be productive unless the function is given solid management support. "Support" means a great deal more than merely enfranchising the OA unit; it means backing the auditor when he—as he sometimes will—runs into opposition from corporate executives or when his findings arouse hostility because of imputed criticism. The operations auditor must be confident of active support against any ill-based resistance to his audit.

The scope of the operations auditor's work must be clearly defined in the delegation of authority that establishes the function. The delegation should be encompassed in a comprehensive job description, a copy of which should be sent to every manager in the company. The description should focus on the results sought and be modified as necessary to keep it up to date.

In determining the scope of the operations auditing function, it must be recognized that the work to be covered will be governed somewhat by the kind and scope of authority given to the executive to whom the function has been assigned. Each management should give careful consideration to the organizational implications of what it expects from operations auditing. The more it expects, the higher its reporting relationship should be.

At the audit level, each auditor will normally be looked upon as a threat to the staff in the unit being audited until he proves by his actions that he is there to help improve the unit's effectiveness. One approach that may be helpful, particularly if it is backed by the policy announcements of OA objectives from top management, is that an operations audit is a regular checkup undergone for reasons similar to those of a medical checkup. In any event, the manner in which questions are asked, how problems raised are treated, and how deficiencies are recorded will determine whether the auditor will meet with cooperation or resistance. The auditor should listen sympathetically to all ideas offered by his respondents, however offbeat they may seem. In fact, one reliable measure of the auditor's effectiveness with his main source of information (people) is the volume and variety of unconventional ideas he is offered. Respondents do not normally risk voicing strange ideas to representatives of management, as they almost inevitably consider auditors to be. That is why only a well-accepted auditor will receive many original and unusual suggestions.

"Participative management" is a current byword, and the concept is useful in OA work. For example, when investigation discloses problems, the auditor will do well to get the assistance of the people involved in identifying and defining them. Similarly, it is advisable to have personnel in the unit being audited collect the data to be used in the audit. By soliciting the help of persons affected by his audit and by identifying the facts gathered with them, the auditor can go a long way toward creating a climate favorable to his work and the audit findings.

Sensitivity to the workload problems of the unit being audited will help warm the reception of the OA staff. Almost every unit has some peak loading, and the OA staff should try to fit their work in so it will not aggravate the affected unit's schedule problems. When audit work continues for a considerable period in one location, the various audit areas should be scheduled for minimum interference at peak periods.

In connection with building positive relations with operating personnel, the OA staff should carefully consider how notification of an impending audit will be made. Although surprise audits were once an almost universal practice, they are now made only when the risks, particularly exposure to fraud, are so appreciable that the surprise element may have value. In general, they should be minimized because a much more favorable reaction from the audited location will be had when advance notice is given. Another reason for minimizing surprise audits is that they are seldom real surprises, thanks to the company grapevine. Finally, by giving a unit advance notice, the OA staff confirms that it is gathering facts cooperatively, and not snooping. Along these lines, it is usually helpful to have a pre-audit meeting at which top personnel of the unit to be audited can discuss areas of concern and the OA staff can alert the unit's staff to data that should be accumulated.

Operations auditing is part of the company's sensory mechanism, and that point should be emphasized in all contacts. An example is in the handling of progress reports. Although most companies require no regular report of progress except on longer audits, there is a certain amount of normal correspondence between the supervisor and the headquarters office, such as preliminary reports of audit findings. The informal reporting in such correspondence also helps to keep headquarters up to date on the progress of the audit. It is important that the supervisory personnel in the unit being audited see the correspondence and pass on the preliminary findings before headquarters is informed.

SCOPE OF AUDIT

Operations auditing focuses on any corporate aspect that is auditable and economically significant. Aspects without economic significance should not be audited; those with such significance are many and varied. Each aspect requires different methods and intensity of effort.

What and how much can be covered in any single audit is necessarily affected by OA objectives: to appraise and to discover opportunities for improvement on a nondisruptive and convenient basis. At any one time OA cannot have a large field of analysis, because a large field will not allow it to reach its objectives—not, at least, within cost and related parameters. For the same reasons OA cannot be a review in great depth over a wide range of activities. The configuration of operational audits depends heavily upon the company served, the audit subject matter, the size and makeup of the audit team, and the level of responsibility accorded the team for their opinions and conclusions. Audit content is especially influenced by whether the audits are of unit or functional activities, the only two options with respect to audit demarcations that OA has.

Not a great deal of information is available on what corporate units and activities are most commonly audited. Internal auditors have conducted most audits with an operational flavor, and a 1968 survey of internal audit programs in 308 companies showed the functions most frequently audited, outside the usual accounting and financial areas, to be purchasing, 89 percent; inventory control, 80 percent; insurance, 66 percent; EDP, 64 percent; construction, 56 percent; traffic, 51 percent; management information system, 48 percent; advertising, 47 percent; production, 46 percent; organization control, 44 percent.[1] The authors have no reason to think that similar distributions of audit attention do not prevail today, whether OA is performed by auditors within the company or without.

The subject matter of OA is limited to what can be observed, measured, compared, or otherwise treated empirically. Accordingly, OA has a rich but not unlimited field of review: statements of intention (goals, objectives, plans, policies); organizational structure (job content, grouping of jobs, relating of groups); systems and procedures (rules, regulations, methods, flows); controls (direct, indirect, quantitative, nonquantitative); operations (physical processes, activities); utilization of resources (financial, material, human); and results, always in terms eventually measurable.

In most assignments, the operations auditor will be dealing with the listed and other elements at the middle and first-line management levels. Operational auditors usually are not asked to audit the plans, policies, and activities of top management, because top management seldom cares for review of its activities by company employees. Another reason is that the work, tools, and apparatus of direction lend themselves poorly to measurement. Top management is usually careful not to define clearly the content of its own purview or working methodology. Consequently, it is difficult to trace results directly back to top-level decisions. When the operations auditor does get to work at that level, it is usually only because the audit is following functional lines. For example, in looking at expense accounting he will get into top management charges only in order to complete his job of determining that policies are or are not being followed throughout.

Operations auditing focuses on results, of course, but in looking for sources of potential improvement the auditor spends most of his time looking at procedures that cause and control operations. That poses a dilemma: becoming familiar with and analyzing the procedures is, relatively speaking, a monumental task quite beyond the scope of the auditor, yet it is the prime source of meaningful findings in the audit. How, then, to solve the dilemma? The answer is to devise audit procedures and train the auditor to think in terms of exceptions. All the tools of audit and the questions asked should be exception-oriented; they should be designed to ferret out things that do not conform to established policies, procedures, or plans. That would be too gross a method of discovery for the other types of services that provide management information (discussed in Chapter 1), but the exception approach serves the purposes of OA very well. The reason is that the objectives of OA are not to find *all* problems, but only those that are becoming or are likely to become economically significant.

Depending on company size, operations auditing can deal with the enterprise as a whole or treat only some specific part or activity of management. Current auditing tends to examine specific aspects of management rather than the whole. There is no strong reason why audits cannot, in some cases, apply to the complete entity, except that even a small company represents, in total, an incredibly rich mixture of elements. Usually, as the scope of the audit expands, the auditor tends to become more subjective, and the reliability of the audit diminishes. Still, the potential usefulness of audit findings tends to increase as the scope of the investigation broadens. Hence, determining the scope of the audit is a matter of finding the point of balance between reliability and applicability of findings—not an easy task, by any means. The following are guides to determining audit scope:

☐ The subject of an operations audit can be any corporate aspect that can be identified to the degree necessary to plan an audit.

☐ Operations auditing should be limited to examinations in which sufficient, competent, tangible, and objective evidence is collectible and criteria are available.

☐ Audits should be limited to areas in which specific findings can be developed and reported.

☐ Audits should be limited to the evaluation of performance rather than individual capacity, since only events of economic significance are subject to audits and they hardly ever stem from the efforts of one individual.

These concepts are not pure, and they have some degree of overlap, but they do have value as criteria of audit scope. Some of the corporate aspects that fall within the purview of auditing of one large manufacturing company are determining whether:

1. Objectives have been clearly defined, are in conformity with sound business principles, and have been communicated to all concerned.
2. Operating policies conform to established objectives.
3. Policies are implemented by specific procedures.
4. Procedures are followed as intended.
5. Productive administrative information is accumulated by orderly methods.
6. Management is provided with adequate, timely, and accurate reports.
7. The control system relates to corporate policies, controls in other operating areas, and the requirements of operating management.

Not all these aspects may be considered in each operational audit, but they do establish the basic audit approach. In total, they show that the most common approach to operational auditing is to analyze the policies, procedures, and controls of a selected function and trace any known or suspected weakness to its ultimate effect on operations.

The broadest aim affecting the scope of any operations audit is to have the audit produce understandable and useful results. But although that is the most important requirement, it is often the least developed. Management is the controlling factor in business organizations, and any evaluation of business actions or results of operations is an indirect evaluation of management. For that reason, the results of OA must, above all, be usable by management.

EXTENT OF THE ENGAGEMENT

Criteria for determining the best size and scope of an operations audit engagement have not yet been standardized, so audit coverage must in each case be determined by careful analysis of the work entailed. The analysis must consider the major risks associated with the activities of the unit or function to be audited. "Risks," in this context, refers both to the amount of dollars subject to the control of the unit or function being audited and to the possibility of loss or gain.

At least four factors affect the extent of an audit:

1. The concept of auditing. Audit coverage will depend heavily on what is expected of the auditor. If he is responsible for finding and defining only major opportunities for improvement, the engagement will last x days; if he is expected to report on and detail all opportunities he encounters, the engagement can last $2x$ to $3x$ days.

2. The urgency of coverage. A company that has an effective ongoing audit program does not need a crash effort or an extensive audit. An experienced audit team can cover far more ground per unit time than an inexperienced one, and an audit preceded by earlier audits of the same unit or activity can be done much more quickly than an initial audit.

3. The resources available. A company that has adequate numbers of trained auditors can audit more extensively than it could if it were short of auditors.

4. The nature of the company's business. A company that only distributes has a narrower range of activities than one that manufacturers as well, and a company engaged in long-term production runs has different auditing requirements than one of similar size with constantly shifting production operations.

Ultimately, two other factors relating to points made earlier (that audits must be nondisruptive and low in cost) affect audit scope most vitally. An audit over 60 man-days in length risks becoming disruptive, excessively costly, or both.

There are at least two reasons for limiting the range of the audit. The first is that the auditor's mind is thereby focused on significant problems. The second is that the larger the audit the greater the number of auditors. As the number increases, the problem of administering the audit work and communicating data and findings is greatly aggravated. One way to keep an audit optimum in size is to put limits on the most time-consuming element of all: the collection and evaluation of evidence. It can be expected that that portion of an OA engagement, as performed by experienced auditors, will require in the neighborhood of two-thirds of the total time. Not, of course, that investigation of significant problems or opportunities for improvement should be curtailed, but each auditor should be conditioned to exercise care that investigatory effort is kept in the highest degree focused on *significant* matters. OA is a poor tool for chasing down the many small problems that inevitably plague every organizational unit and business activity.

DETERMINING AUDIT FREQUENCY

How often a business or a part of it should be audited varies with the scale of the unit or activity involved, the scope of audit performed, and, of course, the resources available for performing the audit. Other considerations are the nature of the operation and recent changes in the unit since—and possibly as a result of—the preceding audit. For example, the need to appraise the effects of major changes usually suggests an earlier than normal return to the unit.

Financial audits customarily are performed annually, and each audit follows pretty much the same program. Operations audits, however, cannot be so highly programmed. The frequency of operations audits should depend on the rate of change and the amount of resources used in the unit. When the work unit is subject to rapid change (for example, EDP) or the total resources engaged are high (for example, R&D), the frequency should be higher than when work processes are not undergoing rapid change and the resources employed are not high in value. In any event, audit assignments should be made often enough to provide protection against growing problems but not so frequently as to result in repetitive work that is of doubtful value.

In most operations, audits on an 18-month basis are adequate to protect the company from problems becoming entrenched or too large. Frequency can be stretched as far as three years, but it should not go beyond. At the other end of the scale, it is difficult to conceive of a situation in which the benefits from audits performed more frequently than every six months will offset the disruptions entailed. When the nature of an activity is such that significant resources are changing on a continuing basis or are being consumed at a high rate, a full-time audit function probably should be associated with the activity. A number of companies make it a standard practice to assign full-time auditors to major projects involving the expenditure of large sums.

SIZING THE FUNCTION

How large an operations auditing unit need be is dependent on the kind and size of the firm and the OA philosophy involved. The latter, of course, entails the scope and frequency of audits as well as the extent to which outside auditors are used.

To the knowledge of the authors, there are no data by which to gauge how large a staff is needed for OA work or what cost averages are involved. Our experience, admittedly thin, tends to show that approximately 0.2 percent is spent by progressive firms for the problem- and improvement-opportunity-finding component of services aimed at corporate refinement and maintenance.

According to that measure, a $50-million firm will spend $100,000 for OA activities.

Let us see what the $100,000 will buy. Operations auditors cost from $15,000 to $20,000 depending on age, skills, and experience. At an average annual cost of $25,000 (including the manager of the unit, fringes, and expenses), $100,000 will provide a staff of four. Productivity of consulting activities typically runs in the neighborhood of 75 percent (allowing for vacation, skills development, departmental activities, and assignment-preparation time). Using that as a standard yields 39 weeks of audit time available per man per year. Four auditors will then have 156 man-weeks available for performing audits, assuming that the manager's time on reviewing results, editing reports, sitting in on audit reviews, and so forth, is counted as audit time. If the typical audit is five man-weeks in duration, all phases being taken into account, in the neighborhood of 31 individual audits can be performed—certainly a sufficient number for a company seriously embarking on an OA function for the first time.

Of course, a great deal depends on how the audits are designed—their scale and content. Even if the audits tend to average six man-weeks in length, however, around 21 can be done annually. For many companies in the $50-million range this number of audits can contribute vitally to improvement.

It is interesting to note here that, when it is applied in a linear fashion, the 0.2 percent rule of thumb implies OA is not for the less than $10-million company (since one man at $20,000 comes to 0.2 percent). That is not the case, however, and the error comes from applying the gauge too rigorously. For firms at either end of the size range from less than $10 million to more than $1 billion, a modified S curve would be more fitting. A $500-million enterprise will not necessarily require ten times as many auditors as the $50-million enterprise, and organizations of below $10 million are not certain, by virtue of size alone, to be without auditing needs.

Two points bear on the question of how large a staff is needed: (1) There are doubtless some units or functions that ought always to be or ought alternately to be audited by outsiders. (2) No company can afford an OA staff so large it can handle any engagement expertly. Illustrative of the first point is the OA unit itself. There is no reason why it should not be audited in a fashion similar to that in which it audits other units. Obviously, it cannot audit itself; it is best audited by outsiders.

An example of an area that should be audited at least alternately from the outside is the upper echelon of management. For a number of practical reasons as well as reasons of principle, wise top management will not shrink from having audits made of its own activities; but it also recognizes the enormous psychological burdens that such audits place on the operations auditor. Therefore, to ease the problem, and to provide a control when the in-house OA unit does do some auditing of top activities, outside audits should be contracted for.

Although, as the text makes clear, the operations audits must be performable by persons skilled in auditing rather than by specialists in the function being audited, minimal degrees of knowledge are required before an auditor can undertake an engagement. When he audits a materials handling or a manufacturing operation, for example, he must have certain principles and standards well in mind before he commences. Acquiring such knowledge often entails a fair amount of preparatory (and nonproductive) time. No firm can afford to be fully staffed with men instantly prepared to go to work whatever the engagements scheduled.

Money spent on operations audits in amounts that accord with the 0.2 percent formula will easily be recovered in savings and improvements in the use of resources. It is difficult to conceive, to repeat the earlier example, of a $50-million company in which $100 thousand spent on systematic problem and improvement-opportunity finding will not at least be recaptured.

Even assuming that the outlay will not be directly recovered, the costs of operations auditing will to a significant extent be offset by savings in accounting and consulting fees, reductions in the need for internal auditing, and, above all, improvement in the utilization of executive time—the most costly, when poorly used, of all company resources.

RECRUITING STAFF

An operations auditing function, like any other business activity, can be no better than the quality of its personnel. Estimates of the capacities and therefore the qualifications of operations auditors tend to be on the high side, as the following statement illustrates:[2]

> In order to analyze the information developed, the auditor must have a broad background of knowledge. This should include not only accounting principles and auditing techniques, but knowledge of organization principles, budgeting and forecasting methods, office equipment, data processing equipment including computers, inventory control methods, statistics, compensation methods, work measurement, production scheduling, sales, and purchasing methods. He must have the ability to bring this knowledge to the problems he is investigating, not necessarily in an attempt to develop improved solutions, methods, or procedures, but with a sufficient level of understanding to identify areas where, with more intensive study and other technical support, he can assist management in its search for improved methods. The auditor may then guide and assist line management in implementing the agreed-upon programs.

Persons with such catholicity of background and abilities are hard to find and expensive to employ for any purpose. To expect to recruit them for operations auditing work is to place excessive strain on both credulity and compensation standards. Realistically, operations auditors must be made of more common clay than that from which the auditor described in the excerpt was molded.

Qualifications for OA work vary with the individual, but they consistently include at least four characteristics: a knowledge of OA principles and methodology, possession of illuminating and unifying convictions that apply to business and management, a capacity to be truly independent, and the ability to express findings. The ultimate measure of a person's suitability for operations audit work is, of course, his potential usefulness in helping his company improve its results.

Experience with operations auditing has yielded more concrete guidelines—though none more fundamental—than the foregoing ones. One is that an operations auditor greatly benefits from familiarity with the theory and practices of accounting. As a result, many companies try to get auditors with accounting backgrounds.

It is true that the operations auditor's burden of work is eased by his being able to digest and interpret quickly the records he is bound to encounter in his work and that accounting experience fosters that ability. Nevertheless, accounting knowledge must not be emphasized unduly, because the connection between it and OA skill has not at all been established.

A limitation of accounting and financial auditing personnel is that often they cannot adapt themselves to the more demanding environment of operations auditing. That is why the top OA manager in one of the largest companies in the country will not hire for OA work anyone who has had more than three years of financial auditing experience, because he has found them to be excessively fixed in their perspectives and work ways. But the new auditor who does not have basic accounting knowledge should be given quick exposure to it when he joins the OA unit.

The most important qualities of the auditor are possession of substantive management knowledge and the ability to think in managerial terms. The auditor must see elements of importance wherever he encounters them and relate any part of the business to the business as a whole. Other important qualities are logical reasoning capability, aptitude for numbers, ability to communicate well, orally and in writing, discriminatory sense, and ability to get along with people.

There is little reason to base recruitment on general intelligence or personality configurations. Competent operations auditors come in all sizes and shapes. They do, however, have in common the ability to reason well and handle numbers accurately. Also, without question, they must be able to converse responsively and relevantly and write clearly and efficiently. Another most desirable quality in an auditor is a keen sense of discrimination—the talent to distinguish between the important and the trivial.

Last but not least, the auditor must have interpersonal competence. The ability to get along with people does not mean that everyone must like the operations auditor. It does mean that he should not, in his demeanor, threaten people and must have a talent for seeing both sides of the question, for giving the other fellow the benefit of the doubt even when he is inclined to disagree, and for eliciting information from reluctant respondents. The auditor with those qualifications will be respected by operating people as an impartial fellow worker who is as anxious as they are to see the business prosper.

The question of staff size when an operations auditing department or activity is to be established is not easy to settle. Some of the factors are the following:

☐ Character of the enterprise in terms of work processes, organizational complexity, and geographic dispersion.
☐ Number of locations to be audited.
☐ Audit philosophy elected.
☐ Definition of audit work adopted.
☐ Frequency of audits decided upon.

These factors determine the number and kinds of people needed.

As to sources of OA personnel, companies commonly recruit from within because the people selected will already have a good general knowledge of company operations and can become effective members of the audit staff with minimal training. Most such recruits come from the company's financial auditing branch, although qualified employees are often transferred from operating departments. A disadvantage of recruiting from within is that company employees may lack the broader background and knowledge of the ways of doing things that can come from outside experience.

When it is not possible for a company to provide the necessary OA staff by transfer of personnel, recruitment has to turn outside. The fact that experienced auditors are in short supply is one of the reasons why operations auditing efforts are being increasingly staffed with nonaccounting personnel. Companies do little direct recruiting of new college graduates for operations auditing work.

TRAINING THE AUDITOR

All auditors, whatever their origin, should receive early indoctrination in the affairs and aspirations of the company. That should include adequate attention to the objectives and operations of the auditing department itself. Next should come a first or refreshed view of management. The ability to view the business as a whole is probably the operations auditor's most valuable competence; it provides the basis of his confidence that, on the basis of a fast review of facts, he can identify the key problems in the areas he audits.

When those broad aspects have been covered, specific training can begin. The best training is on-the-job work with experienced auditors. Usually, the new auditor is given a phase of a regular audit to perform under close supervision. With each operations audit he does, the auditor's awareness of OA's value will grow. In the first few audits he will have many questions and doubts, but each completed audit will give him greater confidence in himself and the technique.

Job-site training also leads to rotation of assignments, a necessity if the auditor is to develop enlarged perspective, broadened knowledge, independence, and objectivity. Also, each audited location then has the advantage of a fresh approach by the newly assigned auditor.

Auditor training in progressive companies is viewed so seriously that it never really stops, and programs for advanced employees receive as much attention as indoctrination training. The objectives of advanced training are usually to help the established auditor (1) acquire new skills and keep up with new developments in the field and (2) keep abreast of developments in or affecting the company. It is not unusual at training sessions to have key executives come in to describe the objectives and operations of their function.

All training and development activities must emphasize the primary objective of operational auditing: to identify areas in which cost reduction, operating improvements, or increased profitability can be achieved. Each auditor must be taught that deciding what changes to make and how to make them is the prerogative of managers but that what managers decide to change often depends upon the problems the operations auditor points out.

STAFFING THE ASSIGNMENT

If recruitment and training for operations auditing have been sensibly handled, staffing the individual audit engagement will not present a great problem. The main factor will be personnel availability. When there are sharp divisions in the capabilities of the audit staff, however, staffing can become a problem. The question of who to put on an assignment must then be resolved by giving close attention to the correspondence between characteristics of the audit field and individual qualifications.

One distinct advantage in assigning auditors with heavy experience in attestation is that, by training and experience, they *tend to be* thoroughgoing and objective. The auditor is one of few people in a company with a truly independent viewpoint in the sense that his interests have a universal quality. His work usually obligates him to follow action lines without regard for organizational barriers. But that background does not necessarily confer the qualities of a broadly usable operations auditor. The financial auditor often experiences special problems in making the shift from attest to operations auditing; he leaves the shelter of a practice that requires comparatively little innovative thinking. He will, therefore, probably continue to be most useful in engagements in which findings will issue primarily from the examination of records.

Auditors whose best qualification is extensive, specialized knowledge of operations must be used selectively. Though good practice demands that a specialist of any kind, including the financial auditor, be helped to acquire general OA competence, it is not practicable to assign the specialist to engagements out of his field. When his assignment does require skills other than his principal qualification, he should be only one of several auditors under the direction of a competent audit manager.

Staffing is vitally affected if some functions of internal auditing and operations auditing are combined, as they can be with mutual benefit. If the two forms of auditing are to be performed by the same people, the auditors must be skilled in financial auditing. That constitutes a constraint that, added to the other qualities needed in an operations auditor, markedly reduces the number of persons available for the work, and the reduction can pose serious problems in staffing OA assignments. On the other hand, simplification of the training problem in some respects should result.

Important projects call for senior auditors of broad experience, and it is essential that they have a working knowledge of the function or the type of operation that is to be audited. When the area is a new one, that knowledge may be rather theoretical, since it will have been gained through reading and questioning. Then the operations auditor may well confirm and supplement his knowledge by being a good listener while the manager of the function under audit explains the plans, operations, and problems of his section of the business.

Staffing the operations auditing project is adversely affected if there is a marked tendency to use either financial auditors or operational specialists exclusively. True, financial auditing is a good background for OA work; and since the auditor deals with matters that often relate to financial or economic data, he should possess some knowledge of finance and economics. But audit engagements can and probably should be staffed from many sources.

The other tendency, to look for OA staff members who have specialized knowledge and experience in certain phases of business operations, is one with which the authors can only disagree. It is undoubtedly helpful to have in an audit department personnel with expertise outside the audit process itself. But to build the department on such expertise is unwise for these reasons:

1. Persons with significant knowledge and experience in selective fields are seldom available for audit work.

2. It is usually impossible to employ auditors with specialized experience and fit them into the existing salary structure.

3. Specialist personnel tend to become involved—whether they want to or not—in recommending and implementing change, which is a violation, from the point of view of this book, of the function of OA.

The spirit of OA as defined herein—that OA is a convenient, nondisruptive technique of information gathering that is reasonable in cost—makes it almost necessary that nonspecialist personnel provide the bulk of the audit staff. Further to this point is the fact that if an analyst's main dependence is on his skill and knowledge in the field he is to audit, he will have to be at least equal to the men who produce the results he is reviewing. It is unrealistic to regard persons of such stature as likely prospects for recruitment.

All this is not to say that specialists will never be available to an audit department or that it is inadvisable to accept them when they are available. Transfer to the audit staff of company employees from operating departments is almost inevitable. When they do join the audit group, however, the special training and utilization they require in order to fit in and grow must be recognized.

When an auditor with specialized knowledge does become available, it makes sense to benefit from his knowledge, but that does not necessarily mean always assigning him to his specialty. A good way to use him is to make him head of a team sent to perform an audit in his field of interest. In that way he can act as a leader of and consultant to staff members.

It should be noted that expert knowledge can be a handicap as well as an advantage. An expert is almost always partisan. Every man is a captive of his knowledge; the more knowledge he has, the more he is limited by what he knows. Finally, it should be kept in mind that a major objective in handling audit personnel is to develop them as broad-gauge business analysts. The specialist should therefore be given as much opportunity to grow as any other staff member by assignment to different fields.

REFERENCES

1. *Survey of Internal Auditing* (New York: The Institute of Internal Auditors, Inc., 1969), p. 5.
2. Francis C. Dykeman, *The Contributions of Management Auditing in Financial Reporting* (Englewood Cliffs, N.J.: Prentice-Hall, Inc., 1970), p. 177.

3

PERFORMING THE AUDIT

The essential ingredient of a successful audit project is research and analysis conducted within a soundly constructed conceptual framework. There can be no simple, get-on, get-off mechanistic procedure. A successful operations audit requires analytical ability, ingenuity, reflective thinking, and systematic procedures. In working to fulfill the objectives of operations auditing, the auditor creates knowledge at three levels:

☐ Verification of the need for and accuracy of the data and reports produced within the information system.
☐ Determination of the degree of compliance with established objectives, policies, methods and procedures, government regulations, and contractual obligations.
☐ Apprasial of procedures, systems, staffing, movement of information, productivity, and so forth.

The first two are factually based. The third comes under the heading of opinion—but opinion that leans heavily on knowledge and on unmistakable, objective evidence.

Each audit assignment has the following phases:

1. *Definition and organization.* The first step in an operations audit is to identify the areas and scope of the study.

2. *Preparation.* The next step is for the auditor to become familiar with corporate plans, policies, and organization as they relate to the unit or area to be reviewed and to acquaint himself with relevant industry information.

3. *Initial survey.* The auditor should become oriented in the field within which he is to work through discussions with key people there. At this stage he samples aspects of the work and environment of the field of inquiry.

4. *Research.* Once he has become familiar with the field of inquiry, the auditor systematically uncovers the facts about the operations, assignments of responsibility, and plans and management of the area. At this stage he

must guard against attempting to dig out all the facts. He will never be able to get all of them, and he should concentrate on getting the key ones and those that are readily available. They will suffice for his analysis.

5. *Analysis.* When he has the key facts and enough additional information to justify the formation of conclusions, the auditor is in a position to analyze and to decide whether the results of analysis indicate true opportunities for the making of improvements.

6. *Reporting.* At this stage the auditor sums up his findings in writing and takes care to define the problems he has uncovered as meaningfully as possible in specifics and costs. Although report preparation is customarily regarded as the final step, the auditor will be well advised to start it on the first day; the surest way to drag it out is to wait until the end of the study. It is also beneficial to discuss findings with the manager of the auditing department before submitting the report to a higher level.

7. *Justification.* This is the last step in a study, often the most critical. At this point such challenges as have arisen to the accuracy or worth of the findings are countered orally by the operations auditor, usually in executive meeting.

Operations audits do not have a common starting place. Each audit is unique and requires individual treatment; hence the approach and factors dealt with will vary as much with the audit as with the starting place. As was noted, the first task in an operations audit is to break the audit down into component areas. The following are some of the investigatory elements that offer a starting place: goals and objectives, plans, organization, operations, controls, systems and procedures, staffing, facilities, reports, policies, and communications.

In his first operations auditing assignments the auditor will have to cope with some novel experiences. He will find, for example, that his presence in operating areas is not always understood or appreciated by personnel in those areas. Accordingly, defenses begin to be thrown up as soon as he makes his appearance. That fact supports the authors' view that OA must be a structured discipline. A formalized activity that is performed in a prescribed manner looks more objective and gives less appearance of being a judgmental process. Thus, the auditors should both use and make the most of the formal aspects of OA work.

INFORMATION SOURCES

The sources of information available to an operations auditor are as many as his experience, training, and intelligence make available. This section will deal only with the sources that are commonly employed. The people in the unit being audited are the prime source. Therefore, a well-conducted interview is probably the most efficient tool available to the auditor. Unfortunately, interviews are not always as well conducted as they should be. Two common mistakes are that they are, in the attempt to be exhaustive, longer than they should be, and interviewees are not seen more than once. Whenever possible, an interviewee should be seen at least twice in meetings of short duration.

Internal documentation can also be a major source of information. Flow charts, organizational charts, staff memos, policy and training manuals, recruiting brochures, and advertisements of the company are some of the documents that may prove useful in addition to the more obvious financial, production, sales, cost, budget, and forecast ones. The auditor should make it a practice to start the accumulation of documents early in the assignment.

Direct observation is another productive source of information. The auditor who consciously *observes* will become aware of many problems that are not recorded or are incapable of analysis through data. Feelings of openness, communication freedom, respect for subordinates, manner in which supervision is performed, neatness, housekeeping, and so forth tell a good deal about conditions in the unit being audited. Observation is also a rich source of specific examples that are useful in illustrating general conclusions.

In the authors' opinion, however, the traditional sources of information are no longer sufficient to business control needs, because the nature of both business and the managerial role has been changing in recent years. Companies have been growing larger, the business environment has been growing more complicated, and the manager's span of responsibility has been broadening and diversifying. More and more managers are operating out of sight of the activities for which they are responsible. One result is that the limit of effectiveness of the familiar tools of management is being reached and in some cases exceeded. Operations auditing has arisen in response to the demand for new tools capable of helping the manager meet the demands of attaining and keeping control over his expanding area of cognizance.

Operations auditing has also arisen in response to the marked acceleration of the pace of activities within business entities. The enterprise, which is oriented to getting out the product and securing and extending its market, acquires profit-absorbing ways that, unless sought out on a regular, systematic basis, quickly become organization fixtures. Every manager, and particularly the one with diversified responsibilities in a highly differentiated structure, must, if he is to maintain his area of responsibility in healthy condition, have a means for readily identifying and accurately defining emerging problems before they become institutionalized.

The real motive for operations auditing lies in the managerial condition touched upon when Jay Forrester said:[1]

> The manager's task is far more difficult and challenging than the normal tasks of the mathematician, the physicist, or the engineer. In management, many more significant factors must be taken into account. The inter-relationships of the factors are more complex. The systems are of greater scope. The non-linear relationships that control the course of events are more significant.

Because the problems facing the manager are so variegated and sophisticated and the threats to survival are so imminent, no company can fail to provide its managers with the latest and best possible information about the present condition of its affairs. Operations auditing is an efficient source of such information.

Also, as more authority is delegated it becomes increasingly difficult for top management to keep informed on how well its programs and policies are being carried out. Operations auditing is a means of gathering intelligence suited to the needs of top managers, whose circumstances prevent them from being personally informed about the state of affairs in their areas of responsibility.

Perhaps the final word on the need for operations auditing is the observation that companies that haven't yet installed some objective basis for measuring their performance can be on their way to the severest kind of trouble. In such companies managers may spend more time on looking good than being good, and unless a technique such as operations auditing is applied, the difference may not be detected until irreparable damage has been done.

TOOLS

Tools of the auditor are his own knowledge, unit documents, questionnaires, flow charts, and sketches and notes. The operations auditor is concerned with all aspects of an enterprise that can be investigated objectively. Accordingly, he must enter each assignment with both general and particular knowledge. General knowledge embraces the scientific method, principles of reasoning, and management science; particular knowledge includes the means and methods for extracting, identifying, and using factual information.

Of course, the auditor is completely familiar with the archival aspects of investigatory work; the bulk of his work is done through the study of documents. But in operations auditing he is going to deal more with people, plants, and systems, and he must make use of tools accordingly.

Familiarity with popular management methods and practices is useful, but its value should not be overemphasized. The company ahead of its competition is probably atypical, and its methods will therefore be relatively unknown. Knowledge that most companies do have charts and tables of organization cannot be used to demonstrate that a company lacking them is thereby deficient. Beware of being misled by currently popular management concepts. Peter Drucker has never run a factory, but managers listen to him. He has extrapolated from a few basic tenets without the hindrance of prior knowledge of managing.

The same cannot be said of specific knowledge. The operations auditor should have prior knowledge of techniques. For example, operations auditing often uses statistical techniques such as sampling methods, and the auditor should therefore be familiar with them. He should know a good deal about probability theory and how to construct samples sufficiently dependable to provide the basis for such recommended actions as investigation of problem areas. The reliability of statistical sampling is extremely important in any comparison of performance with standards.

Operations auditing also obliges the auditor to be familiar with the applications of electronic data processing. Knowledge of the capabilities of data processing equipment will not only be helpful to the audit but may also result in the use of equipment in an actual audit. It is entirely possible that, just as a fuller appreciation of the use of electronic equipment in the field of attest auditing can result in reduced detail verification work, so it can permit more ground to be covered in the operations audit.

Among the tools most likely to be used are documents familiar to the financial auditor. Reports, charts, graphs, manuals, and so forth are important sources of information. The auditor should have sufficient familiarity with charting techniques that he can readily comprehend what is being said in the graphics he encounters and can readily select the right form for what he wants to express graphically. Whenever possible, he should present his findings graphically. Charts have long been recognized as the clearest and most effective way to interpret and present a subject, and a skillfully prepared chart can clarify a complex problem.

Questionnaires. Operations auditing, to be systematic and efficiently performable, involves the use of questionnaires. That tends, to many people, to cast doubt on the value of OA. The charges are that questionnaires restrict the course of inquiry, become crutches and ends in themselves, and involve stereotypes rather than fresh and realistic standards. But operations auditing, as previously defined, cannot fulfill its mission without using questionnaires, regardless of the caliber of personnel employed in the audit. Nothing inherent in a questionnaire precludes the auditor from bringing the full range of his capabilities to bear on the performance of the audit assignment, despite the frequent assumption that the auditor's initiative and judgment are restricted by use of questionnaires. In the view of operations auditing presented here, the questionnaire is an important tool, but only one tool, of the auditor.

The use of questionnaires has many important benefits aside from lending uniformity to the performance of an audit and acting as a checklist to insure that the audit covers all subjects. (After all, even a 10,000-hour pilot uses a checklist in operating his aircraft.) Descriptions of three of the benefits follow. First, the use of a questionnaire helps depersonalize the audit by visually signaling the fact that the audit has form, and where there is form there is also repetitiveness. Thus, personnel being interviewed will not be so tempted to feel they have been singled out for investigation. Second, the questionnaire offers a basis for developing audit time standards. The questionnaire involves a specific amount of work, and the time involved in answering it can be used as a measure of the amount of time that will be necessary for the next audit. Third, the existence of questionnaires imposes a necessity on management to deal with OA in a practical way. The investment of time in developing good questionnaires is significant, and the existence of questionnaires may place limits on what can be expected of an audit.

Nevertheless, there is considerable diversity of opinion about the need for and use of questionnaires. Review of the question with a number of companies that use OA programs shows the following applications.

1. When a considerable number of similar audits are performed by different auditors (audits of geographically dispersed sales branches, for example) it is customary to have a rather detailed checklist or questionnaire to assure complete and similar coverage.

2. When much of an audit is done by junior auditors, relatively detailed questionnaires help guide the juniors and save time for the supervisors.

3. As audit requirements progress to an intensified examination of operations and controls—and are less concerned with routine—the program becomes more general and the benefits of using questionnaires diminish.

The belief that a systematic and effective operations audit can be performed by typical OA personnel only with the help of questionnaires may seem to place operations auditing in the position of being concerned with whether things are "right" or "wrong." That is not so. Operations auditing is practiced solely for the purpose of gauging the effectiveness of operations and discovering opportunities for improving them in the interests of efficiency, economy, or better control. Those goals can be realized only if the auditor is allowed to use all of his experience, judgment, and expertise.

It is true that most progressive internal audit departments abandoned the use of standard checklists and questionnaires some time ago, but those departments are also largely engaged in consulting on a broad basis. In that work, questionnaires are not as useful as they are in the more narrowly defined OA area.

Operations auditing can operate successfully only in a supportive environment and under a franchise given it to operate in a specific way. Granting such a franchise requires management to examine the OA function in detail and face the realities involved. Nothing can be more destructive to operations auditing or the operations auditor than an open-ended assignment, and few devices focus attention more efficiently on what is involved than a questionnaire.

The questionnaires in Part 3 should be used with different respondents to accumulate what might appear to be the same information on the same area or unit. That is not a wasteful suggestion, because "facts" are seldom presented in the same way or equally emphasized by all the people who observe them. The objective truth—which is inherently difficult to find—is more likely to be unearthed if the auditor obtains multiple answers to the same question.

Time studies. In making his observations, the auditor will greatly benefit from having familiarity with some of the standard tools of the industrial engineer. One such technique is simple time study. The performance of time studies is a demanding skill that requires training before its results can be used reliably for setting standards or making changes in production or clerical procedures. Normally, the operations auditor is not qualified to do that type of study—nor is he obligated to be, since his objectives are different. He should, nonetheless, be aware of the value of comparing methods and outputs through informal time study techniques, the main purpose of which is to point out areas of possible cost or system improvements. Random sample observations can often serve the purpose.

The technique is simple: in any situation in which the auditor is in a position to make random observations of a job that would be expected to be worked at in a steady manner, he merely records whether work is being done or not. For example, if he is investigating a billing operation, every time he sees specific clerks he can note whether they are working or not. The definition of work must be clear: it is any task or action directly involved with the function. In a clerical job it would include the sorting of papers, filing entry in the records, use of machines, giving of information, and so forth. Excluded would be obvious absences from the work, being away from the desk, or asking for instructions.

Because of its unscientific approach (like any other sampling technique, its reliability increases with the number of observations) the usefulness of the work, no-work technique is limited to pointing out possible areas of further inquiry, not to making conclusions.

MAINTAINING RELATIONS

In most financial audits the auditor's presence and capabilities are taken for granted; but when the auditor enters an operating department, he is apt to be regarded as an intruder or as lacking competence. And although operating management can usually be convinced that he is not a threat, it may be some time before that idea really takes root. One of the commonest defenses is to question the auditor's qualifications to appraise *"this"* unit."

As far as his personal qualifications to work in a given area are concerned, the auditor must realize that they will always be questioned. He should not respond by defining his qualifications or trying to explain away his lack of knowledge. The auditor's qualifications for any job—aside from the possession of basic tools and training—lie outside himself. It is sufficient to explain that he is there simply to assemble such facts as are available about the particular operation. The object of the investigation is to see whether established objectives are being fulfilled and business standards met—and if not, why not.

The operations auditor must learn to work closely with operating personnel. His work forces him to deal more with line personnel than does the work of the financial auditor, who deals more with documents and with accounting and financial personnel who speak the same language as he. The operations auditor must, therefore, if he hopes to make significant and lasting contributions, make a special effort to create a climate of trust. People are usually eager to cooperate once they are sold on the advantages of the audit to their own job performance.

The management of the area being audited knows (subconsciously, at least) that the auditor is looking for inefficiencies and that some can and will be found. The normal defensive attitude resulting from that awareness requires the auditor to tread lightly while he emphasizes the objective nature of his fact gathering and makes sure that operating personnel are fully informed of the results of the audit before the final report is submitted. Little could be worse for the auditor than to attempt to disguise the objective of his work or to misrepresent the point of his inquiries.

REFERENCE

1. Jay Forrester, *Industrial Dynamics* (Cambridge, Mass.: The M.I.T. Press, 1961), p. 1.

4

MAKING THE FINDINGS USEFUL

By its nature, the audit process is bound to uncover many opportunities for improvements with paybacks too small to justify extensive investigation. They should not burden the audit report but be brought directly to the attention of the manager of the unit being audited.

AUDIT MEMOS

Audit memos should be issued at the discretion of the auditor in charge; they are the ideal vehicle for the transmission of information concerning small problems. Care should be taken, however, in arriving at the decision that a problem is "small." Only the opportunities for improvement that have been clearly demonstrated not to be part of a larger problem or not to signify massive failures in control should be put into memos. An example is the need for upgrading a form that does not arise from total lack of a forms control program. Another is the failure of an employee to fully comprehend his responsibilities that does not stem from a general failure to train people properly or from the complete absence of job descriptions. When the need for improvement does stem from a deficiency in control, the subject of an audit memo is likely to be only a facet of a larger problem.

Putting findings into an audit memo often results in discussion with the people affected. Such a discussion requires the auditor to exercise restraint; he is often asked to supply or recommend solutions. He should limit himself to proving the existence of the problem and not get involved in its exact definition. Certainly, he should leave determinations of what to do about the problem to others.

Audit memos can also be used to inform local management of audit progress. It is helpful to give notification at least of reaching the midpoint and approaching the end of an audit. That suggests progress reports to unit management and the need for an exit meeting or debriefing.

EXIT INTERVIEWS

By the end of his field work the auditor will have amassed information that will form the basis of his appraisals and suggestions. The more important of those findings should be discussed with operating personnel in an exit interview. The benefits are reciprocal: local management gets a head start on the problems disclosed and the auditor gets another chance to test his findings. The practice seems to have a common basis. For example, well over 90 percent of companies with internal auditors require them to meet with representatives of the audited organization to review the audit findings. Though similar figures are not available for operations auditors, the picture is probably the same.

The discussion in an exit interview usually centers on a draft of the audit report that has been prepared by the auditor-in-charge before the meeting. Almost always some points of disagreement are uncovered. Conflicting views, when they cannot be resolved through further investigation or redefinition, should always be included in the final report. Most of the companies that have been surveyed on the matter require inclusion of the reactions of the audited organization as well.

An exit interview must be based on complete frankness and free, full discussion. That is another reason why the audit report should be started as soon as the audit is begun—the omission of major findings is thereby minimized. Nevertheless, there is always danger that items likely to appear in the final report will not be brought up at the exit interview. Misunderstandings due to such omissions will be greatly reduced if the first draft of the final report is ready for the conference.

THE FINAL REPORT

The end product of every operations audit is a written report to the company's management. Hence, the entire conduct of the OA engagement must facilitate the production of the final report. As has already been said, the auditor should start writing his final report the day he starts work. The practice has at least four merits.

1. It helps structure the audit by forcing the auditor to develop hypotheses early in the audit and thereby establishing targets and directions for study.

2. The process of writing his findings and conclusions forces the auditor to be more precise in his investigation than he would otherwise be and thereby fosters analysis.

3. Writing on the job avoids the difficult problems of digesting a large mass of material and expressing findings that would occur at the end of a job.

4. Writing the report while doing the job helps minimize the distortions of fact that creep in for psychological, literary, and logical reasons when a report is prepared after the study has been made.

The recommendation that the final report be started early in the assignment implies nothing about the form and content of the report. Both style and what goes into the report depend on the character of the operations audit function and the degree to which report standards have been adopted.

In preparing the report one guideline should be uppermost in the writer's mind: An audit report is advisory and should—in the way it communicates results, in its tone, and in the way it documents the findings—be of the greatest possible assistance to management. Again, the report has the purpose not of laying down recommendations, but of so delivering results that they can be used to measure the value of taking action.

The report writer should also be guided by the need to be factual and the need to write for the persons who will read the report. The first need stems from the fact that operations auditing, far more than financial auditing, requires interpretation of the significance of information and justification of the conclusions drawn. The report should therefore avoid conclusions based on opinion or judgment alone. When an opinion is unavoidable, it should be clearly labeled as one. The second need relates to the fact that the people who are going to receive the report have parochial interests. The language of the report should be appropriate to those interests.

The most general requirement is that the report be lean, clear, and simply worded, but it should not be so honored that the report is too bare. No report can be complete enough to provide the basis of decision making without additional work. Nevertheless, it should contain all the information needed to define its findings clearly, especially those related to deficiencies and opportunities for improvement. (On the other hand, findings about the things that are going well should not be slighted.)

Above all, the conclusions of the report should be presented in a manner that allows management to take proper and timely action. Since the firm's management services, specialists, and internal or outside consultants may be called upon to implement recommendations, the report's accent should be on specific opportunities for cost reduction and results improvement.

The last point to be kept in mind in writing a report is Dr. Lillian M. Gilbreth's dictum that too many operations have been studied in detail that should never have been studied at all. It is fruitless to waste time on protracted analysis of operations, activities, procedures, and so forth that are of low value or are likely to be dropped.

Defense of the report is an almost automatic requirement on two grounds: (1) the realistic recognition that auditors cannot be expected to be error-free, and (2) honest confusion about conclusions presented. So the report should not rely on words alone in describing examples of existing problems or opportunities for improvement. Exhibits in the form of tables, charts, graphs, schedules, and the like should be used liberally. Visual aids play an important part in telling the story to management by revealing the message briefly and simply. It is important to remember that these exhibits are not to be presented for attractiveness, but are to serve either as an explanation of or as a reference to the text of the report.

The writer of an OA report should keep in mind that there is little telling into whose hands the report may come. An audit report is submitted to various levels of management, depending upon the nature of the audit findings and the management level to which the auditor is responsible. But a report often ends up elsewhere, and since each reader tends to interpret an audit differently, depending upon his background, care should be taken to keep the report as objective and neutral in tone as possible. References to persons by name in the body of the report should particularly be avoided.

The final report should not be shown by the operations auditor to personnel other than the manager of the OA unit or those who authorized the audit. As noted previously, the auditor should have discussed his major findings with the operations personnel before leaving the audit, so there is little question of a need for secrecy. In fact, it is the practice in some companies to give the unit audited a chance to rebut the report. (Reynolds Metals, for example, gives management three days to rebut the report.) Even so, *control* of copies of the audit report is very important, and for that reason the final report should not be delivered by the auditor to other than authorized hands.

REPORT FORMAT

The form and content of an operations audit report will, of course, depend on the charter of the OA function in the company and the scope of the audits performed. The value of an audit is, however, critically affected by the way the report is prepared and written. It is even possible to destroy the value of the very best work by poor writing and organization of the audit report.

Standardization of the report format has many benefits. Among other things, it saves time. Most people, auditors included, write poorly and take far too much time on report preparation, and so a standard format simplifies report writing. It also saves time in reading, especially as experience with the format grows. Finally, standardization eases the problem of acceptance of the auditing function. A standard format goes a long way toward offsetting the feeling that scrutiny is directed against "me" or "my unit." It does so by emphasizing the routine nature of the audit.

Here is a format for a report to be accompanied by a letter of transmittal:

Title display. Name of unit audited, date of audit, and number of copy among total number of copies.
Table of contents. Captions of parts, major sections, and appendixes.
Summary of conclusions.
Body of the report. Details in support of each major finding.
Appendix. Supplemental information in the form of backup graphs, charts, and exhibits.

In some enterprises, the format also includes a section that contains the comments of managers in the unit audited, usually those made during the exit interview.

A well-organized report never combines justification of findings with the summary of the findings. Taken together in summary, the findings paint a picture of conditions in the unit that is dulled by coupling each finding with the evidence supporting it. Therefore, in order to sharpen the reader's attention and concentrate it on the findings, the justifications should be given separately.

No operations audit or expression of its findings can be exhaustive. OA is an instrument for searching out major problems and opportunities for improvement, and therefore both audit and report must stop before all the problem and opportunity finding has been done. Since an audit report cannot be complete and still be factual, the auditor will often feel obliged to present findings that are recommendatory in nature, pointing to matters of less than first rank in significance that merit further attention. In the authors' opinion, that is the only kind of recommendation the auditor should make.

2

AREAS OF ANALYSIS

Introduction

The operations auditor is concerned with the evaluation of both general and specific activities in the company being audited. General activities run from one end of the firm to the other without regard for organizational boundaries. Typical examples are administration, systems and procedures, and communications. Specific activities serve limited purposes and are unique to individual organizational units. Typical examples are purchasing, engineering, and quality control.

Of course, evaluation of the two kinds of activities cannot really be separated. General activities will always be found in specific areas, and specific activities powerfully affect what happens in the business generally. And although an auditor must almost always work in parts of the total, he cannot think in parts. Every organizational entity and process is a part or expression of a dynamism that must be dealt with as the complex entity it is.

Some of the areas of interest to the auditor are treated in this part of the book; they are representatives of activities that lend themselves to auditing. The treatments do not exhaust their subjects nor do they view their subjects from traditional perspectives. Their aim is not to serve as condensed technical treatises for the guidance of area practitioners, but to help auditors who are inexpert in a given field learn something about audit entrance points and opportunities. Finally, the fields described are not necessarily identical with or similar to traditional business functions or organizational units. For example, the principal thrust in auditing the constellation of activities associated with personnel is to see how well manpower is being utilized rather than to measure the effectiveness of a personnel department. Recognition of the distinction has vital bearing on how the audit is conducted.

Part 3, which contains questionnaires, is designed to parallel Part 2, and so its classifications also are arbitrary and have a fair amount of overlap. The chapter on personnel, for example, covers some aspects of personnel development, as does the section on research and renewal. That is to be expected, and undue effort was not exercised to attain rigid separation.

5

ADMINISTRATION
AND MANAGEMENT

The whole of this book, in one way or another, deals with administration and management. This section will treat the two as one process (generally under the term management). The process will be treated as an identifiable segment of the total behavior of every firm.

Each company must have a function, which we will call management, whose primary and unique responsibility is to provide direction and coordination and set the guidelines within which economic progress can be made. The quality of management is the prime determinant of the profit effectiveness of the company. Management reaches through all aspects and to all units of the firm; it must be performed for the company as a whole and for each part according to the needs of the company.

Though in one sense an operations audit is always a measure of the whole management process, it is unlikely that the operations auditor will ever be privileged to evaluate the effectiveness of management in total. For example, there is little possibility that an operations auditor will ever be asked to audit the activities of his own top management. For one thing, though there is growing agreement that top management must be held accountable, the means by which such accountability should be measured are still open to discussion. For another, when top management accepts any judgment of its performance at all, it usually accepts it from peer or superior groups only—from executive committees, committees of the board, and so forth.

IMPORTANCE OF A SOUND DEFINITION
The word "management," in one part of speech or the other, has become one of the commonest expressions in business literature, but its meaning is still not well understood. For the purposes of operations auditing, however, possession of a sound concept of management is vital. Unfortunately, it is not easy to develop.

Areas of Analysis

Lyndall F. Urwick concentrates on management from the task viewpoint. As he sees it, the work of management starts with studying the task and getting individual adjustment to it. Study involves such techniques as time and motion analysis and market and customer research. Individual adjustment involves selecting, developing, and motivating personnel. Tasks must also be arranged and coordinated by forecasting, planning, organizing, directing, controlling, communicating, and the other functions necessary in a particular industry and enterprise. Finally, Urwick sees management as responsible for motivating and directing functional groups by policy determination, executive appointments, allocation of authority and responsibility, and establishment of the right mix of power, duties, discipline, morale, and informality.

Henry Fayol took the functional approach; he was one of the first to point out that management consists in planning, organizing, commanding, coordinating, and controlling. Since his day, names of the functions have changed, but the functional approach is still the most popular one. Not one of the functions is a true entity, however; no single management function can be completely independent of the others. Instead, management emerges from the interaction of all its functions. Terms are useful for the purposes of classification, and they do contribute something to understanding of management. But by themselves, the functional terms fail to describe management as the dynamic process it essentially is. Nevertheless, there is some advantage to thinking of distinctive functions within the management process, particularly to the end of analyzing and directing attention to specific aspects of management problems.

Whichever approach is adopted, effective management in every situation deals with common elements:

Resources. Materials, facilities, equipment, finances, and time adequately balanced with human resources to achieve desired results at minimum cost.

Men. Carefully chosen, adequately trained, suitably placed, and efficiently used, each charged with clear responsibilities and given matching authority.

Organization. Simple and direct as possible; each job and relationship designed to accomplish a given kind and amount of work.

Objectives. Motivating, adequate, and realistic, providing a sound basis for planning and for developing a sense of direction.

Information. First rate in quality, sufficient in type and quantity for all needs, and available to all who need it at costs related to its usefulness.

Systems. Well-written, widely circulated, and up-to-date policies, rules, regulations, procedures, and other devices serving to create common understanding, uniformity of action, and stability of operations.

Measures. Unobtrusive and repetitive readings taken of all major flows, operations, and personal performances for the ready detection of malfunctioning.

Controls. Exercised at vital points, enforceable and enforced, considerate of resources *and* feelings, based on plans and objectives, and operating to conserve the vigor and survival capacity of the enterprise.

That is admittedly a primitive list but each element in it provides the auditor with a discrete and important field for analysis.

DYNAMIC CHARACTER OF MANAGEMENT

Management is undergoing and will continue to undergo changes for reason of the changes taking place in the world:

1. Rising rate of world industrialization.
2. Rising educational level of workers (in the West, at least).
3. Rising levels of automation.
4. Increasing security of workers: rising personal savings, full or close-to-full employment, unemployment compensation, Social Security, Civil Service laws, union contracts, health and life insurance, and annuities.
5. Increasing demand for satisfaction in work.
6. Growing communications network.
7. Growing research in motivation and productivity.
8. Declining labor content: rising first-employment age, earlier retirement age, longer vacations, sabbaticals, rising use of shorter working days.
9. Increasing stability of national economies.
10. Increasing governmental intervention in business affairs.
11. Rising demand for goods and services.
12. Rising labor cost and mobility.

The list is far from complete. Any businessman can think of items to add to it, such as the increasing use of mathematics in problem solving and the rapidly improving education of professional managers.

MEASURES OF QUALITY

The auditor will do well to remember that, despite its critical importance to corporate performance, management is secondary to the purposes for which the company was organized. It should be as small in scale and as low in cost as possible, but many companies are run as if they exist only to be managed and many managers behave as if managerial effort were more important than getting the right product into the right hands at the right time and at the right cost.

Competent management, as good children were once described, is seen but not heard. In the well-run company, administrative activity is an integrated whole that is "conspicuous" by its quiet and modest operating ways. In poorly run companies, on the other hand, management is characterized by the clamor and feverishness of constant crises and emergencies that it both causes and is the victim of.

Beyond the cardinal measure of the bottom line on the income statement, there are three rule-of-thumb indicators of administrative quality:

1. Ratio of administrative managers to total personnel.
2. Ratio of administrative decisions made personally to total administrative decision burden.
3. Timeliness of the decisions provided.

As to measure 1, the most obvious sign of company health is the comparative smallness of the administrative group. No employees are more expensive than managers, and although ratio 1 is here expressed in people, it is more commonly expressed in dollars. That is not to imply there must be no knowledge redundancy. A company that does not provide for adequate succession in critical areas of activity will be severely affected by the loss of a key executive.

With respect to measure 2, the size of the ratio between decisions made personally and those made in total is determined by (1) how good a job has been done in converting repetitive decision requirements into policies, regulations, and procedures and (2) how far management has gone in eliminating false problems. No decision requirement should arise more than a few times before it is considered for proceduralization, but no procedure should be established until the problems it has been designed to cover have been tested for reality.

Many imposing, seemingly real problems are not what they appear to be or are not intrinsic to the affairs of the company. Every business has two kinds of problems: those that are necessary—the real ones—and those that are not—the false ones. The relative proportions of the two are a measure of a company's condition; a healthy business has mostly real problems. Every executive should ask himself whether the problem he is dealing with is genuine or not. And although almost every business executive will agree that one of his important functions is to improve productivity by eliminating waste, it is amazing how many executives waste time in solving problems that shouldn't exist in the first place.

Perhaps a main reason why executives work on the wrong problems is that they measure their value by the number of problems they can handle in a given amount of time; the greater the number the better the job. The wise executive measures his effectiveness by the number of problems he does not have to solve. Whereas the ineffective executive spends a good deal of his time dealing with problems, the effective executive spends most of his time preventing problems from arising. There is a fair chance that when a company has a high-volume problem solver, it may also have a real trouble-maker on its hands.

Another reason why managers waste time dealing with unnecessary problems is that they have not learned their managerial ABC's. The metaphor is not inappropriate. Many managers are not aware that the fewest number of business problems (A problems) cause the greatest amount of loss in dollars, hours, or units and the greatest number of problems (C problems) cause the smallest losses and are usually not worth the effort to cure.

To do his job properly, the manager must be able to recognize which problems he should solve and which he should sidestep. There are many tests of the "value" of a given problem, but the best one is to ask if solving the problem will make any difference in the company's asset, profit, or market position. If the answer is no, ask a second question: If nothing is done now, will the problem disappear for good? If the answer is yes, forget the problem. If the answer is no, ask a third question: What will be needed to keep the problem from arising again? If the answer is that move x or y will eliminate the problem permanently, make the move or moves. If nothing can be done to keep the problem from arising again, you're right back where you started; you've got a problem that must be dealt with.

The real problems of a company are always in some manner the consequence of the business the company is in; they arise, for example, from the necessities of meeting price and product competition, of securing properly skilled workers, and of buying essential material at lowest cost. The false problems are almost always in some manner the consequence of poor management. If management is, among other things, the systematic practice of economy of means, it follows that manpower must be treated as economically as the other resources of the business. The key to using management manpower efficiently is to see that it works primarily on necessary problems. That means that every business should do what is necessary to find, identify, and root out the false problems that waste its executives' time.

As to point 3, decision timeliness is a good criterion of administrative quality because it is easily measurable and important. Late decisions are always costly in both economic and human terms. They cause expenditures of excessive time and effort; and whenever they occur on a continuing basis, they cause unrest and morale problems.

ADDITIONAL CRITERIA

To survive, a company must at least:

- ☐ Establish realistic *objectives* for operations.
- ☐ Make enactable *plans* to reach the objectives.
- ☐ Develop *policies* to govern the implementation of plans to insure adherence to the company's intentions.
- ☐ Establish *controls* that cause necessary adjustment to implementation of and alterations in the plans.
- ☐ See to the preparation of *reports* of actual results suitable for evaluating the effectiveness and progress of implementation.

Each of these items should be of considerable interest during every operations audit. Each is closely related to business success, yet each is the object of much confusion and lack of clarity in the executive mind. The following discussion concerns points relating to the items that are worth remembering.

To be effective, the objectives, plans, policies, procedures, and performance reports of a company must be documented and communicated. Therefore, one of the first things an auditor ought to do is ask for copies of those documents. If they prove difficult or impossible to collect, the auditor is well on his way to a major finding.

Unfortunately, when it comes to the provision of clear, well-integrated, and work-saving policies, most companies do an appallingly bad job. They make the same decisions over and over again at higher levels instead of setting up decision guides for lower levels in the form of policies. Effective policies are in large measure distillates of the many private judgments that are part of the collective experience of the company; they are not a sign that top management takes a poor view of private judgment or individual initiative. Quite to the contrary, enlightened managements provide policies because they realize that, when executive power is absorbed in making the same decision over and over, little time is left for experiencing and investigating the new. In effect, companies without policies are captives of the known and therefore the past. In the failure of its decision makers to be free to acquire new experiences lies a mortal danger to the firm.

The maintenance of policies, as well as their establishment, provides a useful basis of auditing inquiry. Policies can be economically productive only so long as they are current. It is important, therefore, that policies be modified or replaced as soon as experience warrants. Alert companies build regular review into their policy statements either by dating them or setting a review date. Generally, policies should be reviewed at least every two years to prevent hardening of administrative arteries.

Policies should also be examined to see if they are of economic consequence to the firm. They seldom are, and those who are responsible for setting policy must accept the blame. If policies fail to focus attention on profitability, the result will be excessive, stultifying growth in paperwork and communicating. Policies that are not closely tied in with profit planning permit line personnel to operate on their own in the critical areas of the business and greatly diminish the influence of even the best of managers over operations.

PROCEDURES

The bulk of administrative practices issues from carrying out the formal or informal policies of a company. When each policy-related practice is made a standardized procedure, consistency in policy interpretation is insured and the task of administration is considerably simplified. Standard procedures go a long way toward making sure that pertinent information flows to the people who need it and that each person understands what he is to do with it. In addition, standard procedures, when expressive of the policy guidelines established by management, facilitate control of business operations.

It is easier to tell an employee his responsibilities and authorities than to inform him in writing, but it is also riskier. Oral descriptions lead to errors; and when they have to do with any form of automated activity, those errors can multiply beyond belief. Crude as it sounds, the purpose of establishing procedures is to reduce to a minimum interpretations of agreements reached or guessing about repetitive events or items open to interpretation.

Because the importance of providing procedures is well recognized, the auditor will usually not have to spend a great deal of time in finding out whether existing procedures are adequate in coverage, well designed, and appropriate to the unit's circumstances. More difficult will be the determination whether procedures are provided in a timely and understandable fashion. Efforts taken to provide procedures at the outset of activities will spare a great deal of trouble later. Further, procedures should be written from the viewpoint of the users rather than in the language of technical writers, as they so often are. Also, the auditor should check to see how well procedural statements are distributed. No man who has occasion to use the statements should be without ready access to them. Too often, procedures are not established until late in the life of an activity.

To summarize, system, method, rules, regulations, plans, policies, and procedures are absolute requirements in the enterprise; for they are the basis of order, uniformity, and stability. Procedures should be provided to insure consistent interpretation of policy. That eliminates the need to make the same decisions over and over and leaves more time for creative planning, thoughtful analysis, and productive effort.

In routinizing everything possible there is, however, danger as well as benefit. In setting up routines it is possible to repress and prevent action. Then frustration, regimentation, and ultimately failure result. The machine of enterprise requires a functional design that satisfies both the need for *order* and the need for *progress*. In short, the cogs must serve man, not man the cogs!

6

PLANS AND PLANNING

"Plan" is a common word in the managerial vocabulary; and that it is used so often creates the impression that the concepts it involves are clearly and widely understood. The facts are to the contrary. Understanding and application of planning concepts are such that effective business planning is almost as rare as the American bald eagle.

Planning is badly done in most companies mainly because few people know much about it (as a definite activity it is less than 100 years old) and because it stands in the way of willfulness and private interests (which are more common in top managerial ranks than is generally recognized). Nevertheless, because of the work of a few dedicated managers, planning technology has had exceptional growth in scope and application in recent years. It may well be that the most memorable accomplishment of some companies in this decade is the progress they have made in converting planning into an operationally useful management tool. In most companies, however, corporate planning produces little more than after-the-fact measures of how far results exceeded or fell short of established targets.

Skilled planning is rapidly becoming a significant competitive factor and is on its way to becoming a crucial one. That rate of progress will undoubtedly accelerate as management practice continues to mature, with the result that the gap between the few companies that plan well and the many companies that simply engage in wishful thinking is bound to grow.

The following statement will be useful to the operations auditor: Planning is a commitment to action on an orderly, realistic, systematic basis; it is a reasoned choice of courses of action. The statement has the virtue of making it clear that planning is a process of relating conceptual phases in an orderly fashion. In the absence of a simple, singular definition, the statement by Norbert Weiner, the father of cybernetics, is useful: "Life is made up of patterns—thus it is comprehensible. Business must have pattern—else it is irrational and not experienced!"[1]

BENEFITS OF PLANNING
The function of planning in business has many definable characteristics. Planning is an economic and motivational necessity, the beginning of order,

and a form of decision making. It is aimed at designing tomorrow, and it is a call for action. Also, it is a commitment of resources derived from larger objectives and aimed at attainable goals. Other characteristics that can be added, such as that planning has the mission of improvement, must be acceptable to employees, and requires matching controls, are either less important than, or are part of, the ones cited earlier.

The benefits of planning are that it:

Focuses action.
Reduces risk.
Reinforces objectives.
Simplifies coordination.
Facilitates control.
Creates new opportunities.
Vitalizes organization.

Again the benefits are manifold, but none are more important than these.

DEFICIENCIES AND LIMITATIONS

Since good planning is so essential, effective managements have spared no effort to develop procedures that turn out operationally useful plans. That is not to say that all the problems that can still bedevil planning efforts have been solved. The following are the prime deficiencies in the planning process today:

1. Planning often suffers from lack of genuine top-level interest and support.

2. The degree of involvement needed frequently leads to executive avoidance and consequent dilution of the quality of the planning process.

3. The actual work of building the plan is often left to subordinates who usually are comparatively inexperienced and formalistic.

4. Planning is more often done for the approvers than for the doers.

5. Planning done by headquarters usually reflects top management's views but seldom is realistic to the people in the field who have to carry out the actions called for.

6. Planning is usually conservative, with the result that opportunities are seldom fully exploited and the firm is seldom committed to targets that extend it.

7. Planning too often is rich in relevant information but poor in resources for critically evaluating projections and assumptions.

8. The process becomes traditional or habitual, with the result that it responds more to philosophy or perspective than to economic or market opportunities.

9. Plans are too general; they have insufficient detail to permit the establishment of selective controls.

Plans, like all tools, have natural limitations. It is not always possible to plan effectively in all areas that could benefit from planning. Reasons why plans cannot, or perhaps should not, be formulated are:

☐ The future is not sufficiently determinable.
☐ The cost of planning is not justified by the results attainable.

☐ Planning diverts too much time needed elsewhere.

☐ Plans limit flexibility.

☐ Organizational inertia is sometimes greater than the rate of changes called for by the plan.

☐ Plans call for courses of action that limit initiative.

☐ Personnel may not always be available to implement plans.

TEN MEASURES OF A PLAN'S WORTH

Perhaps the most important thing to know about planning—after the fact that it is a business necessity—is that all plans cause change whether or not they have been designed to bring it about. Plans that are designed to keep things the same inevitably produce change because, among other things, they activate the machinery of control. Hence, plans always produce change of some kind, sought or unsought.

That point, so simple and unimposing, holds powerful implications for business planners: (1) If you want to keep things exactly as they are, leave them alone. (2) Unless you know exactly the kind of changes you want, don't bother to plan. If you ignore those two injunctions, you will lose what you want to keep and become enmeshed in changes for which you are not prepared. It may be said, therefore, that the first measure of the worth of a plan is that it calls for change. In companies that do not plan to change and do not change as planned, no planning worthy of the name takes place.

The second measure of the worth of the plan lies in the kind of change it seeks. A worthwhile plan always aims at a particular kind of change—the improving of results. No other plan justifies the necessary, and always considerable, effort and expense.

In determining the kind of changes that are worthy of being planned, one starting place is the choices available. In a competitive world a business has three choices: it can do nothing and die, it can merely adapt and limp along, or it can innovate and prosper. The third choice is, of course, the only worthwhile one and the one most managers espouse. But it is astonishing to see the number of companies that reflect only the first two choices in their actions—among them are prominent companies with sound reputations.

Innovation is not necessarily a means of improving performance; it is not an unalloyed competence. In an environment in which it is not controlled, it can be as damaging as it can be beneficial. Just as gold in his pockets can purchase a man's wants in a city or drown him in a sea, so innovation can lead to business prosperity or extinction. There is therefore a need for an instrument with which the creative process (which tends to overreach, be irrelevant, or be insufficiently detailed) can be tamed and made applicable. Planning has arisen specifically in response to that need.

Because the improving of results is the only kind of change it should pursue, planning can be regarded as the process through which the generation, protection, and amplification of profits are systematized. It is such a process because of its special ability to introduce change in an orderly, systematic, and practical fashion.

What constitutes an improvement in business can be determined only on a dollar basis. However we view it, business is an economic enterprise, an activity whose existence and survival are predicated in terms of least cost. Hence, the third measure of a plan's worth lies in the values with which it is connected. A sound plan always leads to the production of a significant number of added dollars, profits, or savings.

That point touches on the fact that plans should be formed only when they are necessary. That, oddly enough, leads to a good deal of confusion, because one man's necessity is frequently another man's luxury. Necessity for planning, more often than not, is based on vague or highly subjective considerations. It is given a solid foundation, however, when it is based on dollars in the form of savings or profits. Necessity, so construed, naturally focuses attention on repetitive, high-unit-cost events and major opportunities for improvement, including exploitation of events occurring outside the company.

If one measure of the worth of a plan is the values with which the plan is concerned, another is the plan's cost. Every plan, regardless of the values at which it aims, has a minimum cost of production. A sound plan is one whose cost is well below the dollar amount it aims at producing. A fourth measure of the worth of a plan is the kind of dollars the plan uses or aims for. A good plan never uses resources more badly needed for other purposes, no matter what the plan costs. In other words, good plans never commit the company to smaller risks while larger risks go untended. For example, a plan to enlarge shipping facilities cannot be a good one when the company's market is going to hell and there is no plan to improve it.

Of course, not all risks can be seen or correctly assessed, and planning is limited to dealing with the risks that it can identify and do something about. Accordingly, plans must be laid with the recognition that the stakes in dealing with risks often run higher than predicted. Survival of the company is the highest of all stakes, and sound planning never puts it forward except when the clear alternative is business extinction.

The fifth measure of the worth of a plan is the degree to which the changes it calls for tie in with the changes called for by other plans of the company. A worthwhile plan always dovetails with other corporate plans, and the prime benefit is that resources, objectives, and activities are brought closer together.

Probably no quality of effective planning is more important to an enterprise than integrative capacity. That companies are beginning to recognize this is shown by a growing tendency to plan for the corporation as a whole rather than for divisions, departments, or subunits and to put planning in the hands of specialists. Further evidence is the fact that demarcations between short- and long-term plans are becoming progressively less distinctive. An interesting result is the relating of budgets to long-range intentions rather than current need.

These points highlight the fact that business planning is essentially hierarchical; each plan ought to be formed within the framework of a larger one. That means organizationally that the plans for each unit should be laid within the plans of larger units or as the framework of smaller units. It means managerially that the plans of each manager should be closely linked to those of his supervisors and his subordinates. It means administratively that tactical plans should mesh with strategic plans and unit plans fit with mission plans. Thus, a real test of the worth of a plan is the connection it has with other plans. A plan that has no connection with other plans is worthless.

Identification of the kind of change that justifies a plan is fostered by recognition of the fact that companies cannot safely leave the reaching of their markets to chance. A can of beans eaten is an appetite filled; a suit of clothes sold is a period of wearing lost; empty seats in a plane taking off are gone forever. The company that has not crystallized its intentions and embodied them in a plan before the foodstuffs are eaten, the clothes put on, the plane's door closed, loses out.

The sixth measure of the worth of a plan, therefore, lies in its scope. Effective business plans always have influence beyond the units in which they originate; they always affect primary business functions. Speaking simply, effective plans always reach out and make themselves felt at the company-customer interface. Progressive companies recognize that and spare no effort to make their plans useful at the operational level. No pie in the sky for them. Wherever in the enterprise the changes called for by the company's plans are designed to be made, the effects of good plans will be felt—somewhere, somehow—in the company's marketplace.

But although a sound plan reaches across organizational lines, it does not do so by spreading like a fog. A good plan has laser-like qualities; it pinpoints its intended accomplishment. Therefore, the seventh measure of the worth of a plan lies in its focus.

That is far from an academic or self-evident point; it clearly spells the difference between a plan and a hope. It reminds us that plans are poor devices for creating general conditions and for dealing with broad organizational aspects such as attitudes, morale, and climates. Such characteristics are, without question, deeply influenced by the kind of planning a company does. But they are not fit objectives of the planning process because their relationships to productivity cannot be clearly seen, much less described. The objectives of good plans, on the other hand, can always be defined in one sentence.

The eighth measure of the worth of a plan lies in the resources allocated to it, including the assignment of personnel responsible for implementing it. A plan is more than a statement of intentions; *it is a commitment to action*. And, of course, actions cannot be taken without using resources. Therefore, no plan is complete without a coupling of assets. In other words, determining "where we are going" (strategic planning) is a waste without determining "how we will get there" (tactical planning). Typical business plans fall so far short of this standard that they are only daydreams.

The surest sign of a bad plan is a negative answer to the question, "How much money, time, and materials have been set aside for this plan?" A bad plan is a sales quota that is not coupled with money allotted to customer or salesman development, a budget that does not have an associated sum for insuring that it is followed, a market venture without funds to support the missionary or penetration period, a control designed without the naming of a controller. A respectable plan always specifies what will be used, when, and by whom to bring about the results the plan calls for.

The committing of resources is a test as well as a characteristic of a good plan. One of the best ways to check the practicability of a plan is to ask, "How do we get where we say we want to go?" Manifestly, when the answer is "Don't know" or "Can't tell you," the plan ought to be redesigned or dropped.

The ninth measure of a plan lies in the stuff of which it is made. A sound plan is always constructed out of factual information. When we think of planning, qualities of imagination, ambition, creative thinking, and optimism spring to mind, nor can their necessity in planning be questioned. Less frequently, however, do we recognize the equally vital planning element—knowledge—without which planning becomes an exercise in speculation. And in this connection, we are talking about not only knowledge upon which to base plans, but also knowledge of how to use knowledge in the planning process.

One view of the manager is that he is a fellow who makes things happen. That is fair enough if we also understand that he makes things happen because he (1) is not satisfied with present results, (2) intends to improve on them, and (3) works systematically to implement the intention. Adding 1, 2, and 3 to the preceding definition immediately makes the manager the employer of knowledge. The manager is a person who makes things happen because he knows recent performance, knows wherein improvement is possible, knows the means available for making improvement, and knows the benefits likely to flow from using the means. The manager who makes things happen in the interest of the company has considerable knowledge of the state of his company, the general economy, and the discipline of management.

Because the manager is an intensive user of knowledge, such knowledge-amplifying tools as mathematical techniques, econometric models, and computers are being increasingly employed in planning—especially in such areas as forecasting, facilities planning, plant location, distribution, production planning, marketing profitability analysis, and determination of alternative investment choices. Evidence to that effect is the fact that many companies are discarding objectives by edict in favor of goals arrived at by deduction and analysis.

Knowledge of how to use knowledge in the planning process is a subject that could fill a book, but it can be summarized in a few general propositions. Meaningful planning:

- [ ] Begins with knowledge of the present position, condition, and opportunities of the business.
- [ ] Proceeds with the knowledge that most available information is historical and probabilistic.
- [ ] Takes place with the knowledge that not all risks can be foreseen.
- [ ] Is tempered by the knowledge that costs permit the use only of truly relevant information.
- [ ] Is facilitated by the knowledge that human experience and judgmental capacity can be productive sources of planning input.
- [ ] Is refined by the knowledge that basing a plan on facts does not necessarily make it workable.

Some of these points are self-evident, others less so. Take, for example, the point about costs and information relevance. The successful planner knows that because the volume of information usable in planning is so enormous, no company can afford to assemble and analyze all the information related to the aims of the company. The planner, in short, must choose and use information selectively.

Because the costs of information can, under the impact of stepped-up planning activities, easily get out of hand, progressive companies are striving to cut back their information requirements. Companies already skilled in planning are limiting their planning to areas most in need of change and reducing the time span covered by each plan. In those companies emphasis has moved from planning for functional areas to broader business planning (for example, for products, markets, profits, and investments), and the period of time covered by typical plans has been shortened.

The tenth measure of the worth of a plan lies in the degree to which it arises out of deliberate, controlled effort. A sound plan is never a gratuitous event; it is the result of calculated intentions operating through the agency of skillfully designed procedures.

A main reason why the cost of planning has received so little attention is that planning has usually been regarded as a nonlinear activity, a unique activity, an activity that ends with the production of a plan. That is a dangerous and costly view. If it is true that business planning is critical to business survival and progress, it is equally true that the planning process must be organized and run as a continuous operation.

Planning also suffers from fuzzy organizational thinking. Because all managers have something to do with the production of plans, planning is often left to somebody else, somewhere else. In other words, planning more often than not is an amorphous function with no organizational focus. That is absurd. True enough, every manager has planning responsibilities, and his work benefits to the degree to which he develops skill in contributing to the building of sound and realistic plans governing his actions and the activities of those he directs. But planning seldom has a chance of success when it takes place outside a system of tight planning procedures followed by persons with precisely defined planning responsibilities. Thus, the idea that every manager should produce the plans affecting his area of cognizance is not necessarily a good one. Generally speaking, planning should be centralized and performed, or at least controlled, by specialists.

Corporate planning is in fact becoming more formal, although less complicated. As noted earlier, planning is becoming increasingly more systematic and strategic—a trend made possible by the establishment of procedures, assignments, and schedules. That the corporate planning office is becoming a common feature in all but the smallest businesses is testimony to the fact that planning is increasingly viewed as a formal and specialist function.

The corporate planning office must not only have an identifiable location but be plugged into well-defined channels of communication as well. In other words, planning must have a clear organizational position fed by prominent informational pipelines. Only when it is richly connected within a soundly engineered communication network can planning function effectively and efficiently. When planning does not occupy such a position, it is uninformed and mute.

INGREDIENTS OF SOUND PLANNING

The ingredients (tools and motives) of planning are wants, information, knowledge, experience, insight, imagination, judgment, ambition, optimism, courage, and realism. On the last point, plans are justified only when they afford better control over the future than mere chance. The following lists suggest the kinds of knowledge that may be needed in planning.

FINANCIAL

Sales volume
Sales trend
Gross profit
Net profit
Profit to sales
Breakeven point
Return on investment
Inventories, aged
Inventory turnover
Profit by product
Per share earnings
Selling cost per sale
Accounts receivable, aged
Accounts receivable turnover
Budget performance
Cash turnover
Product line profitability

PRODUCTION

Costs per unit
Purchasing costs
Cost variance
Standard costs
Production lead time
Production backlog
Overtime costs
National costs
Manufacturing costs
Value analysis
Shipping costs
Labor performance
Labor availability

MARKETING

Economic trends
National sales volume
Competitor products
Competitor practices
Competitive pricing
New products
Sales cost per salesman
Frequency of sales by class of
  customers
Distribution costs
Advertising and promotion costs
Market penetration
Territory penetration

PERSONNEL

Size of workforce
Distribution of workforce by age, ex-
  perience, training
Personnel requirements
Benefits as a percent of compensation
Arbitration costs
Negotiation costs
Training costs
Recruitment costs
Lost time
Ratio of staff to workforce
Retirement forecasts
Personnel turnover
Employee morale

FACILITIES AND EQUIPMENT

Acquisition cost
Gross floor area
Space per person
Area utilization
Construction costs per area
Maintenance costs per area
Book value
Machine capacity
Machine utilization
Age

ADMINISTRATION AND DEVELOPMENT

Total administration costs
Administration cost as percent of sales
Ratio of administrative to production
  force
New methods
Communication costs
Employee attitudes
Corporate image
Total R&D cost
R&D cost trends

In reviewing the planning function, the operations auditor must sooner or later take into consideration corporate objectives. Though it is generally well recognized that successful performance in the enterprise begins with the setting of objectives, the designated targets, goals, and aims to be reached in most instances fall short of their purpose, because in establishing goals and setting up objectives most executives end the job there. They fail to carry the job to completion. They fail to see that much more is required than merely deciding where "we want to be by the year x" or what "we want to look like in 1982."

The job of setting attainable objectives begins with two things: an idea or ideas about the business and an assemblage of factual information relating to the idea or ideas. Probably no observation about business is more true than the one that holds that the mainspring of enterprise is an idea. In every going, healthy business there is one factor at work that overshadows all others—the factor of powerful, mutually reinforcing ideas. Behind the founding and building in competitive society of any successful enterprise there has been a prime mover in the form of an idea or group of ideas so overpowering that no contrary idea could survive. The idea or group of ideas commanded obedience, impregnated the functions of the enterprise, and annihilated all contradictory ideas. Ford (low-cost, high-volume manufacturing), IBM (lower information unit costs), Litton (systematic entrepreneurship), GENESCO (specialization in everything to wear)—each is an example of a company arising out of and so far sustained by a compelling idea or group of related ideas. When any of these companies faltered on their way to becoming the giants of their kind they are now, it was because some contrary, unintegrated idea took root and began to flourish, as when Henry Ford confused product stabilization with competitive efficiency.

That businesses are built and sustained by compelling ideas is a popular notion. But one seldom sees it in operation; that is, recognition of the notion seldom goes beyond lip service. Very few managers ever in their lifetimes engage in searching out and putting to work the massive, life-giving ideas appropriate to their businesses.

Yet nothing contributes more to the building of corporate strength than identifying and giving force to the ideas capable of dominating the energies of men. Companies without such ideas are like medieval clocks without springs. Gears only transmit power; they do not generate it.

The most commonly employed measure of business success in a free economy is sheer survival, but business continuity is not necessarily a sign of health. Remaining in business is usually taken as evidence that a company is fundamentally sound, that none of its ailments is deadly to continuance in business. That view is invalid, because every business has capital, product, or market momentum that can keep it going a remarkably long time, even when it is dying. Products continue to sell though their heyday is passed; salesmen continue to book orders though prices are out of line; profits continue to be shown though investment is not paying off. Many of the signs normally taken to be those of success continue to be shown by companies that are no longer competing healthily.

The best assurance of business health lies not in material assets such as capital, plant, or produce—although these are the gears of the enterprise—but in the driving force of ideas that direct the energies of the enterprise in the direction of clearly defined targets. These ideas, characterized primarily by the fact that they direct behavior, are called values. The word "value," in turn, connotes compelling belief, which itself is a useful idea because a business—no less than a man—needs beliefs and convictions in order to live successfully.

Ideas, to be compelling, must have breadth and scale. Compelling ideas are not small things, and for that reason they must be rarities. Neither men nor companies can be motivated simultaneously by a wide range of stimuli. Persons simultaneously driven by hunger and sex end up starving and unloved!

Hence, for each of the major functions or action areas of the business one and only one value should be established. For the business as a whole one central idea is usually sufficient to create understanding; if it is truly compelling, it is enough to support its purpose in life. Some measure of the truth of that statement is contained in some of the mottoes now being promoted by major companies: "Progress is our most important product" (GE), "You can be sure if it's Westinghouse," "Quality goes in before the name goes on" (Zenith). These are not public relations gimmicks; they are recognitions of the need to create compelling and easily understood ideas about their companies in the minds of employees, stockholders, and the general public.

What more is required to make the setting of objectives meaningful and productive? The answer is that sound management has unity, continuity, and consistency. Merely setting objectives does nothing to promote those qualities. In fact, failure to do more destroys the essential harmony.

Let's look at it this way. An army convoy made up of jeeps, amtracs, and tank carriers has a given objective—town x. Jeeps can go by the most direct route, straight through villages and cities, because they are small and make little noise. Amtracs, on the other hand, must take a different route because they are noisy and disruptive of traffic. Tank carriers have to go by yet another route, one that has bridges strong enough to carry their weight. Will the convoy arrive at its given destination if the lead jeep contains the man—*and the only man*—who knows the destination?

As our analogy illustrates, it is not enough to *develop* sound objectives. The objectives, once established, must be so communicated and so divided that every member of the enterprise has his share of them in the form of subobjectives. In other words, objectives should be looked upon as an elected job of work that, to be done, must be apportioned to each unit and individual in the whole organization. Therefore, each manager has the responsibility of knowing what his share of the work is and, in turn, giving to each of his subordinates an understanding of what his share is. All business planning is hierarchical, which means that each organizational unit must plan within the framework of the plans of the larger units and as the framework of the plans of smaller units.

GUIDES TO EFFECTIVE PLANNING

Planning is a managerial function that too often is left to somebody else or to specialists. Every manager has planning responsibilities. His work will benefit to the degree that he develops skill in constructing sound and realistic plans that will govern both his activities and those of the people he directs. The following are some tips for effective planning.

1. Planning *shapes the future;* it must not be a case of simply being in tune with the times. Had Henry Ford followed the advice of pundits, he would have remained in the bicycle business instead of remaking America. Planning that is a mere adaptation to trends or to forecasts of the future is dangerous because it does not make full use of the creative elements within the company.

2. Effective plans are *company-centered;* they are based on considerations applying to and arising within one company and no other.

3. Plans issue from *central ideas.* The worth of a plan derives as much from the ideas held about the business as from the target of the plan itself.

4. Good plans *have positive goals;* they always aim at creating something rather than stopping something. For example, a good plan does not seek to put an end to machine idleness; it tries to raise utilization to levels of profitability. Negative plans cost more to implement and control than positive ones because they fail to capture the interest of those whose work is affected.

5. Sound planning *is based on careful appraisal;* vital to it are knowledge of company needs, the probability of reaching a given objective, and the cost of attaining that objective. That is not to say that plans should be laid only to achieve objectives that are certain of attainment and are reachable at low cost. On the contrary, some needs are so pressing that there is little choice but to take risks at high cost. The real point is that, before he commits the company, the skilled planner knows both the odds for and against a course of action and how badly the action is needed.

6. Plans call for *specific results.* Since plans should be aimed at the attainment of given results, the results sought must be specific. Numerical relationships are especially desirable; when they are lacking, the desired results must be carefully described. When it proves difficult or impossible to state exactly what results are sought, take another look at the necessity for the plan. There may not be any.

7. A plan has a *timetable.* Every business is an economic enterprise, from which it follows that its principal terms are rates, productivity, and other words defining units in time. It is not enough that plans stimulate results; they must stipulate by when. It is also useful to have checkpoints so designated that progress in attaining results can be monitored.

8. A sound plan *identifies the executor.* The surest way to achieve the results sought by planning is to assign responsibility for results to one man. That is not as simple as it sounds; it forces planners to deal with many questions besides immediate objectives. There will be times, therefore, when planning will prove impractical, even when objectives seem realistic and attainable, because secondary considerations make them uneconomical or too disruptive to organize.

9. The plan must lay the *basis of control;* only that should be planned which can be controlled. This is a broader and looser requirement than the others, but it is no less vital. When unacceptable or excessive deviations cannot be corrected or the corrections cannot be enforced, planning is a waste of effort. Part of the planning job is therefore consideration of the types and extent of controls required for the plan's realization.

Probably no injunction holds greater implications for the planning process than this one from Senator J. W. Fulbright, as quoted in *The New York Times:*

> Maturity means the acceptance of permanent responsibilities of continuing tasks, or enterprises that advance imperceptibly toward fruition with neither climax nor completion. It means ambiguity when we would prefer precision, tedious labor when we would prefer dramatic action, infinite patience when we would prefer immediate rewards. Above all, maturity requires a final accommodation between our aspirations and our limitations.

This quotation points up the fact that the man who continues to aspire in a world full of limitations is a worthy man indeed. But it is the man who expresses his aspirations in a selected, detailed, and scheduled way—that is, in plans—who does best in coping with the limitations of the world.

REFERENCE

1. Norbert Wiener, *Cybernetics,* 2d ed. (New York: John Wiley & Sons, Inc., 1961).

7

CONTROLS
AND CONTROLLING

No single function exemplifies the spirit of modern management more than control; in fact, the efficient fulfillment of business objectives and needs stems directly from its exercise. But although control is recognized to be an absolute prerequisite to the achievement of results, it is actually as little understood as its function is familiar.

The main facts about controls are these: effective accomplishment demands effective controls, few companies have even a faint notion of what their controls cost and what they produce, and even fewer companies know how to design controls properly. Controls are taken too much for granted. Because they are necessary to accomplishment, they are thought to be fixed requirements that offer few, if any, cost alternatives. That view is usually the first block laid in the foundation of many business failures.

Control began to emerge as a distinctive subdiscipline within management in the last half of the nineteenth century. Henry Fayol was among the first to put his finger on its essence:[1]

> Control is the examination of results. To control is to make sure that all operations at all times are carried out in accordance with the plan adopted, with the orders given, and the principles laid down. Control compares, discusses and criticizes. It tends to stimulate planning, to simplify and strengthen organization, to increase efficiency of command and to facilitate coordination.

For operations auditing purposes, a control is action taken to make sure that plans happen. More exactly, control is established and exercised when significant deviations from planned occurrence are systematically and directly detected and corrected. A much better definition is that a control is an environmental element that operates on feedback falling outside the standards established within the parameters of the objectives sought.

Each of these definitions implies at least two things: (1) controls have no life of their own and (2) they are future-oriented. Controls are derivative, and as such they are transient and impermanent. Controls are future-shaping devices, and as such they operate according to views of what tomorrow can and should bring.

MISCONCEPTIONS

The primary misconception associated with the control function is that, because it is essential to successful accomplishment, its costs are unavoidable and therefore are not to be counted. The truth of the matter is that both the effectiveness and cost of controls vary greatly and seldom in direct proportion. Some companies have good controls at least cost; others have poor controls at maximum cost; and there is every possible combination in between.

Business control and the cost of doing business have powerful relationships. The costs of control are always among the heaviest incurred by any business, and they can damage the best of businesses unless they too are controlled. Though it makes little sense to have controls that do not return at least their cost, many such exist simply because the relationship between costs and savings is not known. An example is a company that spends $10,000 to catch a thousand $2 losses and so has to sell $50,000 worth of goods at 20 percent gross margin to support a control that produces savings worth only one-fifth of its costs. The company that knows the costs of its controls, and uses that knowledge, has a competitive advantage equal to the best.

A major misconception is that control is aimed primarily at keeping things from happening—preventing theft of finished goods, keeping unbudgeted funds from being spent, or restricting the use of vehicles to company purposes. The worry behind that view cannot be ignored, but it is often based on erroneous assumptions about potential losses. Take, as an example, the accounts receivable area. Companies frequently have invoices checked by a second employee after they have originally been typed or prepared by a clerk because it is believed that customers will report only the errors made against them and never those made against the company. Actual study may show that errors are made randomly, that is, as often for as against the company, in which case the number of complaints received from customers can be used as a test of the accuracy of invoice preparation and invoice verification can be dropped until complaints disclose the need for procedural change.

The real purpose of control is to make things happen—to raise the profitability of a product, to achieve an objective within budgeted cost, or to move into a new market successfully. The point is not academic. Controls that do not have a positive purpose, that are repressive, and that do not appear to support the higher aims of the business invite evasion by employees. Controls that invite evasion can lead to a false sense of security, which in turn can lead to decisions that have disastrous consequences. In plain language, many controls, because they are negative, lead to greater losses than would occur if they didn't exist. The chances are good that the auditor can find examples in the company he is in now.

Another source of problems is that controls are often isolated from other functions of the business. That is a major error. *Effective* controls cannot exist in isolation. When they contribute to a business, it is because they are vitally linked with other functions such as planning and directing.

RELATIONSHIP TO PLANS

Plans have an especially close relationship to controls. Plans are commitments to action. The life and design of controls should therefore be based on the obligation that the commitments will be carried out at the least cost and within the time allocated. Thus, when controls fail, so do plans, and when plans succeed, so do controls.

Controls that are plan oriented have shorter lives than those that are viewed as tools in themselves. One sign of an unhealthy control is long life. It will be very helpful to make a list of the controls in use and put down the dates of their installation. The exercise, when it can be done, is most revealing.

Do not be overawed by controls. They are more simple than the average person thinks, and you already know more about them than you realize. In order to work, controls depend on information that arises out of the activities controlled, the kind of information called feedback. The practical implication is that a control is not an end in itself but is part of a system of some kind. Thus, a control is inseparable from the activity it is set up to govern and acts through comparisons of system output against the performance desired. A familiar example of control based on feedback is the household thermostat. As the heat provided (the plan) rises past a predetermined point (the standard), it activates a thermocouple (the control) that shuts the heat off (the return to plan).

This model reveals a number of facts about controls that can serve as sound guides to the operations auditor's investigation and evaluation of controls:

1. Effective controls use only as much of the primal energy as is needed to assure that the tasks of the activity monitored are accomplished as intended.
2. While they are in force, effective controls are energized continuously but operate infrequently.
3. To operate infrequently, controls must be activated by exceptions only.
4. Exceptions come into being when there have been set sensory thresholds that are exceeded only by the actions that threaten to destroy the objectives.
5. When the activity being monitored ceases, the control should become inoperative.

Each of these guides has powerful implications for control design. Take the second one, which seems to imply that a poor control operates frequently. But what about a plan that happens to be monitored by a well-designed control? If the plan is going sour, isn't the control going to operate frequently? The answer must be no, and the reason is that a well-designed control has a cascade feature. When unacceptable performance under a plan becomes commonplace, the control triggers another class of receivers that causes alterations in implementation of the plan, alterations in the plan itself, or abandonment of the plan.

Manifestly, if that process were to be automated, it would become too rigorous; also, in view of the transient nature of controls, the equipment investment would be unjustified. Hence, the most responsive and adaptable element of business—an individual human being—is employed as controller at one control level and as interface medium between control levels. Economic cost alone (there are other kinds of cost) decrees that business controls be designed with a place in their loops for the exercise of human judgment.

Among the myths about control is that merely setting it up guarantees that a control will work. However, the inescapable truth is that most plans can and quite often do go awry without causing undue disturbance. But controls, once invoked, produce either the results sought or all sorts of other results that are serious and costly. In short, the results of misapplied controls are always consequential. Therefore, no control should be established unless there is reasonable assurance it can work. To attain that assurance, always follow three basic rules:

1. *Necessity*. Always make sure that the control contemplated is necessary to the achievement of the objectives chosen. Controls are not ends in themselves; they must always be an answer to the question why.

2. *Measurability*. Institute control only when some form of measurement can be employed. The ideal one is exact; and although it is not always possible to find such a one, the departure from it should not be too great. Controls diminish rapidly in effectiveness, both organizationally and psychologically, when measurements become inexact.

3. *Enforceability*. Employ only controls that are enforceable. The astute manager recognizes that exceptions that cannot be acted upon constitute avoidance of control and thereby cause erosion of control.

BUILDING BETTER CONTROLS

In addition to the three basic workability requirements, there are other desirable control characteristics. They are implied in the following summary of tips for building better controls:

1. Control positively. Control is exercised not so much to keep things from happening as to make the right things happen; realization is the highest purpose of controlling.

2. Control decisively. Control does not end with detection; it is completed when corrective action that leads to the elimination of faulty performance is taken.

3. Dovetail plans and controls. Plans alone can tell us what, where, and how to control, and they should therefore identify and specify the controls needed. A plan that does not contain provisions for controls is not a viable plan.

4. Keep controls simple. Make the controls no more elaborate than they need be to detect and correct significant deviations from plans. Testing for deviation significance is a good guide for control design.

5. Combine responsibility for execution and control. Many problems are avoided and coordination is simplified when the manager responsible for executing a plan is also made responsible for the associated control.

6. Control through variance. Control is simplest when it acts on evidence of departure from standards. On that basis, attention should be given primarily to the definition and detection of exceptions.

7. Control at points. It is impossible to control processes throughout their operation; control must be exercised at the points where change occurs.

8. Locate controls advantageously. The exercise of control should not

place strain on organizational relationships; the machinery of control and the organization must be compatible.

9. Continue the control for the life of the plan.

10. Give control only to qualified managers; therefore, design controls as much as possible to fit the capacities of the individual manager.

When all is said and done, self-control is the best basis of control. The wise manager gives his people the means for controlling their own activities.

Establishing the controls. Four steps are essential to establishing a successful control.

1. Developing effective standards.
2. Setting the standards at strategic points.
3. Creating feedback for performance comparison.
4. Setting up the machinery for correcting destructive deviations.

These steps, though generally recognized as essential and separate moves in building an effective control, are seldom taken. More often than not, controls are established on the basis of felt rather than proven need. The ideas embodied in the four steps must be followed if successful controls are to be built.

Take the idea of developing standards; how often are controls thought of as inconstant things, mechanisms that operate only intermittently? An effective control operates only in the exceptional circumstance—as a door closer operates only when the door is opened. The rest of the time it is there but inactive. For a control to operate in that fashion, standards must be set; further, they must be such that control operates only when events take place that are, by their nature, undesirable. The setting of standards is often the weakest part of control design.

As to step 2, setting standards at strategic points, it must be realized that processes as such cannot be controlled. Just as measurements can be made only at points, so controls can be actuated only at points, junctions, or interfaces. That being so, the best place to insert control is where something is likely to happen—where a purchase order becomes an invoice, a petty cash voucher becomes an outlay, or a picked order becomes a shipment.

In step 3 the idea of creating feedback is made explicit. The reason is that controls are more often than not set up as definitions of what is undesirable and seldom contain a mechanism capable of the information generation, processing, and utilization that enable the control to operate. Thus, most controls are verbal and little else. A control with so insubstantial a character usually requires a sizable and wasteful portion of an employee's time to make it work.

Another vital idea is associated with the word "destructive" in step 4. The great bulk of repetitive activities—and they are the ones to be most carefully controlled—vary in some degree from the standard. To act on every variance is to invite economic disaster; controls must—if they are not to eat the company out of house and home—operate only on the occasion of a variance that threatens to prevent the established goal from being reached. Finding the degree of variance that can be tolerated is a cost-critical task that must be carried out with considerable skill if the control to be set up is to serve the purposes of the business and not vice versa.

If it is accepted that controls are system-based, then a number of systems engineering principles apply to business controls. One illustration lies in the design of control display; it has been found that the simpler the tasks imposed upon the operator of a control system, the more precise the execution of control will be. Hence, a control should give the operator the simplest possible evidence on which to act.

That there are various kinds of controls is shown by the following list.

☐ Direct; for example, the countersignature that validates a check.
☐ Indirect; for example, the periodic auditing of accounts to verify their accuracy.
☐ Quantitative; for example, the hash total of check numbers in a computer program.
☐ Nonquantitative; for example, the experience requirement built into the specifications covering a particular job.
☐ Objective; for example, the statistically derived variance standards set up to flag only the ± 10 percent variances.
☐ Subjective; for example, the controls we speak of as among the goals of training and development, the controls that lie within the individual.

AREAS OF CONTROL

The criterion for setting up controls is quite simple. Whenever significant sums or expenditures of effort are involved or whenever lesser scale is involved but there is repetition, there is justification for setting up a control. Some examples follow.

A manufacturer processed 1,500 accounts payable invoices monthly. Two clerks checked the invoices for the normal things—extensions, footings, agreement with purchase orders, and application of proper discounts. As a first step toward control, the clerks were asked to record the errors they found both for and against the company by size of error and size of invoice in which the error was found. At the end of the year the net error was calculated to be $22. It took little effort to convince the company of the futility of spending $7,000 (the cost of the two clerks at the time) to find $22. Instead a random sampling procedure that involved stratification of invoices by amount was set up. All invoices from new vendors and from vendors whose invoices had in the past been found to contain errors were checked closely. By that procedure, the company was able to reduce its control costs from $7,000 to approximately $500 a year.

Another major area in which the control cost and value relationship may show the way to cost reduction is in payroll preparation. It is a common practice to have manual payroll computations checked by a second person. Just as in invoice preparation, it is usually assumed that only errors against the payee will be reported. Study may show that to be an unfair assumption, and it may also show that the errors made against employees are sufficient in incidence and value to disclose whether the cost of payroll errors justifies setting up a control.

Inventory controls also invite comparisons of control cost and value, but they are not so easily made. They require not only that the auditor analyze the records maintained for major item activity but also that the marginal income of lost sales and the cost of maintaining excess inventory be estimated. Rarely is the cost of inventory control segregated as an item and related to the value of that control. In this case the value is not that of the total inventory, the total storage cost, or the cost of stock-outs; it is the value of the changes in the inventory decisions that the control procedure triggers into action.

There are other areas of control common to most businesses that are ripe for control cost analysis. The checking of salesmen's expenses and petty cash vouchers is an example. Establishing suitable budgetary controls usually justifies the elimination of detailed checking. An application of the exception principle should offer sufficient protection, as can be seen in the following example.

A manufacturers' representative with approximately forty salesmen on the road and incurring variable expenses spent a great deal of time and effort on checking the mileage between cities, the invoices from restaurants and hotels, and toll tickets and parking receipts before preparing the reimbursement expense checks. The elaborate checking not only was time-consuming but also created poor relations between the company and the salesmen.

It was recommended that the automobile allowance be set up as a standard weekly amount for each salesman. Also, basic mileage allowances for each route were worked out with each salesman. Additional mileage allowances were covered by a record of the towns the men visited; the mileages were determined on a standard basis from oil company maps. Standard rates for hotels in different parts of the country (including all minor reimbursable items) were also established. To receive reimbursement for hotel costs, the salesman merely had to submit bills in evidence of the number of nights he had been out of town, and that figure was multiplied by the standard rate in his area. These simple procedures eliminated a large part of the control cost and, more importantly, also eliminated the major cause of friction between management and the sales force. The cost-to-value relationship in this case benefited to the tune of $8,000 in control costs eliminated at an additional cost to the company of a $1,500 increase in reimbursement to the salesmen.

Conversely, the value of installing a control where no need exists can be discovered by control cost analysis. An example follows.

In one mammoth ore-processing plant where the maintenance force numbered several hundred, most work was assigned as jobs were completed; an exception, of course, was emergency work. In other words, the main control over nonproductive time was job completion. The control was vigorously enforced; not to report completion of a job immediately was a major offense. Nevertheless, as might be expected, productivity was poor—so poor the company felt impelled to institute effective control. The company then shifted from control through job completion to control through job standards; that is, job time standards were calculated and exceeding the allowed time standard became the signal to check on job progress. Productivity rose over 25 percent, which was equal to adding the services of 15 extra men to the maintenance force, worth at least $99,000 a year. The cost of the control? After the standards were developed at a one-time cost of $80,000, one scheduling clerk and another supervisor (for maintenance of standards work) were added at an annual cost of $18,000. Hence, after the first year, the company was ahead at least $72,000 annually because it instituted effective control. (Actually, the saving was substantially larger because the maintenance force had been working overtime on a fairly consistent basis.)

IMPROVING THE PRODUCTIVITY OF THE INTERNAL CONTROL AUDIT

Every independent public accountant's opinion audit is preceded by an internal control audit the purpose of which is to ascertain the scope of the audit and obtain foreknowledge of procedures, flows, and authorities. This section deals with how to get the facts about controls needed when operations auditing is combined with a financial audit.

Although the internal control audit is informative and valuable, in only a few cases does it provide all the insights it is capable of. An audit of internal controls can be made to supply a great deal more information with no more than a modest increase in total effort. We seek to prove this thesis by taking the example of management controls. If it can be shown that much more knowledge about controls, valuable apart from the asset protection the controls produce, can be yielded by the internal control audit, the hypothesis can be assumed proved.

Neither auditors nor managers are often concerned with control cost and effectiveness. Controls in general are not, of course, as easily explored as control *results* are, but the benefits can be of major significance.

Audits of internal control are customarily documented by the use of a questionnaire. If the audit is to produce added value, that is, specific information about individual controls, a control audit data sheet should be added to the questionnaire. The purpose of the data sheet is to collect in one place information that will be usable in evaluating the effectiveness of the control apparatus as a system element, that is, as one separate whole of the total management system. It is best presented in tabular form with the following as column heads:

Control Title
Control Objective
Date Control Was Established
Initiating Authority
Total Yearly Man-hours
Frequency of Operation
Yearly Value Recovered
Yearly Cost
Ratio of Cost to Value Recovered

Here are a few notes of explanation of some of the headings. The first four collectively ask for information on the intent and history of each control. With that information in hand, it is possible to review each control against sound business practice (what was once vital may now be obsolete) and provide a picture of the total situation (controls averaging three years or more suggest administrative sluggishness).

Under Total Yearly Man-hours will be recorded the hours spent by all persons involved in the functioning of the control. A control that requires more than one man-year of time is probably grossly inefficient.

Frequency of Operation refers to the number of times the control operates. A control operates when someone acts because the control says a significant deviation has taken or is taking place. If the frequency of action is high and the value involved is low, the control is probably set too finely.

Areas of Analysis

Yearly Value Recovered provides a place for recording the dollars actually recovered or prevented from being lost. In some instances that amount is difficult to calculate, but without it, the cost of controls is a blind item and rational estimates of effectiveness cannot be made.

Yearly Cost is included to measure the effort as well as the expense and to indicate whether the control is being handled by the lowest-level person available.

Ratio of Cost to Value Recovered is self-evident and is the payoff. In the accounts payable invoice example cited previously, it was the 1-to-320 ratio ($22 in errors measured against the $7,000 cost) that prompted change.

Obtaining the information for the spread sheet will seem to most auditors to be a formidable task. It need not be one, however, and the data can be accumulated through interviews and direct observation such as sampling and time studies. Personnel in the department being audited can often be used to collect the data after the auditor has designed a program for collecting them. Review of the spread sheet after it is prepared may highlight major areas of expense over which there is no control.

REFERENCE

1. Henry Fayol, *Paper on the Science of Administration* (New York: Institute of Public Administration, 1937), p. 103.

8

ORGANIZATION AND ORGANIZING

Organization has been an object of fascination ever since large numbers of men were first involved in common causes. Before the Industrial Revolution, large-scale organizations generally reflected military power or the power of ownership, and some of the principles of organization still in use are based on coercive power. Those principles do not serve us well in industry—not, at least, in the industry of the free world. Whereas ancient large-scale organizations were usually simple and undifferentiated and had relatively few levels from the supreme commander to the soldier or slave, modern industrial organization is complex, specialized, and multilevel. Part of the change is due to technological complexity; a greater part is due to man's newly acquired personal freedom and raised aspirations.

Management thinkers and practitioners have, in the last 100 years or so, tried to develop general principles of organization that would have predictive value. To date their efforts have had meager results, but that is not to say they have been in vain. A vast amount of practical know-how has arisen, and much of it is incorporated in the management philosophies of present-day companies and managers. Included is recognition of the importance of assigning responsibility and delegating authority, of matching the two, of placing each unit of work under one person's responsibility, and relating activities and functions in a sensible framework of objectives.

The most important idea about organization for the auditor is that structure makes a difference. Organization is a tool to help accomplish a company's objectives; hence, it is a competitive element. Not many people think of it that way, but there can be no doubt that sound structural design, although it cannot insure success, is essential to successful accomplishment in business.

DEFINITIONS
If we look for a definition of organization and for an insight into the process of organizing, we can't do much better than the words of a pioneer in the field:

Organization . . . refers to more than the frame of the edifice. It refers to the complete body, with all its correlated functions. It refers to those functions as they appear in action, the very pulse and heartbeats, the circulation, and respiration, the vital movement, so to speak, of the organized unit. It refers to the coordination of all these factors as they cooperate for the common purpose.[1]

A simpler definition could go something like this: an organization is a means by which resources can be accumulated, mixed, integrated, coordinated, and motivated to achieve a desired objective.

The term "organizing," as applied to a function of management, must have limited meaning if it is to be properly understood and employed. Too often the work of organization planning is extended into areas of management, where its principles and methods of problem solving do not work properly. To say it another way, too many problems are labeled organization troubles when they really result from other types of deficiency. Generally speaking, organization planning must be limited to the following activities:

1. Defining the function.
2. Properly classifying the function.
3. Grouping the functions.
4. Establishing sound relationships between groups.

Defining the function does not mean merely setting up the function; instead, it means examining the function from the viewpoint of its being necessary to the accomplishment of given objectives or goals. In other words, the true test of organization planning is that of making sure that each function and activity in the enterprise is tested for relevance to the objectives at hand.

Classifying the function means examining or analyzing it for the purpose of finding where in the organization it can function to the greatest advantage of the enterprise as a whole.

Grouping the functions means identifying all activities that support a function and are closely related to it and then placing the function in a group assembled to achieve maximum coordination and synergism.

Finally, the most productive relationships between groups are established by so placing each group in the organizational structure that its informational sources are close at hand, communication channels are kept as short as possible, and the chain of command is as simple as possible.

In dealing with organization, the tendency to oversimplify must be avoided. There are many aspects of organization besides the formal or structural ones. They include:

1. *Job-task relationships,* the official and legal relationships that form the foundation for the others.

2. *Personal relationships* based on desired and rejected relations; the so-called social relations.

3. *Functional relationships* that are important to but are different from job-task relationships; the professional and staff specialist relations.

4. *Decision-making relationships,* which seldom follow the job-task relationship decision lines and are highly variable and unstable.

5. *Influence relationships,* a variant of 4.

6. *Power relationships,* epitomized by "You'd better clear that with Jack"; power is not synonymous with delegated authority and replaces authority.

7. *Communication relationships,* epitomized by "If we had to go through channels, you'd never get it done"; patterns of communication are at variance with official relationships.

DETERMINANTS OF STRUCTURE

Of the many factors that have bearing on how a company should organize, the following are the more important ones:

- ☐ Nature of the business, the characteristics of market served, nature of technology employed, rate of change in market and technology.
- ☐ Product, geographical, technological, and manufacturing diversity.
- ☐ Size, average product life, and average price for product.
- ☐ Growth strategy and rate and the frequency of mergers or acquisitions.
- ☐ Governmental regulations.
- ☐ Culture.
- ☐ Management philosophy.
- ☐ Computers.
- ☐ Techniques for handling information.

MEASURING ORGANIZATIONAL EFFECTIVENESS

It is not easy to measure organizational effectiveness. Objective, commonly accepted standards are almost nonexistent. Nevertheless, there are certain broad criteria. A company with an effective organization plan has some or all of the following characteristics:

It has better earnings per share, return on capital employed, market share, innovation, and public image than its direct competitors. It has satisfied customers. It is adaptable to change, is able to grow, is responsive to changes in market and technology, and is feasible to staff.

It attracts and holds management talent, lends itself to effective motivation of managers, effectively integrates effort, and produces effective successor managers.

It uses its resources economically.

It effectively coordinates effort with minimum of duplication, lack of mutual support, and nonproductive internal conflict.

It facilitates applying the firm's management talent to high-priority opportunities and problems, and it helps company managers to apply their highest skills to the opportunities in their areas of responsibility for the largest proportion of their time.

To measure organization effectiveness, the auditor will be forced to look for indications of deficient organization. Among the signs are frequent plan changes, lack of arrangement for succession, late decisions, inadequate information, impossibility of accountability, excessive tenure, excessive communicating, tolerance of incompetence, wage and salary inequities, and purposeless redundancy.

When it comes to organizational guidelines and principles, there is a strong feeling of "there's one best way to do each thing" abroad in industry. In organization planning particularly, that attitude has led to serious mistakes. Like most generalizations, it occasionally appears to be true, and so most people tend to lose sight of the fact that organizational characteristics are more important than organizational form. Also, organizational balance, simplicity, and clarity are more important than fulfillment of "principles."

A major truth about organization is that the so-called principles of organization are not absolute, but relative, not to be applied purely, but practically. On the other hand, there can be no soundness of organization when balance is lacking, complexity exists in place of simplicity, or confusion takes the place of understanding. Those characteristics are absolute, even though the means for achieving them vary with work, time, and place.

Once that point of view is accepted, it becomes easy to see that time is better spent on making the organization work than in selecting the form of organization. Some people regard organization as shoppers regard a purchase—the job is done when the selection is made. The critical element in organization planning is not selection but installation. Given results can usually be obtained in different ways, as Du Pont discovered in a study the company made in 1919. The ten criteria of organization adopted by Du Pont at that time include a statement that many things can be done in more than "one fashion without loss of efficiency."[2] It is a fact of managerial life that organizations are growing larger and more complex—and are likely to keep growing that way for some time to come. To the customary reasons for sound organization planning must therefore be added those of anticipating the effects of such trends and preventing them from seriously adding to the managerial burden.

Coordination and integration. Traditionally, as the work force has been enlarged or more complicated production processes have been employed, managers have been added proportionately. That is not the way to carry the increased managerial load, however, because adding managers without changing management methods merely adds to the work of managing. Coordination and integration, for example, become bigger problems than ever. There are many sets of principles, guidelines, and commandments, and almost every organization specialist has a set of his own. The following is a typical and generally useful one:

1. Organize to solve problems of organization. Correct structure can solve only problems of organization; it cannot solve problems rooted in procedures, communications, or motivation.

2. Shape organization to objectives. Company aspirations control the kinds of work that must be done, and structure must be designed to facilitate their realization.

3. Minimize the gap between the designed and the real structure. Every design distorts the going organization and tends in the long run to be modified by it.

4. Structure from the bottom up and from the top down. Short of the top level, the content of each position arises out of the decision needs of jobs reporting to it. The style of leadership exercised at the top level strongly determines job content.

5. Arrive at span of control analytically. The number of jobs that should come under the same supervision depends on the nature and content of all the jobs and the capabilities of those in the jobs.

6. Give decision making an upward thrust. In each superior-subordinate

pair, the subordinate should make the bulk of the decisions while the superior focuses on finding, identifying, and describing problems.

7. Distinguish between authority and comunication. Each right of direction should be given to one man, but the right to communicate should be given freely.

8. Divide and assign work in wholes. Every class of activity should have one person in charge, and an activity of the largest class should be the full-time responsibility of one person.

9. Separate the powers of execution and review. Evaluation of results should always be made outside the activities audited.

10. Work toward organizational effectiveness, not form. Most jobs can be accomplished effectively in more than one organizational format.

11. Provide purposeful documentation. Assignments of responsibility should be made in writing to afford a basis for training, review, and appeal.

12. Establish controls over organization. Structural design is a plan, and plans are never fully implemented in the absence of standards, evaluation, and adjustment.

Organization is neither the beginning nor the end of the management process, and so there is no special time for organizational change. Instead, like the improving of management itself, refining the organization is a never-ending task. Improvement should be made when and where benefits result, and they should not have to wait longer than necessary. It is therefore likely that there will always be organizational lag. The auditor should be discriminating; only the obviously significant lags should bear comment.

Major problems are caused by lack of understanding of responsibilities and authorities, an extremely common condition in most companies and one that is easily corrected. A description of the job incumbent's responsibilities and authorities will do much to communicate clearly what is expected of each employee and to promote effective performance.

Intensive study of managers who, in the long run, achieved high productivity, low costs, reduced turnover and absence, and high employee satisfaction has been made under the guidance of a social psychologist, Rensis Likert. His study shows that high-producing managers encourage *participation* even in those usually specialized activities of setting standards and budgets, cost control, and organization of work. As a result, the organizations of top-rank managers are characterized by high employee motivation, cooperation, and coordination. That can be achieved when the work shared by people makes them feel that they are needed and are important and well used. Every member of an organization will work more effectively if he sees his role as difficult, important, and meaningful.

Evidence increasingly supports the view that an organization is more effective when its personnel work not as individuals, but as members of highly effective groups with high performance goals. Management should seek to construct such groups and develop organization by making the superior of one group a member of at least one other group. Span of control is one of the concrete things the auditor can and should look at. The spans exercised in a company have a direct influence on the way the company operates and the results it achieves. Harassed supervisors and frustrated subordinates often say that spans are too broad.

Areas of Analysis

The proper number of subordinates cannot be generalized, however; too many factors—such as the kind of decision making practiced, the existence of adequate written policies, and the characteristics of the information flow—affect the appropriateness of the spans in being. For example, the number of executives reporting to the president in 100 companies with over 5,000 employees was found to vary from 1 to 24. The complexity and number of theoretical direct and cross relationships increase astoundingly with an increase in the number reporting, as Table 2 will verify. If the number reporting is 24 instead of 12, the number of possible relationships is multiplied, not by 2, but by over 8,000 to 201,327,166.

A span of control of ten men is by no means wide. A recent study showed that in 83 companies the span of control of the president over principal subordinates was most often seven or eight. A tabulation of study results is shown in Table 3. The table shows that 60 percent of presidents have between six and nine subordinates. Only 5 percent have fewer than four, but 17 percent have between twelve and fifteen.

To the question whether any one man can effectively supervise and coordinate more than six persons, the answer is yes if the supervisor is skilled in administration and his subordinates have similar jobs. But if they have extremely specialized areas of activity that do not bear on one another in a highly interlocked way, the answer must be no. Since most management functions are much interlocked, executives in many companies can comfortably supervise no more than six to eight people.

Table 2 **Theoretical direct and cross relationships of executives reporting to company president.**

NUMBER REPORTING	NUMBER OF POSSIBLE RELATIONSHIPS
1	1
2	6
3	18
4	44
5	100
6	222
7	490
8	1,080
9	2,376
10	5,210
11	11,374
12	24,708

Sources: Ernest Dale, *Planning and Developing the Company Organization Structure* (AMA, 1952), p. 77, and Luther Gulick and Lyndall F. Urwick (eds.), *Papers on the Science of Administration* (New York: Institute of Public Administration, 1937), p. 186.

Table 3 **Chief executive's span of control.**

NUMBER OF COMPANIES	SPAN OF CONTROL
1	2
3	3
2	4
6	5
9	6
19	7
13	8
9	9
7	10
2	11
4	12
3	13
4	14
1	15

Keeping spans of control short carries with it one form of penalty: it increases the distance between the topmost and lowest levels in the organization.

AUTHORITY AS A MEASURE

The way authority is distributed, used, and respected has a lot to do with corporate success and is another aspect the operations auditor can use as a measure of organizational effectiveness. Every manager, sooner or later, faces the question, "What is authority?" When that is answered, a further question is raised: "How shall I use it?" The answers he gives to those two questions greatly affect his way of doing things and the profit of his company.

Probably no word in the manager's vocabulary is more misunderstood than "authority," and probably none has more emotion-arousing connotations. That is not hard to understand; in most minds, authority is linked with such disagreeable words as command, order, coerce, and force. Yet almost all of us are convinced that, however much we may dislike it, authority is indispensable to organizational success.

One of the toughest problems for managers to handle is proper use of authority. Without authority it is pretty hard to get things done, yet the very use of authority is dangerous to the purpose for which it is used. Failure to take people's feelings into account can adversely affect group objectives. On the other hand, authority that is too concerned with feelings may also result in failure. We have seen that authority does not work well without a system of rewards and punishment, yet authority that emphasizes such a system fails to enlist the best efforts of people.

Careful analysis of the nature and use of authority is called for before any decisions about authority are included in management philosophy. Such an analysis makes a number of characteristics immediately apparent. Authority

Areas of Analysis

(1) always involves at least two people—the person who uses it and the person who accepts it, (2) is used to bring about desired actions, and (3) in and by itself, does not always succeed in achieving its objectives. Now, if these characteristics are measured against the common view of authority— that it originates with ownership, a board of directors, or the president of an enterprise and then simply flows downward—some real problems result. In the common view, possession of authority is in itself sufficient assurance that orders will be obeyed, yet we know that authority breaks down quite often. Therefore, either the common view or our statement of the characteristics of authority is wrong. To choose the latter alternative is to ignore reality, so it may be well for us to scrap the common view and start over again to try to redefine authority.

To begin with, we must separate formal or legal authority from real or accepted authority. We have seen too many people in formal authority whose orders are consistently disregarded for us to think there is no difference. Furthermore, we have seen too many managers who have given up their authority because they don't know how to get their orders obeyed for us to believe that formal authority alone will get orders accepted.

Obviously, something besides from-the-top, formal, or legal authority is needed to get the job done. That something is acceptance of authority by the people toward whom it is directed. To put it even more strongly: *Authority cannot produce results unless it is accepted by those who are subject to it.* In a totalitarian system, formal and real authority are fairly close to being the same thing. But when a man has the free choice of working to reach his personal objectives, the acceptance of authority rests in those personal or inspired objectives and not in a charter of incorporation, bylaws, or the chief executive of the organization. Hence, the acceptance of and the source of authority rest within the person subject to the authority.

The problem does not end with that realization, however; there are good, indifferent, and bad reasons for accepting authority. The following are the basic reasons why authority is accepted.

Social good. Authority is obeyed because it is recognized that the common good requires it.

Corporate benefit. Authority is accepted because the company needs it.

Individual good. Authority is obeyed because the person subject to it realizes some benefit.

Respect for superior. Authority is accepted to gain approval of the supervisor.

Pay. Authority is obeyed because income depends upon it.

Moral standards. Authority is accepted because the person subject to it has been taught to accept it.

Power. Authority is accepted because it is backed by coercive power, variously based.

Prestige. Authority is accepted because it confers a vicarious sense of importance.

Avoiding responsibility. Authority is accepted because it relieves the subject of the necessity for making his own decisions.

Some important guides for the wielder of authority can be stated briefly as follows:

Get to know the people you supervise well enough that you recognize their personal objectives, motivation, and capabilities.

When giving orders, blend the objectives of your organization with those of your subordinates to the fullest extent possible.

Base orders on organizational objectives, not private ones.

Place as much as possible of the responsibility for fulfilling orders upon the person subject to them.

Make orders universal—don't permit exceptions to be made.

Make the language of authority as conversational and mannerly as the everyday speech of your shop or social group.

Whenever possible, invite subordinates to assist in framing policies, rules, and orders that will affect them.

Recognize that sound leadership helps avoid most of the problems for which the use of legal authority—by itself—is a last resort.

In short, all who exercise authority must realize that ability, knowledge, title, and position do not in themselves assure the acceptance of authority. Whenever the men supervised have choice, they set the limits of authority.

The usual basis of distributing authority is the scalar principle: decision-making powers are thought of as granted from the chief executive downward to subordinates. That seems clear enough, yet many of the problems intended to be cleared up by delegating authority continue to remain or create new kinds of problems.

The trouble with many principles is that they are inadequate descriptions of complex ideas. Delegation of authority is an example. Though it appears to be a sensible way to handle increasing numbers of situations calling for decisions without adding to staff or making the executive groups comparatively top-heavy, many managers are dissatisfied with the way things work. Why? One of the basic reasons is that people are different and therefore do things differently. To state it more exactly, the person who delegates must expect decisions affecting him with which he will differ, and he *must* accept and support that as long as he delegates. It is here that the principle, in its fullest meaning, is most often violated.

To delegate properly, one must have an understanding of the management process and realize that, however it may be defined, management is ultimately a special application of economics. It is particularly concerned with increasing the efficiency with which decisions are made and lowering the costs of making decisions (its true objective). But the gains to be made by placing authority and responsibility at the lowest level compatible with decisions to be made cannot be realized unless the delegatee is convinced that he will be appraised on the basis of the net effect of all the decisions he has made, and not on each one.

To make delegation work, managers have to surrender in part a privilege they have worked hard to obtain—the power of judging and overruling subordinates. In short, delegation calls for a suspension of that power on a daily basis, and human nature rebels against giving up something it has worked so hard to get. To keep in check our natural inclination to criticize is always something of a problem, but it is certain that, unless we do keep it in check, delegation cannot bring with it the savings and efficiency for which it is designed.

How is the company to be protected from the harmful results of bad decisions on the part of the delegatee? The competent executive insures that proper controls in the form of SOPs, policies, regulations, and job descriptions are in effect before he confers the right to make decisions. Above all, he sees to it that the person to whom he grants decision-making rights has always before him a statement of the objectives, preferably jointly set, toward which he is to work.

Having given a subordinate the right to make decisions and having set over his actions the proper controls, what then? Is the manager free to turn his attention elsewhere, safe in the knowledge that he has put a principle to work and need concern himself no longer? Not unless he wants his own head on a platter! It is true that delegation calls for suspending judgment and withholding criticism of specific decisions, but periodic review of the net effects of exercising responsibility and authority is certainly called for. Delegation is always contingent, never permanent. Continuance of it is always based on satisfactory performance.

NEW TRENDS

The hierarchical organization is historically old, unresponsive to current change, and therefore vulnerable. New ideas are coming in. One new idea is the profit center, which includes the product, market, or brand manager and the systems approach, the organization that emerges from integrating men, money, facilities, materials, information, and methods. The profit center has grown in favor as an organizational tool for a variety of reasons:

1. The nature of marketing has made it sensible to put authority for all aspects of the product, cutting across engineering, design, market research, sales, and related staff functions, under one man. He is the product, market, or brand manager.

2. Direct costing has made it both acceptable and possible to segregate controllable costs and related income so that the planning and control of an operation can be measured and the performance of the manager can be computed on the basis of his profit contribution.

3. One approach to the training of new men that contrasts with specialist background developments is to have them manage smaller entities in total before turning over larger responsibilities to them. The profit center is ideal for the purpose; it serves to expose a manager to the whole management process in a restricted, controllable area that permits full responsibility within limited areas of asset risk.

4. The profit center can be used even for the service function that does not create income by transactions with the outside world but does have controllable costs and measurable information as to quality and quantity of service. The term "cost center" may be appropriate to such activities as personnel, accounting, maintenance, and quality control. The concept of having the manager responsible for developing plans and standards of performance for his operation can be tied in with a compensation plan that rewards the contribution these services make to the company.

The problem of survival makes it clear that a better approach to insuring the company's future existence is needed than is now commonly used by United States firms. Many firms will aim to survive by improving products, manufacturing productivity, marketing, resource utilization, and management control. Some of them will not survive, however, because those intentions are the common ones of top management and offer too little competitive advantage. The firms that do survive to the 1980s and 1990s will be those now at work in search of a goal so rational and pervasive that it compels complete integration of resources and early identification of the distinctive capacities required to achieve its aims. A goal of that kind is bound to cause organization to be viewed as a resource essential to its accomplishment and the matrix for the effective application of men, money, machines, materials, and methods. That is the systems viewpoint, and at this time it promises to be the most powerful influence on organizational design.

There is a wide gap between the common type of organization and the most systematic one. Studies of social systems reveal that systems concepts can be applied to organization structure with consequent improved stability, manageability, and growth. The impulse to organization planning has traditionally stemmed from management directives as to how the firm's organization should be structured and principles of organization developed through the years. That will not suffice in the future. Even now it results in situations such as this described in a recent article:

> Primary reliance on the more pure form of functional organization has given way in recent years to patchwork organizational structures, which reflect management's desire to maintain as much of the traditional concepts as possible.[3]

What is needed is a singular view, fundamental and broad enough to provide the basis for building an organization capable of matching the dynamic complexities of the environment of which it is a part. The systems view meets that requirement.

Viewing the organization as a total system has some massive implications. In the first place, the systems approach is not a suitable vehicle for current managerial viewpoints. The bureaucratic structure represents a serious constraint to the systems view and the new management technologies. In the second place, the systems approach will require the manager to shift from considering himself a leader to thinking of himself as the auditor and controller of a plexus of integrally related activities.

It is too early to guess when the full weight of the systems view will be felt competitively, but that it will be felt is certain. That systems designers now occupy so many significant positions in companies is proof enough; there is no reason why this new breed of technologist will not make significant marks on enterprise and its organization. One thing is sure: When the systems view has had its impact, many of the old, tiresome, line-staff, centralization-decentralization quarrels will disappear for good.

Traditionally, work has been accomplished through organizations that were more or less fixed. In recent years the organizational unit tailor-made for reaching a specific, limited objective has made its appearance and seems to be growing in popularity. Many companies are now setting up work on a project basis, particularly those in construction, R&D, and engineering. Even companies primarily dependent on mental skills find that organized effort is more productive than effort expended in isolation. There is evidence that the decisions made by groups are superior to those made by individuals in many projects with high intellectual content.

The practice of setting up temporary groupings of personnel from different organizational units to provide a given product or service first arose in World War II. The special-purpose task force was found to reduce the communication and coordination problems involved in complex, multispecialty missions. When business firms began to experience difficulty in dealing with greatly increased rates of economic and technological change, they were compelled to abandon their predilection for static organization and seek new organizational formats. That is why project management, as it is customarily called, has become a fairly common organizational feature of American business.

In addition to its being a response to change in technology and marketing, the task force serves a subtle psychological need. Job satisfaction comes from challenge, a sense of growth, responsibility, and peer acceptance, and the person asked to join a task force has an unusual opportunity to experience those satisfactions. Task forces cut across hierarchical lines; people are invited to join because of what they know rather than because of their status. A person who leads a task force in his area of specialization may be a consultant to another task force, one led, perhaps, by a junior member of the company whose leadership is based on *his* knowledge. The changing membership, interchange of knowledge, and sense of movement created by task forces may be symptomatic of a dynamic organization. Equally significant is short life. When the task is done, the group is disbanded.

REAL TOOLS OF ORGANIZATION

Organizing activities and people into a pattern most likely to yield the results sought is an important and separate work of the manager. Each manager organizes his work in relation to the work of his subordinates, and he must contribute to the establishment of sound relations between the work of his and other units. He does so not on the basis of theory or principle but on the basis of judgment, experience, objectives, common sense, and a respect for people and justice. Those are the real tools of organization.

REFERENCES

1. James J. Mooney, *The Principles of Organization* (New York: Harper & Row, 1947).
2. Ernest Dale, *Planning and Developing the Company Organization* (AMA, 1952).
3. Howard M. Carlisle, "Are Functional Organizations Becoming Obsolete?" *Management Review*, January 1969, pp. 2–7.

9

INFORMATION
AND COMMUNICATION

Every enterprise depends on the knowledge it has available as much as it does on the money it has available. In turn, knowledge can be valuable only if it is quickly and understandably dispersed. Since knowledge arises from the mind acting upon information, it is no exaggeration to say that the success of any company is greatly affected by the quality of information it has and the efficiency of its internal communications. A company reacts to emerging conditions and exploits opportunities in direct relation to the quality and the availability of its information. Only recently, with the advent of electronic data processing, has a great deal of attention been given to information and communication. But we are talking not of EDP information only, but of the entire information-communication network that an organization needs.

Chester Barnard, one of the first to give information and communication prime places in business, noted that there are three main elements in organizational success: communication, a willingness to serve, and a common purpose. As he saw it, communcation performs the critical task of relating the other two. By means of communication, common goals are passed from one member of the organization to other members so that cooperative effort can be attained and the willingness to serve can be directed to varying circumstances. Communication becomes a primary basis for interacting decisions within the organization.

The current importance of information and communication to American industry is indicated by the following:

☐ Somewhere near one-quarter of all money paid out by United States companies for salaries in 1963 ($71 billion) went for paperwork.

☐ By 1980 the American labor force will have reached 100 million, more than half of whom will be white collar workers.

☐ By 1980 the number of computers, reproduction departments, and automated information storage and retrieval systems in business will have at least doubled the number in the 1960s.

Areas of Analysis

☐ About three-quarters of a million words—in the form of reports, letters, and memos—are piled atop the typical president's desk every month; he spends a minimum of five hours *per day* just reading.

These facts and forecasts show that management is moving steadily away from the position in which a business can be managed by making decisions solely on the basis of first-hand observation. To the degree that personal observation declines as the basis for decision making, dependence upon environmental information and the systems that supply it grows. The basis of the auditor's evaluation of information-communication effectiveness consists in closely examining information generated, communicated, processed, retained, and discarded for integrity, consistency, and usability.

So important has information and communication become that "information systems" have emerged. They are so large in scope and so complex and costly that, in the best interests of the company, they must be audited. Many authorities feel they must be audited on a continual basis, but at least they should be audited once during each of the major stages of planning, development, implementation, and post installation. That is particularly important when managers are removed from first-hand observation and when the resources of the company committed to an information system are a significant portion of the total resources.

The auditor will find analysis of the communication system a rich source of symptoms in companies with serious underlying problems. Also, because a communication system cannot be reviewed in neatly bound organizational units, it is an unconventional audit subject that offers the auditor undreamed-of possibilities to innovate beyond the traditional audit exercises.

PRIME FUNCTIONS

Evaluating the information-communication systems begins with understanding what information is and why it and its communication are needed. Information takes many forms; it can be raw or processed data or factual, subjective, or deductive material. C. E. Shannon, one of the founders of information theory, probably enunciated the most fruitful idea about it when he said that information is that which resolves uncertainty.

The need for information is common to all business, but it begins to assume critical significance when a company grows beyond the administrative capacity of one man. If a highly differentiated company is to be run effectively, there must be a basis for focusing effort. The prime means is through the downward communication of corporate plans and directives and the upward communication of information that requires management action.

The problem generated by the information explosion that has taken place in all but the smallest companies is that decision makers cannot possibly digest information fast enough. It is commonly held that an information-communication system constitutes a problem when an organization is unable to furnish the executive with up-to-date, pertinent information he requires to plan, control, and manage by using cost-effective resources. But just as great a problem exists when the executive receives more information than he can handle or receives material in an unrelated or disorganized fashion.

An information system is a means to an end and not an end in itself, a fact that is not always kept in view when a system is designed. Further, not only are true user needs ignored but only current need is considered. Today's information needs must be satisfied with tomorrow's needs very much in mind, and that entails open-ended design techniques. Otherwise, the system is obsolete even before it begins to operate. Information needs fall into three major classes, each of which is dependent on the others.

1. *Strategic information,* which relates to the decisions that promise the biggest payoffs.

2. *Tactical information,* which relates to mainline activities such as engineering, procurement, and manufacturing quality control.

3. *Operational information,* which relates to day-to-day needs and is most useful in assessing status at the lowest organizational level.

DESIGN CRITERIA

A prime consideration to the operations auditor is that an information system cannot be successful unless it is designed for the direct needs of the user and with his full involvement and participation. Too often, systems people think they know what the real needs for planning, control, and management are, and in their designing activity they take as models and standards the systems configurations used elsewhere. The information user and his needs fall into three general groups.

1. *The generalist* is one who has unpredictable needs and whose decision responsibilities require a large store of information; among the generalists are chief executives and managers of administration. This kind of user is probably the most demanding of data base, question formulation, and retrieval techniques.

2. *The mission-oriented user* is probably the easiest to satisfy. His needs are limited, and he can define them pretty well. Information storage and retrieval that will satisfy him can be achieved without too much trouble compared with that for the general user.

3. *The managerial user* is characterized by the urgency he must impose on the availability of the information. Decision-supporting information must not only be quickly accessible but provide a great depth of supporting information.

The higher the position of the user, the more general are his interests and therefore the more difficult it becomes to satisfy his needs. The determination of the proper category into which the information user fits and how the system must be structured to suit his needs must precede any system design.

Some of the main system design elements concern factuality in reporting data, completeness of data received, and correctness in data handling. Additional factors are control over data flows, scheduling of data handling, and communication of processed data. Even accurate information is of little value when it is not readily available to and understandable by its users.

Knowledge can be held back or distorted by organizational influences. Staff specialists, for example, are often better informed and more innovative than operating managers. The specialists are free to spend the bulk of their time on selected problems and are not held responsible for specific results. Staff people can afford to be liberal. Line personnel tend, however, to resist listening to recommendations for change made by staff people, and they continue to depend on established sources for control information.

In gauging the availability and application of information the auditor must keep in mind that information is a resource and therefore a form of power. The possession of power can corrupt; for example, it can cause managers to serve private motives rather than those of the firm. Therefore, the auditor should pay particular attention to the freshness of the information and the readiness with which it is shared.

Little information in a company should be closely held; so if an audit reveals a tendency to treat a great many things as confidential, a major problem has possibly been uncovered. Because information confers power on its possessor, information itself can be a barrier to effective communication. Information tends to flow in direct proportion to its unimportance; people tend to hang on to information that has importance of one kind or another and pass along information that has little value.

Information and knowledge are often confused; most people conceive of knowledge as capable of existing out of mind, in paper stored somewhere, and of information as a form of knowledge. That is not so. Information can be stored; but knowledge—which is propositional in form and immediately applicable—exists only in the human brain. In effect, knowledge, which is what an executive must have in plentitude and relevance, exists only in individual human beings. Looked at in another way, information is an identifiable commodity that is stable but is also inert. It can be transferred; but until it is transformed into knowledge and takes on dynamic and pragmatic qualities, it remains inert.

One measure of the effectiveness of information and communication lies in the efforts made to reduce and simplify data to their lowest common denominators. Proper evaluation involves consideration of both the users and the action results sought from information.

As an example of the uses of information and resulting action, consider the losses that occur when customer complaints are not immediately analyzed as to their origin—slow delivery, inadequately trained personnel, product defectiveness, or whatever. Most companies have neither a formal method of dealing with complaints nor the machinery to analyze complaints to see how their market position can be improved.

In summary, the auditor must recognize that knowledge includes the possession of information, that information is made up of data brought together and operated upon, and that communicating is the process of conveying information. The quality of each provides an excellent measure of the future prospects of a company.

TYPES OF INFORMATION AND COMMUNICATION

The operations auditor deals with three basic types of information.

1. *Identification information,* which is used in detecting and describing matters that call for management decision.

2. *Decision information,* which is used to help the manager formulate the nature and content of decision options and decide.

3. *Action information,* which is used in translating decisions into activity.

Information can also be classified by whether it is single- or multiple-use, that is, unique or applicable to repetitive situations. Information of the first class is likely to be short-lived; that of the second class, long-lived. Information of the first class is in the nature of operating information; that of the second class is in the nature of policy information.

The auditor also deals with information-communication flow.

1. Down the line of corporate authority to provide overall direction and to establish objectives, programs, approved plans, and policies (usually via organization charts, approved budgets, policy directives, manuals, and so forth).

2. Upward from operating units (usually in the form of reports of operating results).

3. Into the corporation from outside sources (usually from customers and vendors and often from government agencies and industry sources).

4. Outward from the corporation (to customers, vendors, stockholders, government agencies, and so forth).

Problems caused by lack of understanding of individual responsibilities and authorities are so common that they can almost be thought of as inherent in a business entity, but they are not only unnecessary but very costly. Such failures of information-communication should be relentlessly sought out and systematically eliminated. There is no reason why everyone concerned with a given job should not know all that it entails. That information can be supplied in the form of job descriptions, and many unnecessary, unreal, and totally wasteful problems can thereby be eliminated.

Management consultants are often asked to find executive personnel for clients, but experience shows that the clients seldom know what the hiree is to do. Defining the job and communicating the assignee's responsibilities and authorities through a job description will do much to make the job tenable and the employee effective. In fact, a company will do itself a great service by preparing suitable descriptions for all key jobs. Although no description can cover everything a job entails, a good one will cover every important responsibility, and that will eliminate 90 percent of the misunderstanding.

The operations auditor should consider the relevance of results by looking into the effects on performance of certain simple, immediate feedback information. Although performance can differ from standards or expectations for an almost infinite variety of reasons, in many cases the only change that has to be made to improve performance is to give to the people doing the work immediate information on how they are doing compared with what is expected of them. This approach eliminates questions of training and assumes that, if the standard is reasonable and has been communicated, most people will be able to improve their performance if they are merely told how they are doing.

In one case, operating personnel from the vice-president of operations to the men actually doing the work all felt that a certain performance standard was being observed 90 to 95 percent of the time. This company enjoyed a substantial rate saving in shipping costs when items were combined in a certain way. The investigator checked the number of times that the performance was actually achieved and found that, in truth, the compliance reached only 40 to 45 percent. The simple change that resulted in a dramatic improvement in performance was to have each of the workers keep track of the number of times daily that the special rate was available and the number of times that he actually used it. *In one day* the performance went from

40 to 45 percent up to 90 to 95 percent and was maintained for several years.

There was no change in the standard, in training, or in supervision. The only change was the immediate feedback of the difference between expected and actual performance.

In another case, an airline measured on-the-ground efficiency by the speed with which planes were serviced—fueling, cleaning, and baggage and food loading. A station that had ranked 40 out of the 80 stations the airline maintained raised its level of efficiency to first in the world by the same procedure: merely informing service personnel of the standard that was expected of them (information that had long been disseminated and accepted) and how they actually performed against that standard. Although the change in this case was not quite as dramatic, it took only three months for the station to move from 40 to first in overall efficiency.

The general applicability of this finding should be evident to the operations auditor. When performance is not up to standard, what may be lacking is not training, supervision, or more sophisticated and expensive management techniques, but merely *information* provided to the people who are responsible for the work, fast and clearly enough so that they can adjust their work. There is a further implication—in many cases the individuals involved in the work are capable of adjusting their performance without any supervisory intervention.

REPORTS

The auditor must particularly find out whether the information generated and distributed in the company signals significant deviations from preestablished targets and important internal or external changes. An information-communication system that does not alert management to departures from plans and point out unforeseen potential threats is of little value. One type of information reporting that has uniquely significant action-inducing value is the exception or discriminatory report. The following examples of reports indicate the use of the exception principle.

Percentage rejects in items received.
Percentage shortages in scheduled production material.
Significant variances between number of requisitions per month and forecast.
Significant change in average total costs of issuing a requisition.
Significant difference between supplier's performance and promised quality and delivery.
Significant change in flow time from request to purchase to purchase order issuance.
Rate of absenteeism and turnover.
Number of grievances.
Number of accidents.
Below quota sales by man, outlet, or territory.
Budget variances exceeding x.
Gross margins below x.
Customer payments not received.
Minimum, maximum, and low-limit inventories.

Hours worked exceeding x.

Aged accounts receivable trial balance showing only balances over x days.

Inventory report of all items below minimum point.

Cost analyses of all inventory items with dollars in excess of x percent of total inventory.

Order status report of unshipped orders in plant over 48 hours.

Order status report of all orders held by credit department over 72 hours.

Sales versus budgeted sales by product for any item over or under budget by x percent.

Sales report showing any items that represent more than x percent of total month's sales and less than x percent of total month's sales.

The professional approach to reporting systems, whatever their nature or level of sophistication, is not to have each user design his own report but to coordinate the development of reports through the agency of staff specialists working within the framework of an overall plan.

A very lucrative source of information and communication in a large organization, and one that is often overlooked, is the employee suggestion system. In addition to the obvious morale information, a wealth of systems information can be generated from it when it is supported by rewards for accepted ideas and explanations of rejected suggestions. It must be controlled and monitored and have a two-way flow of information from and to employees.

THE ULTIMATE FACILITATION

Of all the factors bearing on information-communication effectiveness, perhaps none is more powerful than the values recognized and absorbed or transmitted by the prime information receptor: man. This is touched upon in the following quotation:[1]

> Effective communication . . . suffers when management fails to sense that in a free society a man good enough to make a strong contribution is good enough to have his own scale of values, and that goals which he has established . . . are not necessarily parallel with those which management has proclaimed for the company. Only when an intelligent effort is made to recognize and appreciate his objectives and to integrate them with those of the company . . . does communication . . . become a significant exercise.

REFERENCE

1. Clarence B. Randall, *The Folklore of Management* (Boston: Little, Brown and Company, 1960), p. 7.

10

RESEARCH AND RENEWAL

Every company, regardless of size, must be able to discover and utilize new concepts and procedures if it is to survive. The company that merely keeps current is in fact sliding back. And regardless of size or market served, every commercial enterprise exists for the purpose of spending money to create values in excess of the money spent.

Since the values involved are those of the marketplace and therefore relative to what competitors do, it follows that every company must be able to discover ways to meet or beat competition. No company has ever escaped having its fate determined by its capacity to do something better than its competitors. Maintaining that capacity always calls for deliberately changing what the company does.

IMPORTANCE OF INNOVATION

The danger of obsolescence is greater today than ever because the rate of change is greater. If the 1960s have conditioned us for anything, it is the speed with which yesterday's vision becomes today's reality. They have taught us that nothing can be casually dismissed as impossible—be it the way work is done, the way firms are managed, or the way people act. The company that wants to survive in the 1970s will have to come to grips with the ideas behind forecasts of what business life will be like in the following ten years or so. Does that seem extreme? A decade ago, most managers would have ridiculed the idea that business survival depended on that sort of coping. Today, managers understand the fact and are also beginning to understand that change is a constant feature of business activity.

To put it another way, change cannot safely be dealt with these days on the basis of accommodation, on a reactive basis; it must be recognized that change can and must be anticipated and prepared for. Every company must, of course, deal with the changes thrust upon it, but when that becomes a preoccupation and precludes creative work to keep the company abreast of the market, organizationally lean, and operationally effective, it can be fatal. Finding out how a company *should* change is a good deal different from deciding how best to deal with the changes forced on the company. Also, it entails the exercise of an entirely different set of competences.

The abilities needed to react well to change can often be provided by managers and personnel with line or other responsibilities. High orders of analytic and synthesizing competence are needed to identify and deal with coming changes, and they can seldom be provided by personnel with operating interests or responsibilities. Profits from business activities in the future will most likely fall to firms that take pains to provide those competences and allow them the purview and scale and variety of resources required for them to make their unique contribution.

Conditions of the kind needed to provide a contributory and economic innovative activity do not arise naturally or accidentally. Survival needs impose on companies the necessity to take formal steps to force information across organizational lines and coordinate the work of managers across a wide range of functions.

In small companies, work usually takes place within a framework of understanding so complete as to minimize the need for formal action to achieve coordination. That feature of managerial life in the small company is not all on the plus side, however; the very fact that it reduces the need to "work to make things work" diminishes awareness of the information and control requirements of innovation efforts.

Correspondingly, most companies that seek to maximize their chances of prospering by improving at the best rate are more likely than not to benefit from formalizing their innovative efforts. In the company that does not expend its creative energies within a structure of effective planning, close control, and organizationally recognized responsibilities, resources gravitate toward daily activities and problems and never get to be applied to building a better future.

INNOVATION GUIDELINES

The executive who intends to make his company optimally innovative needs to know that innovative companies are characterized by freely moving knowledge of what's going on. Non-innovative companies, on the other hand, are highly stratified; there are sharp breaks in the character of knowledge and information flow between the executive, middle management, and lowest supervisory levels in the firm. A traditionally organized and run company is least likely to be or become innovative. Successful innovation inescapably involves changes in procedures, policies, systems, management philosophy, and organizational relationships, and for the average small company to accomplish it takes steely resolve and patient thoughtfulness.

The manager interested in innovating also needs to know that the most creative firm is one that has the most interaction between its members and the outside world through professional organizations, consulting, teaching, and other activities that bring men and ideas together. The key people of innovative firms are generally open and, at least as related to change, inclined toward participative decision making. In any but that rarest of companies headed by a creative genius who also possesses a keen administrative and marketing sense, team effort is vital to successful innovation. The aspects to be worked on should be chosen with care, since not every company can afford to innovate on a broad front. The following are small-company characteristics:

1. Small size is a special disadvantage in a number of operating areas. A small company's innovative efforts should be directed to projects likely to yield above-average payouts. In most cases, they are size-related.

2. A small company makes its living by producing products or services in response to variables inimical to large-scale production, such as short delivery time or custom featuring; the big company prospers best when it produces products that can be sold in high volume without frequent production line changes.

3. A small business that must continuously fight product obsolescence has picked the wrong product, but product obsolescence favors the large company as long as it does not prevent high-volume production between product changes.

4. The small company is favored by products that have short production runs; the longer its production runs, the more vulnerable a small company is.

5. Great variability of demand, seasonally or volumetrically, favors small-company operations and hurts large-company ones.

6. Small companies should look for products that are required in high quality. High-volume methods favor large companies but often leave something to be desired in the quality of the article or service produced.

7. Opportunities for small business relate to the stage of maturity of the industry or product involved. Small businesses tend to be important producers or suppliers of components and of products in early stages of development, whereas large firms tend to dominate the markets for older, established products.

8. Increasing product variation and complexity creates new opportunities for exploitation (piggybacking) by small companies.

9. Companies that serve markets highly sensitive to product features must take pains to avoid getting trapped into product stasis. (Market stability at times results from design mobility.)

10. Small companies should strive to maintain recognizable degrees of exclusivity in their products or services. Because their finances do not permit them to invest heavily in equipment, small companies benefit less from freezing product designs than large companies do.

11. Small companies should resist having a full product line if to have it would detract from having a distinctive line. The small company competes most effectively when its items are appealing because they are distinctive rather than because of gradations among them.

12. Small firms are sheltered when their products or services cannot easily be combined with other products or services, either in production or sales.

13. Small companies that risk large portions of their resources in projects that do not offer the possibility of an early indication of success take unjustifiable and possibly deadly risks. (Seven out of eight hours of technical time devoted to product development in this country are spent on projects that do not reach commercial success.)

14. Small companies should avoid and large companies should seek products that require heavy investments of time. Risks for small firms rise but competition for large companies declines in direct proportion to the stretching

out of time between the first investment and the earliest possibility of money coming in.

STRUCTURE AND DIRECTION OF RENEWAL EFFORT

The size of the research effort and the structure of the research department, if there is one, will vary with the size and type of industry. The advisable size will be indicated by answers to the following questions:

1. What kinds of innovations are needed?
2. Where should innovation start?
3. How much can the company afford to put into it?
4. What phases should be made into checkpoints?

A company's search for better ways of doing things should not, of course, focus exclusively on the company's products or services. The real answer to the question "why innovate?" is "to do something better." "Better" can mean cheaper, higher quality, or earlier entrance into the market. In turn, the implication is that innovation should be extended to the methods of manufacturing, marketing, inventory management, record keeping, data processing, organization, and all other aspects of the business. In short, a firm must search for better methods in every area in which it acts. Otherwise, it risks many losses, not the least of which are its bright, aggressive personnel. People with imagination soon become bored with and leave a company that is set in its ways, and the result is that the firm's innovative capacity is further depleted.

Some of the key areas in which a company might look for profit improvement through innovation are marketing, sales methods, products or services, packaging, manufacturing processes, administrative methods, employee utilization, and clerical procedures. Innovations can also take the form of changes in the methods of keeping records of inventory, sales, and the like.

Regardless of the form they take, innovations should be handled in the same manner. Innovators must constantly add to their store of knowledge; they must continually make a conscious effort to tap the many sources of new thought:

Libraries. Most libraries have good business sections, and librarians will help get material through interlibrary loans once a specific line of inquiry is outlined.

Government agencies. The federal government has a vast storehouse of knowledge on a variety of subjects, and it is available to any businessman.

Salesmen. The company's sales personnel can be of great value in obtaining new ideas and devising better ways of doing things. They should be motivated to stay alert to new ideas during their visits to customers. Also, vendor salesmen can introduce new concepts into a business.

Trade shows. Both industrywide trade and other-industry trade shows are sources of ideas. Certain equipment, with moderate modification, may be just what is needed.

Brainstorming. An organized group session in which free expression of all ideas is encouraged may produce useful ideas among the crop of suggestions.

Areas of Analysis

Long-range plans. To fill the gap between where the company is now and where it wants to be in five or ten years may require new ideas for products or services, markets, and sources of people and money. It is usually wise to develop two or three times the number of ideas that are at first apparently needed because the attrition rate is high when the time comes to implement.

Universities. The faculty usually have continuing and close contact with significant changes in their various areas of interest. A company may be able to tap that knowledge source through a consulting relationship.

Employees. Many employees, including those in nonexempt positions, can make valuable contributions because of their knowledge of the product or the manufacturing processes. A good suggestion system can encourage the receipt of those ideas.

In gathering information, an innovation file can be helpful. In it facts and ideas can be listed under such headings as product, production methods, packaging, advertising and sales promotion, financing, and personnel.

SCOPE OF RESEARCH

Our society is becoming more professional and technical. One result is that the innovation and discovery important to companies will come increasingly from basic research. That is one reason why total United States R&D expenditures have doubled in the last decade and now are running around $16 billion annually. A fair portion of that sum is spent on original research. The implication is that every company must seek some original solutions, not just piggyback on others' discoveries. There are times, in fact, when it is cheaper to develop a unique solution or improvement than to look for answers in what others have done.

That is not to say that innovations should always be completely new, which would be as remarkable as it would be unwise. The renewal problem—whether the company should survey the field or go it alone—always has an economic side. Sometimes the innovation amounts to minor changes in a mechanism or design. Deciding how much innovation is needed is a difficult and cost-critical task. The operations auditor should check carefully to see what changes have been made, when changes last occurred, and why changes were made.

The direction that innovation should take varies with the company and its manager. One approach is that a better way of doing things should be adopted if it can be afforded. That requires someone to keep constantly alert to new developments in his field. He should also be aware of financial and other risks. The operations auditor must find out which choice or combination of choices the company is exercising and in what degree. In the process of finding that out, he is measuring the company's chances of survival.

To search for better alternatives—the action aspect of a willingness to learn and absorb new knowledge—is far from being a universal inclination, even among top executives. As long as things look all right, many executives not only leave things as they are but do not search for other ways of doing them. Only when things go wrong is the search for alternatives triggered. The other side of the coin is that, when they are forced to decide in a hurry, managers often produce better decisions than when they have plenty

100

of time. Under the pressure of a crisis, the normal organizational processes and vested interests have no chance to react.

The auditor should find out if there is a set procedure for processing new ideas. Whether or not the idea is practicable is immaterial at this stage. It is important that there be an avenue down which suggestions will come to the attention of management and that the employee be given full credit for his ideas. Evolutionary improvements are constantly possible, even when revolutionary research breakthroughs are evasive or their pursuit is too expensive.

In today's competitive economy the value of initiative in management is extremely high, even though it is more recognized in speech than in fact. Intelligent planning is, beyond question, of immense importance, but intelligent efforts of top planners will be fruitless unless they are coupled with the exploitation of new ideas and approaches.

One of the prime benefits to a company genuinely interested in change is to set up a climate in which people work more for themselves than for others. That means finding ways to fulfill goals with less supervision, and they must be the objects of research that is as effective as is that for products. Finding new things to do should be placed on an equal plane with finding new ways to do things. A better method of production may not reduce the cost directly but instead reduce the boredom involved in the job and thereby increase quality.

CONTROLLING RESULTS

To stay competitively strong, organizations will have to become mission-oriented and know not only how to handle today's breadwinners but how to identify tomorrow's. The first will encourage the company to concentrate its research resources; the second will guide it in the deployment of those resources. The following are guidelines for determining whether research will keep an organization young:

1. The company should at all times have a sense of how much innovation it needs to stay or become competitive.

2. A definite portion of every company's income should be set aside for renewal activities regardless of whether the need is specifically felt or not.

3. Innovation and research dollars should be directed toward tomorrow's needs, not toward dressing up old workhorses.

4. Research concepts should be sufficiently broad in spectrum that new or emerging trends with possible relevance to the company's capabilities can be recognized and are not screened out.

5. Go, no-go decisions on innovations should be based on team analysis; one-man decisions are too risky.

6. The group charged with innovation should know specifically where they are going, what resources they will use to get there, and when they should arrive.

7. The innovative needs that can best be filled by in-house capabilities and those that have to be filled by outside resources should be so identified.

8. Innovations should be tested in some sort of pilot program, whenever

possible, before a full-scale commitment is made. Testing keeps the price of failure down so that company resources are not fatally strained.

9. Innovations should not be evaluated against narrowly defined possibilities of growth. Traditional expense notions should not keep the company from occasionally trying a cost-borderline innovation.

10. No resource affects the future configuration of the enterprise more directly than manpower. The company must identify its renewal needs and the in-house capabilities that can be put to renewal work, and seek, through the adjustments within its reach, to match the two.

These points strongly imply that a company deliberately engaged in innovation should embody such activities in a planned program. The program need not be elaborate, but it certainly should entail assigning responsibility for it to a single individual or a group, depending on the size of the company. It should lead to reasoned decisions on what will and will not be done. Innovation without a prescribed plan is worse than none at all. Therefore, basic ground rules must be established.

CONCLUSION

One of the skills to be measured in a company is knowledge of how to bring about change. Change brings genuine fears of loss of status and security, especially in a company already in trouble. Add to that the prediction by William Haber, University of Michigan economist, that in the next quarter-century half of the American work force will be relying on skills not yet developed, and you get some idea of the enormous challenge that lies ahead for management.

One factor the operations auditor must be conscious of is that the need for conformity affects the rate of change possible in a company. Every company needs conformity to a certain degree, and that need causes no problem. The problem comes in when conformity is made into conformism—systematic refusal to think.

One final note on the subject may be appropriate: It should be kept in mind that change in business is constant. Because it is constant, change tends to anesthetize. The whole point of renewal activities is not to introduce change but to bring in productive changes. The alternative is to be the victim of change.

11

PERSONNEL

Most of the difference between an effective company and a defective one often lies in the quality of manpower and the intelligence with which manpower is used. It is therefore vital that a company know where it stands with respect to both. Audits of the activities that have to do with the employment of personnel can provide many of the elements that make up such knowledge.

SIGNIFICANCE OF THE MANPOWER RESOURCE

Before financial or physical resources can be used to the best advantage, people have to be employed to the best advantage. When they are not so used, money and machines cannot be. Those views have general acceptance, but it is incredible how small a part of the capabilities of personnel is used in the typical company. For that reason, the company that strives to excel in the employment of personnel enjoys a significant competitive advantage.

Up to now, the employment of human beings has been largely an art, mainly because the means for establishing and maintaining close contact with this dynamic and complex resource has not been technically or economically feasible. But times are changing. Though objective, research-proven information on human behavior has been slow to filter into business and the means for processing behavioral data has been slow to be developed, the rate of absorption of the first and evolution of the second is now stepping up. The time is not far off when behavioral science will become a leading source of business knowledge and more fully reflected in the accounting and control technologies. (Even now, human resource accounting is becoming practical and accepted and human factor research is beginning to be utilized in designing business controls.)

Probably no harder job faces the operations auditor than appraising the effectiveness of corporate activities relating to human employment. The activities are not always readily available for investigation; their influence is not always discernible; they very frequently extend far beyond the boundaries of a single unit of organization; and they are often great in number and variety. It may be that the quality of manpower utilization efforts will always lie beyond measurement with anything like the accuracy possible in, say, physical production. Nevertheless, because of its great importance to corporate improvement, it is vital that appraisal of the personnel function be made.

These points touch on a consideration vital to audits of the function variously called personnel, personnel management, and manpower utilization. If conducted within the framework of traditional concepts, the audit performed will be of the personnel department or analogous unit only. But so restricted an audit touches mainly upon the mechanical aspects of human employment and reveals practically nothing about the environment in which human resources are used. The authors regard such an audit as a waste of time.

That personnel departments are so common and direction of personnel is so ubiquitous a managerial task has led to fragmenting the approach to what is essentially a single, unitary function. But an audit cannot take a fragmentary approach; the personnel function cannot be meaningful in itself. All the standards worth applying to employee-centered activities relate in some way to employee productivity, and personnel activities that have no actual or potential effect on how well manpower resources are used are valueless from the viewpoint of corporate purpose, no matter how well designed or fashionable they appear to be. The most fundamental measure of the worth of a formal personnel function lies in the degree to which the function's activities extend into the rest of the organization.

Hence, sound appraisals of the manpower function cannot be reached solely by judging the quality of activities internal to personnel departments. Appraisal of a personnel function (which may be defined as a complex of activities aimed at serving the needs of a firm's manpower in order that it may produce at essential and desired levels) will certainly involve an audit of the personnel department where it exists, but it will also be an audit of effects permeating a large organizational landscape.

Experience tells—and the foregoing remarks are intended to show—that an assignment in the personnel-manpower utilization field requires much of an auditor. Few areas are more complex or sophisticated, nor do the common measures of effectiveness apply as well here as in other business areas. Pitfalls for the auditor abound in the personnel-manpower field.

Take the example of a personnel department that is impotent with respect to how employees are regarded, treated, and employed. It would not be difficult for the auditor to label it a failure, but he should not take lack of influence as proof that the department is inherently deficient in direction or programs. Personnel department practices that reach out so far as to have real influence on manpower utilization should be looked upon as a resultant of long and patient striving and not as a measure of success at any one point of time. A good department, in short, is not necessarily recognizable by the influence it currently exercises over manpower utilization.

The reason for a personnel department's failure to bring about productive employee relations may indeed lie mainly within the department, but often it does not. In many companies the personnel function is treated by operating management as necessary for window dressing but actually superfluous. Thus, the auditor must concern himself not only with whether the personnel department has positive and constructive ideas and programs aimed at improving manpower productivity but also with whether those ideas and programs are being successfully promoted and adopted and, if not, why not. Investigation along these lines may expose some of a company's principal managerial flaws, but that would constitute one of the auditor's best contributions. He should not hesitate to pursue his course simply because the investigation may turn up some painful facts.

PERSONNEL FUNCTION: MISSION AND ORGANIZATION

The mission of a firm's personnel function is to maximize return on the company's investment in personnel. That does not mean an exploitative approach; it means the establishment of a climate in which the best available talent is brought into the company and developed and utilized to its fullest extent. In such a climate personal and corporate goals can be brought together through a process of adjustment and accommodation that fosters both personal and company growth.

Often, in smaller companies, the personnel function is not separately organized. Even so, it is important to review the activities periodically as a unitary corporate function. It is certain that *someone* is handling the continuing tasks of finding people, training them, paying them, handling their problems, selecting them for promotion, evaluating them, and terminating them. Because those activities are both critical and costly, they cannot safely be ignored.

The existence of an organizational unit created to deal with personnel matters is not *prima facie* evidence that the personnel function is being properly recognized or handled. Personnel departments vary greatly in effectiveness. Some are little more than paper-processing mills that add little to corporate progress; others contribute significantly to the achievement of overall organizational goals. In the first instance, the personnel department spends most of its time performing clerical tasks, recruiting, and keeping records. In the second, it is as much or more engaged in helping provide and maintain documents, such as job descriptions, that contribute to management of human effort, providing or aiding in training, counseling in human relations problems, and helping achieve improvements in manpower utilization. The most effective personnel departments are extroverted agencies in their companies whose work ties in closely with the effort to fulfill established objectives.

The following is a list of activities common to most formally organized personnel functions. It will, of course, be incomplete when applied to any particular case, but it can be used as a checklist to provide quick familiarity with a given department's activities:

1. EMPLOYMENT
    Selection
        Requisition (including job specifications)
        Recruitment (use of personnel agencies, advertising, executive search, colleges; specialized and executive recruitment; minority employment)
        Interviews
        Tests
        Reference checks
        Physical examinations
        Job offer and acceptance

Placement
Induction (plus new employee orientation); legal contracts, bonds, patent agreements
Counseling
Transfers
Promotions
Termination
Exit interviews, checklist
Severance pay
Records
Reports

2. WORKING CONDITIONS
   Sanitation
   Ventilation
   Lighting
   Heating
   Rest periods
   Food service

3. COMPENSATION
   Job descriptions
   Wage scales
   Incentives (management by objectives)
   Bonuses
   Profit sharing
   Executive compensation
   Periodic performance review

4. TRAINING AND EDUCATION
   Exploration of the basis of learning in work situations
   On-the-job training
   Apprenticeship
   Vestibule school
   Conferences
   Technical training
   Management training and development; modern techniques
   Library
   Manuals, programmed instruction, audio-visual tools
   Bulletins
   Tuition assistance program

5. HEALTH
   Examinations
   First aid

6. SAFETY
   Inspection
   Education
   Programs
   Workmen's compensation

7. WELFARE AND SERVICES
   Insurance
   Unemployment
   Hospital
   Life
   Other
   Retirement and pensions
   Savings and loans
   Credit union
   Bonds
   Social activities
   Athletic programs
   Employee periodicals and communications
   Employee purchases
   Transportation
   Legal aid program
   Suggestion system

8. EMPLOYEE RELATIONS
   Grievance procedure, day-to-day union contract handling
   Female workers
   Handicapped workers
   Minority groups
   Contract negotiation, administration, labor law
   Policy indoctrination

9. SECURITY
   Procedures
   Guard service
   Investigations

10. RESEARCH
    Job analysis
    Turnover
    Absenteeism
    Accidents and accident records
    Employee morale
    Wages and living costs
    Community-industry wage levels
    Application of behavioral science findings

11. PLANNING
    Staffing requirements
    Training program
    Departmental budget(s)

The personnel function at its most contributory level does far more than perform the foregoing services; at its best it has influence at top planning levels. It places its skills, knowledge, and contacts at the service of the company generally, and in that way it often contributes significantly to organization planning, public relations, attracting and keeping high-potential personnel, keeping compensation balanced, maintaining productive union relations, and putting new knowledge about human behavior to work.

CONDUCTING THE AUDIT

As previously noted, appraisal of the personnel function is rewarding but difficult. Successful completion of the appraisal will depend in large measure on the auditor's comprehension of the function's general aspects and more significant classes of activities.

Taking the latter first, activities relating to manpower may be considered to fall into three classes: supply, employment, and administration. Two of these, supply and administration, are customarily entirely within the province of the personnel department and sometimes constitute all the work of the department. But an *effective* department has a lot to do with the quality of the third class, employment, and, to the degree it does, the auditor has an indirect measure of the worth of the department. Each of the three classes of activities is dealt with separately following this subsection.

The balance of this subsection deals with several general aspects of the function, inspection of which supports the appraisal. The aspects are primarily reflections of a firm's attitudes toward and understanding of the use of manpower as a resource, and the control philosophy it pursues.

The aspect that should concern the auditor early in the audit consists of what might be called the grounds or foundation of the personnel function. Before manpower can be truly effectively used, positive, realistic, and integrated concepts of human behavior and potentials must exist, but convictions of some kind always underlie how it *is* used. They can be identified and defined, and they offer points of evaluation in making an appraisal. The auditor will often encounter convictions that are neither acknowledged nor consistent; convictions about people are often negative and therefore unfit for public acknowledgment. The auditor will do well to retain the following research-supported views of the needs and thrusts of business employees. They are derived from current behavioral science investigations.

☐ People want to work.
☐ They do not want to be unduly regulated.
☐ They want to know, to be informed.
☐ They have different needs at different ages and stages of their careers.
☐ They need to be given a basis for self-respect.
☐ They need to see that their work is important.
☐ They need to have their work recognized.
☐ They need the familiar.
☐ They need something fresh.
☐ They want to retain individuality.
☐ They want to be treated on an equal basis.

With these work-relevant findings about people in mind, the auditor will have a frame of reference for his work and benchmarks in appraising how well manpower is being used in a firm. To the extent the principles actually in force are negative, restrictive, or repressive, they are unlikely to permit high employee productivity in the long run.

A second aspect of personnel that an auditor should examine is the relative flexibility built into or allowed the function. Since convictions of considerable power almost always underlie manpower practices, it is fair to assume that considerable inertia is apt to be built into personnel functions. Therefore, it should not be taken for granted that the function will anticipate and bend with the changing manpower requirements of the firm. Special awareness and effort and, probably, specifically designed procedures are required to make it do so.

As both the scale and character of a company's manpower needs change, the personnel function must be sensitive to the adjustments in, for example, recruitment and training that follow. The function can sensibly respond only on the basis of knowledge, however. Hence, research is an activity natural to the personnel function, and its existence and directions are indications whether the function has sufficient flexibility and virtuosity to serve the longer-range aims of the company. It is certain that when research is lacking, such service is impossible. Causes of employee turnover, the implications of job tenure, determining the lead time to train new skills, identifying the factors affecting the competition for labor, and determining promotability of employees are subjects of research at least as useful as the more common ones of staffing requirements and recruitment specifications.

A third aspect the auditor should attempt to check out is the cost effectiveness of the personnel function. How well personnel activities justify their cost is seldom an object of concern, partly because personnel is considered an absolutely essential staff function with unavoidable costs and partly because checking cost effectiveness is a difficult job. But there is no reason why the personnel function should not be treated as a cost center and controlled through the use of budgets and the application of such economic yardsticks as comparisons with costs in the same industry and perhaps other industries.

On the other hand, there are many reasons why treating the personnel function as a cost center and controlling its costs should not aim at producing the lowest costs, whether unit or absolute. Few companies have so mastered their affairs that they can afford to be primarily cost-conscious where personnel activities are concerned. The great majority of companies have objectives affecting manpower that require far higher priorities than that of keeping the costs of the personnel function in line.

In spite of this two-horned situation, progressive personnel departments usually have a good deal of interest in and a fair amount of knowledge about the costs involved in their work. For example, they often know the costs of fringes, training, and grievances and how they compare with industry averages. Many departments also know such specific things as recruitment costs on a department or per-hire basis and the costs of indoctrinating new employees, preparing workers to assume supervisory responsibilities, and training employees of various classes.

It is noteworthy that personnel departments that bother to find out what their costs are usually tend to act on the information gathered. For that reason, when the auditor has evidence of cost keeping in personnel work, he usually has evidence of the quality of administration of the function.

MANPOWER SUPPLY

A firm can fulfill its manpower needs internally by identifying, training, and developing promotable talent or externally by identifying skill and talent needs, determining which are not resident in the firm, and recruiting from the outside. Comments on each of these auditable elements follow.

Fulfilling manpower needs from internal sources of supply is not a simple activity and, for that reason, is not often well done. It embraces a number of separable, identifiable activities. At the least it embraces the search for and identification of promotable persons, description of the talents of such persons, identification and description of arising job openings or work requirements, and the preparing of persons to be put into jobs new to them and/or new to the firm.

The tapping of internal manpower sources begins with the identification of promotable persons by activities that should be a part of every personnel function: personnel or skill inventories and the appraisal of performance on a scheduled and uniform basis. Both activities are important even in small operations, in which they are informal or even subconscious. Without them, the possibility of poor decisions in filling jobs is greatly increased.

Training and development. Once promotable talent has been identified and accurately described, the process of preparing it for the new tasks that the personnel function also should have identified and described in advance begins. Training and development activities are vital to a company's interests and for that reason provide a worthy field for audit investigation. Usually they fall miserably short of goals—despite high hopes and high costs—for the reason that most of the conditions for their success are either unknown or ignored.

Not that valid guidelines are lacking. There are available plenty of facts and sound hypotheses upon which to construct programs with a better-than-even chance of producing at reasonable cost the competences and orientation needed in the sponsoring company. The failure is based more on what almost seems to be willful, deliberate refusal to face up to what is needed to develop people than on lack of knowledge.

Requirements for productive training. Among the requirements for making training productive, the following are important and offer the auditor some checkable aspects:

1. Training must be recognized and treated as a complex function that requires the same intensity of effort and attention to fact that is required of, say, systems engineering.

2. Personnel development must be systematic; it must be a total program within which all parts are interrelated and integrated with specific corporate aims and objectives.

3. Training should be approached as a teaching function and not as mere conditioning; development involves the learning of things usable in business.

4. Persons who receive formal training must be known to the company in the fullest range of their capacities so that the developmental effort can bring those capacities up to the needs of the enterprise.

5. Training is effective only when it prepares manpower for the fulfillment of future as well as present needs.

6. If training is to succeed, it must be carried on within an environment of values that is consistent with and reinforces the benefits sought.

Each of these points will now be dealt with at greater length.

1. The statement that training is complex amounts to a truism, but it points to an important fact: more often than not, training is treated at much too low a level of sophistication. Many simpler problems are rated as more complex and given far more attention, although few have more profound or persistent effects on a business. That the omission is common makes it no less grave. A company that ignores the problem of developing its people is truly indifferent to its future.

2. That training must be a total program is evidenced by a comparison of manager development and worker training. At least, workers are given a good deal of training on the job, whereas manager training often consists of little more than an occasional course or seminar. The idea of training as a continuous, systematic, and specific activity would be far better served by designing training and development elements into all lower- and middle-management jobs. That can be done by making specific provision for subordinate training in the responsibilities assigned to all supervisors and leaving room in all jobs below the chief executive's for the assumption of more or broader responsibilities as the capacities of the incumbents grow. Taking those two steps would violate some canons of conventional business theory, but they must be taken if managers are to be prepared to meet tomorrow's problems.

3. That training should be approached more as a teaching than a conditioning activity has largely been ignored in designing training programs. Development is seldom thought of as a learning process; it is usually regarded as some sort of high-level seduction or wooing. That is wrong; in business, it is what a manager knows that counts. Most training programs teach little that is specific and can be used by the participant for the benefit of the business. Too often only the spurious aspects of education rub off, such as the special vocabulary acquired without any accompanying understanding.

One reason for the situation is that few persons connected with training bother to acquaint themselves with the requirements of optimal learning or the facts of the company environment as they relate to the learning process. For example, it is known that the speed of learning is related to the removal of distractions and the penalties that are attached to mistakes made, yet programs are continually being designed and implemented without consideration of those factors. The problem here is that most businessmen spend too little time on *how* to teach and too much time on *what* to teach.

The emphasis must be reversed. Determining what needs to be taught is, of course, vital and is actually sometimes skipped or poorly done. But it does not deserve the amounts of time it usually gets; it is, after all, fairly obvious—being virtually tied in with the management process in general and as it is practiced in the specific company. But how best to impart that which is to be taught needs far more time than businessmen customarily give it. The reason is that it involves unfamiliar areas of knowledge, such as the discoveries of the behavioral sciences, and the barriers to change specific to each situation and company that require a good deal of intelligence and sensitivity to acquire and put to use.

4. If it be accepted that management development is a learning process, success will be achieved only if the needs of each person to be trained are factually and considerably known. Probably no single requirement of sound training to make the individual more broadly and fully effective in the company faces more formidable handicaps than this. Measuring human capacities is difficult enough without the problems of interpreting personality and experience, the defenses of individuals and organizations (which also have personalities), and the inexactitude of what we know about motivation. It is, in fact, beyond doing in the absence of accurate and reasonably complete information about employees.

Thus, it can be said that effective management development starts with the accumulation of information about a person. That kind of information takes a lot of time and effort to get and is therefore rare. Almost all companies know far more about their money and their physical assets than they do about the people who work for them, and that is probably more true of big, amply staffed companies than of small, thinly staffed ones. (The brave talk about computerized personnel information systems has remained mostly talk.) Adequate information, when it does exist, is almost always limited to higher-level employees with five or more years' tenure and is hardly ever available on production or clerical employees or on personnel recently brought in from the outside.

The situation is undoubtedly changing, however. There is evidence that companies are beginning to think of computer applications in the areas that have always suffered from information deficiencies, that have always been viewed as being, by nature, incapable of generating objective data. Personnel selection and development are prime examples. As understanding of and accommodation to computers moves forward, automated data processing will undoubtedly be extended first to the assembly of employee information data banks and then into staffing, organization planning, and similar areas.

5. If training is effective only when it prepares manpower to fulfill future as well as present needs, then management must provide an organizational climate in which the learning can most effectively and efficiently take place. Experiences become significant when they are relevant to the learner and the tasks assigned to him or the seminars he attends relate to his desires, motivations, and drives. In other words, unless work and training provide the individual with experiences that are meaningful to him *now*, learning will not take place. Providing a man with a learning opportunity and not providing him with the opportunity to use or benefit from what he has learned renders training and development sterile activities.

Effective learning requires an environment that supports an individual's strivings and is tolerant of his mistakes. Unless failure is understood and dealt with as a learning experience (among other things), it will only inhibit initiative. The trick is to structure situations so that the opportunity for making truly critical errors does not arise. Assignments should therefore be consonant with but somewhat beyond the learner's background. Challenge attaches not so much to the novel as to the experience partly known.

6. The last point in the list stresses that values determine what is learned. As a rule, merely telling a man what is right is not sufficient to assure that he will do what is right; for that to happen, something in him will have

to be changed. A change in behavior, which is what personnel development really aims at, requires that new facts be recognized and accepted. To state it differently, personality cannot be changed but behavior can be. New knowledge, information that is understood and accepted, holds the best possibility for changing behavior and therefore performance on the job.

If knowledge is to be imparted systematically, it must be recognized that information is most quickly and durably assimilated when it accords best with the values it bears upon. It is almost impossible for knowledge to be imparted if it conflicts with the existing values of the individual or those that he perceives to underlie the behavior of his company. The main reasons why training so often fails in its purpose is that all learning takes place in a value environment and that what people learn and how they use it depend heavily on the values they hold or are responsible to. In industry the term "value" is used most often in the economic sense, and that meaning has a well-defined and almost classic status. As used here, however, "value" can be described as anything that functions as a directive force in action or behavior.

Values act as filters in the learning process. In a free society they are in many ways the ultimate conditioners of perspective and action. In the corporation they influence the kinds of knowledge that will be employed and that will be taken up in a formal training program. Establishment, refinement, and maintenance of an effective value system, then, becomes one of the top jobs of top management. Yet the auditor will find that it is one of the most neglected jobs of all.

Before a company can benefit from training, it must put into practice the lessons of modern management: to the greatest degree possible it must discard hackneyed measures of contribution, rewards to those faithful to safe ideas, promotions for the adherents of company stereotypes, and laurels to the no-mistakes manager. In their place must be put adherence to objective-centered values, realistic measures of contribution, rewards to the creative mind, promotions for the successful innovator, and laurels to the effective manager without limitations in the nature of personal, social, or cultural bias.

The benefits of a program of sound training go beyond immediate results; few activities are richer in side benefits. For example, training activities provide a natural forum for discussion of company practices, policies, and objectives. There is probably no neater way to eliminate bad decisions and poor practices than to expose them to the scrutiny of the training group. Further, few activities refine a firm's management philosophy and processes more efficiently than training. That follows from the old dictum that no one learns better than the teacher. A firm that makes a serious effort to teach management—to pick one among many subjects—cannot fail to improve the quality of its management.

Recruitment. The alternative to the internal provision of personnel is recruitment. There is hardly a company that does not have recurrent need to bring in people from the outside, nor are there many corporate activities that have greater effect on manpower productivity and human relations. Recruitment practices are therefore deserving of the auditor's close scrutiny.

Growth probably occasions the major need for recruitment, but even without it there is usually enough employee mobility and change in technology and procedures that people have to be brought in from the outside. The move to computers is a prime example of a change that can create needs for new skills that are not resident in the firm or cannot be developed.

Bringing people into the firm is costly, and it can seriously affect the future of the company. Therefore, it should be subject to formal control. The first thing the operations auditor should look into is the control process. Each position should be reviewed and approved for filling before recruiting begins, and there should be safeguards that each job to be filled is accurately and fully described.

Next, the auditor should see whether recruiting avenues are being properly exploited; they include references by employees, walk-in applicants, private and state employment offices, newspaper and trade publication advertising, and college and high school recruitment.

Screening. After he has reviewed the recruitment avenues, the auditor should look next at screening, which can have far-reaching effects on corporate welfare. Unintelligent screening can cause the loss of the best-qualified candidates; insensitive screening can create hostility toward the company. Because far more applicants are *not* accepted for employment than are, the company procedures should insure that unsuccessful applicants will be left with a good impression of the firm. Being considerate costs nothing but a little care and effort, and good public relations have considerable value.

In that connection the operations auditor should check whether persons handling recruitment and screening are up to date on the laws bearing on hiring, particularly in relation to nondiscrimination. For practical as well as legal and moral reasons it would be hard to justify rejection for any reason than incapacity to fill the job. That points to the need for the auditor to investigate standards in use during screening. They are of many kinds, but at the very least they include clear and factual specifications of the job to be filled. Others are governmental hiring standards and aptitude tests.

If tests are used in screening, the auditor should investigate whether they are appropriate to their application. He should also check for proof of validity—that they test what they are supposed to test and are sufficiently free from cultural and like bias that they can give reliable insight into the true qualifications of candidates. Test administration is also a matter for audit. Aptitude tests are probably best administered by professionals or by specially trained personnel.

Effects of recruitment. Investigation of recruitment offers insight into many facets of the corporate personnel function. Recruitment cannot effectively serve corporate interests if it is construed simply as a people-picking activity; its effects on employee morale, productivity, turnover, policies, and promotions are too far-reaching for that. The effects on morale are significant when hire from without rather than promote from within is standard procedure. That can undermine the effectiveness of employees by diminishing their incentive to produce well and, in that way, affect corporate profits and growth. Especially when company growth creates opportunities for increased employee contribution should the personnel function investigate the possibilities of promotion from within. Only when it has been determined beyond doubt that the qualifications do not exist in the company should talent be recruited from the outside. Seniority alone, however, cannot qualify for the next level of responsibility, despite many contract provisions to that effect. (Consider the supersalesman whose star dims as sales manager.)

Another way to look at recruitment is to see each vacancy as an opportunity to upgrade the position being filled. For example, if an office manager has to be replaced and the decision has been made to look outside the firm, the personnel department has a chance to find someone better qualified by knowledge, experience, and skills than the incumbent. When such a person is hired, the opportunity arises to expand the job's scope or consolidate activities currently shared.

Size of organization is a major factor in the choice between internal and external search for personnel. The 5,000-person company is normally better able to produce personnel with proper experience than the 500-person company, in which certain skills are likely to be found in only one or two people. On the other hand, the smaller organization is in a better position to gain when personnel are brought in from the outside. The importation of new ideas from other companies can have relatively greater effects.

Though promotion from within is almost always beneficial when the skill or experience needed is available, it cannot be a sound practice when it is done gratuitously, that is, when it is not planned. Therefore, the auditor should determine whether there are standards and policies, written or not, relating to advancement and whether they serve the firm's interests. For example, he should determine whether the policies emphasize capabilities rather than seniority. Emphasis on seniority can signify an historically bound, locked-in condition with respect to employee utilization that is wasteful and detrimental to the growth of the firm. On the other hand, failure to respect seniority *after* capabilities have been duly weighed can also be harmful.

Investigation of a sample of recent personnel changes will shed light on whether promotion is based on the possession of specific skills, perhaps detected through performance appraisal or testing activities, or on more or less subjective considerations. If there is no documentation to examine, the auditor has good reason to suspect that advancement takes place on an ad hoc, private judgment basis. Only a little more research will be needed to confirm or allay the suspicion.

Of course, in respect to manpower supply a progressive company usually does more than find out what skills are available to it; it also seeks to create additional skills according to plan. For example, it encourages self-development through reimbursement of tuition for courses employees complete on their own time. The promotion policies of progressive firms reflect the consciousness that useful knowledge is a company asset.

Advancement. Finally, in his review of policies affecting advancement, the auditor should review the state and distribution of policy statements. Most companies have not taken the trouble to have policies properly written and communicated. For some reason, policies regarding advancement, even when they have been well-promulgated, are usually considered unfit for wide distribution. That position is indefensible, and the auditor can use, as one measure of policy effectiveness, the extent to which promotion policies have been disseminated and are being carried out.

When advancement is made on a rational basis, there is almost bound to be some kind of evaluation system that precedes promotion. When it does exist, the system itself should also come under audit review. There are many ways to evaluate people, and the techniques are constantly changing under the impact of behavioral science findings. The operations auditor should first find out what is the system in use and then determine its quality. Indications of quality are whether the system gives each employee a chance to contribute to assessments of his performance, helps determine his own rate and direction of growth, provides a joint basis, between supervisor and employee, for setting goals and measuring progress, and supplies management with the information needed to assess personnel for reassignment, training, succession, salary adjustments, and so forth.

EMPLOYMENT
The direction of people at work is normally viewed as little of the personnel function's business, but that attitude is far from being reasonable or defensible. Although accepted business principle places the highest value on the worth and privileges of operating management, to leave manpower utilization solely to line supervisors is to leave it to considerably less than tender or productive mercies. Operating managers too often are production-oriented and lack the ability to handle people well. A line manager must have unusual sensitivity, understanding, and self-detachment if he is to supervise in the best interests of the company.

No progressive company can take a laissez faire attitude toward human relations within the firm. The company that is alert to the possibilities that inhere in getting line supervisors, at every level, to work productively with their associates has a leg up on most of its competitors. A good instrument for improving supervisory (and subordinate) styles is the personnel function. One measure of the effectiveness of a personnel department is how much influence it has on the way people are dealt with on the job.

In assessing personnel's influence on employment, the auditor must recognize that, in conducting business affairs, cost considerations dictate the avoidance of personal direction as much as possible. To put it another way, a company prospers to the degree that its employees act in support of the firm's objectives without being constantly told to do so.

Following is a list of the principal means, aside from personal ones, by which action can be directed. As can be seen, most of them are documentary in character, but a few, such as indoctrination and training, involve some human interaction.

Business creed	Procedures
Management philosophy	Rules and regulations
Goals and objectives	Bulletins
Detailed plans	Job descriptions
Programs	Indoctrination
Policies	Training
Systems	

These and similar means should be checked by the auditor as they relate to heading employees in the right direction, stimulating supportive activity, forestalling the necessity for supervisory intervention, and providing readily accessible answers to repetitive decision-making questions. No company can long stay in business without resorting to the use of such tools, but few companies have succeeded in learning how to produce and use them on an integrated basis. A company that has succeeded in doing so will be recognizable by the progress it is making toward superior manpower utilization.

MOTIVATION

Another personnel aspect the auditor should investigate is the firm's motivational efforts, perhaps the best single indicator of the worth of the personnel management function. Getting people to produce more effectively than their industry peers is an exacting, exciting, rewarding, and never-ending task. No exceptional ability is needed to get ordinary performance from personnel, but to get people to produce consistently near the top level of their competence takes persistently attractive and output-centered action. The second stipulation is made because many of the confusions that attach to motivation arise from objectives of motivation that are not always realistic. Though it is commonly held that motivation must be people-centered, that view is counterproductive when it implies that the prime objectives of motivation are other than the attainment of effective production (whence the current high interest in motivation through the work itself).

Few words in the management vocabulary have been as worked over or overworked as "motivation," and so there is a tendency not to think or act incisively about motivation. Such flaccidity is usually very costly and may even be destructive. At their best, planning, direction, and control are sufficient only to get minimal production out; it takes motivation to get production to effective levels. Somewhat surprisingly, the provision of pleasant working conditions has little effect in getting employees to do a better job. Opportunities for advancement, bonuses, profit sharing, and stock purchase plans are usually more effective, but even they can fall short of getting people to produce to the best of their ability.

The findings of Frederick Herzberg of Case Western Reserve University, Cleveland, Ohio, indicate that the best and most durable motivators are not money or fringe benefits but those aspects of the work that satisfy the needs of people. When jobs offer an opportunity for growth, peer recognition, increasing responsibility and challenge, in digestible doses, people find satisfaction—motivation—in the work.

Motivation through work is not a simplistic formula to be universally applied; instead it is a rather sophisticated technique that requires management to be sensitive to the individual needs of people and their different priorities as age and career goals change. It also requires management to be so responsive that every employee can believe that his suggestions will be thoughtfully reviewed and, when useful to the firm, accepted. The idea that he can somehow influence the destiny of his firm does much to motivate an employee to better performance.

The auditor should therefore seek to gauge personnel's awareness and use of motivational findings, what the results are, and the flexibility of management in adjusting its methods on the basis of the results. The auditor should also look to see what studies are being made in order to identify the factors that are most effective in motivating the personnel of *this* firm.

Areas of Analysis

The auditor must resist the temptation to base his evaluation of motivational effectiveness on his impression of the level of morale. Loyalty, morale, and team spirit defy being measured and meaningfully interpreted in an operations audit. They are too complicated and prone to subjective interpretation.

Morale and those states of being gropingly described under the terms "loyalty" and "team spirit" are not useful indicators of either productivity or the working climate. Even assuming that morale can be accurately measured and the meaning of its measure understood, the fact that it is low does not necessarily indicate unfavorable conditions. Morale, for example, can be low because effective control is being exercised for the first time.

Rensis Likert, of the University of Michigan, has discovered that the type of organizational or managerial climate can be identified and that it can be predictive of productivity and such factors as employee turnover. Through the use of specially designed questionnaires, managerial styles were classified along a four-step continuum ranging from autocratic to participative. By analyzing the results of using the questionnaires in hundreds of companies, Likert was able to show the long-range effects of prevailing managerial styles on the operations of a business, as well as the results of changing those styles. His findings point to the significance of a personnel department's being aware of the consequences of the managerial style that the firm's management applies.

ADMINISTRATION

The employment of people imposes on every company a burden of activities beyond directing the employees on the job and helping them enlarge their capabilities. Those activities, which range widely in scope and character, constitute a principal segment of the personnel department's work. Elaboration of all the administrative details is beyond the scope of this section, but discussion of manpower information, compensation, and communications will widen the perspective of the auditor. The starting place, in auditing personnel administration, is to look into the information gathering, record keeping, and reporting procedures. They are basic to the work of all personnel functions.

Manpower is a unique business resource; no other requires as much or as varied knowledge to use it wisely. The resource cannot be understood in one dimension of time or behavioral pattern. For example, its maximum value may reside not in its present, but in its future usefulness. To estimate that requires knowledge of the past. Such knowledge comes mainly from well-kept records and analysis of the records, but historical and statistical information is not enough.

Just as employee behavior is capable of being predicted, so it is also capable of changing, and knowledge of manpower as a group, though important, often tells little about individuals. Therefore, skilled management of human resources requires not only an accurate and comprehensive body of relevant information about individuals and classes of employees, but also information about what happens to employees as the result of exposure to new experiences such as those involved in job rotation, training, and education. No company has enough of that information today, and therein lie the potentials inherent in improving the quality and quantity of information relating to manpower.

Manpower information. The deficiencies in use of manpower by many companies are in some measure due to information methods that have been stretched to the limits of their capacities. The key to improved management of manpower lies in improvement in the availability and utilization of manpower information. This is an economic as well as a technical problem. If discernible improvement in a company's capacity to manage its human resources can be wrung out of the methods now involved, it will be only through a great increase in employee information costs. The only tolerable course open to the company is that of adapting or changing the methods involved. Only in that way can information volume and quality increase without comparable cost increases.

The company that fails to aim at creating this excellence now is endangered because the capability of dealing economically with the immense complexities of a large-scale manpower information field is rapidly becoming an accomplished fact. Possession of this capability will do much to nullify other advantages in the hands of competitors who do not have it also.

In the past the matching of manpower needs with factually detailed and predictive information about personnel was simply not possible; the information could not be put together at tolerable cost. However, the behavioral and computer sciences are now yielding techniques and economies that make large-scale manpower information systems feasible for the first time. Creating such a system will pose many problems, some of them almost as stringent as those encountered in initial efforts to explain behavior on the job and to computerize. It cannot be doubted, however, that reliable behavioral yardsticks and integrated manpower information systems will be commonplace within a decade and will introduce new factors in the competitive situation.

Regardless of how sophisticated or automated record keeping has become in the department or unit he is auditing, the auditor should see whether the information collected can provide sufficient basis for current decisions with respect to manpower. Collecting detailed census information may, for example, serve manpower development purposes poorly.

Because the managerial acceptance of suggestion systems and participative management aimed at improving human relations has been so widespread, there has been little willingness to challenge the effectiveness of those programs and examine their influence on managers' growth and corporate profit. The programs have the sanction of being the "right thing," and measurement is handicapped by the absence of generally accepted standards. Therefore, the operations auditor will find getting answers to his questions about the effects on personal growth and the company's fulfillment of its manpower needs through training and education frustratingly difficult.

The minimum elements in a manpower information system are:

- ☐ Basic biographical data on present and past employees.
- ☐ Classification of employees by sex, minority group, educational level, and so on.
- ☐ Turnover and absenteeism statistics by class of employees.
- ☐ Skills inventory (currently of great interest for computer application).
- ☐ Individual evaluation and test data.
- ☐ Performance appraisal data, especially for management, including estimated prospects for future progress.

Areas of Analysis

☐ Direct labor costs.
☐ Overhead cost data, notably fringe benefits.
☐ Accident costs and detailed records.
☐ Bargaining unit and grievance data.
☐ Projections of increasing or decreasing need for personnel by class of employee.

Communications. Concern for the quality of communications within the firm is seldom thought of as a personnel department responsibility; but unless it is specifically assigned elsewhere, the progressive personnel department will concern itelf with the transmission of information among employees. Communications quality can, of course, never be the sole responsibility of the personnel function, but the company without a formal assignment of responsibility for it cannot hope to have efficiently informed people.

Although it is known that information flow among employees has a powerful impact on profitability, information in business often comes through garbled or not at all. Frequently, despite tremendous efforts, there is little relation between the intent of transmission and the effect of reception.

When investigation shows there to be no other agency concerned with communications quality, the auditor should review communications within the company as part of his audit of manpower utilization. These are some of the questions to be answered: Are messages sent through the selected communication media effectively received? Are the selected media suitable to the character of messages sent? When employees talk, does management listen? What feedback do employees get from communicating with management? Does management spend sufficient money on employee publications? How effective are they? Is management aware that nonverbal means of communication can have greater impact on employees than verbal ones?

Many companies maintain, usually in loose-leaf fashion, collections of policies and standard procedures that can go far, if objectives-based, realistic, and well written, to reduce the burden of decision making, the need to communicate with and train supervisors and managers, and the cost of personnel administration. If the company has such a staff or supervisor's manual relating to personnel, it will reward the auditor to review it intently. That a company or division of size does not have a relatively complete and up-to-date manual will reveal a lot to the auditor. Such a company is likely to be as exceptionally well or poorly run in respect to the personnel function as in respect to any other function.

The auditor should look at manpower planning, which is rapidly becoming a corporate topic of considerable interest. There are many reasons for that interest: the rising rate of changes in the skills demands of industry, spreading recognition of the need for planning on an integrated basis, and the longer lead times required in all planning.

Compensation. Lastly, the auditor should have a look at the rewards and incentives in force. The very efficiency of the industrial society has given man many blessings—unprecedented security, comfort, and leisure. On the other hand, it contains serious threats to human individuality. There is real danger that personal autonomy will be eliminated and mass mentality substituted.

Man invented machinery to serve him. He created great industries to pour out goods at a price within his means. The lands in which industry has reached maturity are showcases of physical satisfaction and plenty.

Within industry itself, employee behavioral patterns are—and since the beginning of industry have been—subject to formative pressures. Left unchecked, those pressures will inevitably produce a race of employees more noteworthy for their similarities than for their differences. That constitutes the most real danger in industry today. Fortunately, there are sound reasons for thinking that high efficiency arises more from making use of individual differences than from making use of likenesses.

According to the Herzberg theory of compensation as a motivator and nonmotivator, pay should be at least equal to that in competitive situations so the employee doesn't feel exploited. In that approach, pay is a maintenance policy—enough to keep people quiet. To be a motivator, however, pay must be appropriate to significant differences in performance. The operations auditor who has access to pay records should try to determine if special performance is specially rewarded or if all pay is routinely percentage-increased without individual rewards.

When possible, a compensation package should be tailored to the individual. Executives, for example, need different things at different stages in their lives; they need insurance and family dependency benefits when they have young children and security, retirement benefits, and long-term disability coverage when they are older.

Changing tax laws require frequent revisions of compensation policy. The 1969 Tax Reform Act made direct cash payments more attractive and gave the recipient choice as to investments. Incidentally, *is* there a compensation policy? There should be a range of pay, for *each* class of job, that is comparable with local competition. Differences between jobs should take into consideration education, responsibility, uniqueness, profit contribution, and the length of time a decision made by a person affects the company.

Regular review of performance should accompany salary revisions. There is some difference of opinion over whether compensation review should be separate from performance discussion, because performance review might be eyed as justification for salary adjustments less than the employee expects. In any case, the overall compensation climate should be audited from the basic point of view of its impact upon employee functioning.

12

CLERICAL OPERATIONS

The auditor should investigate clerical operations quite closely because they are amenable to analysis, they are seldom well controlled, and such waste as exists in them is usually repetitive and therefore costly in the long run. On top of that, clerical operations are not rising in productivity as rapidly as other operations such as manufacturing are, and they are taking an increasing portion of the revenue dollar. Evidence is the disproportionate rise in the white collar work force; between 1950 and 1970, manufacturing payroll costs held steady at about 23 percent of sales and white collar costs rose to 8, from 5.4, percent of sales. Further, opportunities to streamline office systems are widening as the computer becomes more broadly used and stress is placed on information rather than on pieces of paper.

Support for the view that clerical operations offer rich opportunities for improvements is not difficult to find. Manufacturers formerly did not have to think much about laying off white collar people to cut costs because there were relatively few of them; now they've become a tempting target. Because of the 1969–1970 recession, a lot of companies examined their office staffs closely for the first time. They found quite a bit of fat.

Generally speaking, business firms do not reach for the full benefits of new or improved technology on a routine basis. They wait until they have been forced to go through the cost wringer; then they develop crash programs for improving productivity. In evidence is a survey of companies employing a total of nearly 10,000 people conducted by Serge A. Birn Company, Inc. They found that in the normal 37½-hour office workweek only about 20 hours of actual work was done. They further found that performance rose to approximately 30 hours of actual work after controls were installed. In the case of one firm that meant a clerical cost reduction of $204,000 in a period when the volume of business rose 25 percent. Companies that recently laid off sizable numbers of white collar workers almost unanimously declare that they do not intend to hire all of them back even after their businesses return to past levels.

The costs of many clerical operations remain unknown and of little interest.

The cost of the average dictated letter is an example. It was $1.17 in 1953, $2.49 in 1967, and at least $2.74 by the time it was in the mail in 1969 when dictated by a $10,000-a-year junior executive to a $110-a-week secretary. Today, it's $3.05 for every page of paperwork that requires dictation and typing. There is no reason to think the rise will not continue. Here's how the Dartnell Corporation of Chicago said the $2.74 broke down in 1969:

Stenographic expense	$0.91
Overhead	0.67
Lost motion	0.23
Mailing	0.16
Filing	0.11
Materials	0.08
Dictating time	0.58
Total	$2.74

Each of the items offers an opportunity for saving. Take the item of lost motion, priced at 23 cents. It is probably greatly understated because it no doubt involves only time lost in the dictating session and in setting up for typing. It can sharply rise, when, for example, an executive goes looking for someone to take his dictation—a not uncommon event. But to get back to the 23 cents per letter. At an average of 100 letters per day, a not very large number, the losses amounted to $23, a major bite out of whatever profit improvement issued from the correspondence.

Major considerations in the area of clerical operations are work controls, personnel and organization, space and facilities, and services and equipment. The operations audit of clerical work can be successfully structured along those lines as well as any other.

WORK CONTROLS

Although the average program to trim clerical costs usually yields about 20 percent improvement, the benefits in getting the required work out accurately and on schedule are even more important. Employee resistance to efforts to improve control over clerical costs is usually easy to overcome once a sales effort is made to dispel the "efficiency expert" image and promote the positive benefits to the individual employees. Lip service in this area will be quickly resented and the auditor will compound his difficulties unless he is careful to solicit and consider the views of the employees who will be charged with implementing recommended changes. On the other hand, most people can't or won't work efficiently unless they are helped or asked to. Above all, people dislike inequitable and fluctuating workloads. The problem of productivity is especially difficult when there is a fluctuating workload and the office workforce also performs a wide range of tasks.

The start of every sound effort to detect a clerical productivity problem lies in determining what the output of activities should be in terms of so many documents processed or reports issued per hour or other period of elapsed time. The flow of information should then be charted to indicate sources of data origination, the flow of information between various organizational units, the need for manual manipulation of data, the tie-in to mechanized processing facilities, the distribution of system output, and the filing of all documents and reports. The next step is to review the design of the output report. The flow medium, whether mail, manual transfer, or data transmission equipment, should also be indicated, and so should the timing requirements.

Simplification and standardization in administrative practices can be achieved in three basic steps. First, establish policies consistent with the broader objectives and plans of the company; second, design the information system; and third, develop the standard procedures. In the United States the number of transactions and the records they generate are growing faster than both population and production. The numbers of phone calls, checks, bills, receipts, technical papers, stock certificates, and reproductions of everything that will fit on a photocopy machine are all increasing at rates ranging from a barely digestible 8 percent to a staggering 15 percent a year. Even the computer, which some expect to be the instrument of salvation, has turned out in most cases so far to be only a better-than-ever printing press. The flood of data sent over telecommunication lines, presumably to be printed or at least noted somewhere, has been growing at a rate of 25 percent to 40 percent a year since the mid-1960s.

Great ingenuity should be used in the design of the information system, for it is in streamlined design that the foundation is established for simplified administrative practices.

PERSONNEL AND ORGANIZATION

Despite the emphasis upon minimizing costs, there is a widespread tendency in many companies for managers and supervisors to take their organizations pretty much for granted, as fixed complements, regardless of the changing demands of the business. They do not seem to appreciate that the foundation of cost control is manpower control and that the control of manpower goes right back to an examination and appraisal of the *work performed* and the *man-hours* required or committed to its performance.

The fact that people are busy does not necessarily assure that all the things they are doing are vital and profitable. In almost any operation a thorough, searching review of all the functions performed will disclose many activities of questionable value to the business. A substantial proportion of the total work would, if our own business and our own money were at stake, usually be characterized as nice but not necessary. But such work is not more obviously dispensable than essential work is, and it is usually no less formalized. One must look closely at work content to find the difference.

WORK MEASUREMENT

The simplest way to reduce clerical cost is to reduce the number of personnel doing clerical work. And although it often happens that there are too many people to handle the work involved, staff reductions are, unfortunately, seldom followed by increases in productivity. The reason is that the work is organized by the persons doing it in accordance with notions of importance, prestige, and convenience and to satisfy one of Parkinson's laws: that work fills up the time provided for it. To increase productivity it is usually necessary to completely reorganize the work, and the best way to do that is through empirical studies such as clerical work measurement.

An unsophisticated technique for determining whether there may be a large imbalance between workload and workforce is the work, no-work observation. Whenever he looks up or walks past or visits a work location, the operations auditor makes a note of whether the clerical worker is working or not. If fewer than 70 percent of the observations are work, he will probably have found an opportunity for further study and improvement.

Motion and time study is a systematic analytical procedure to eliminate unnecessary work, arrange the workplace in the best manner, standardize the work methods, and establish time standards for the work. The auditor may have to perform some quick studies to ascertain whether the work is being expeditiously performed as presently organized.

Standards based on systems analysis do not guarantee adequate performance. What are needed are communication of those standards (education or training) and feedback to the worker of how he is performing in relation to the standards. To get the most out of a clerical standard properly set up at 25 units an hour requires that the worker be trained to perform the tasks and that he know, at least daily, how many units he is actually handling.

In measuring clerical work, he should keep in mind that the majority of office tasks are governed by the worker and that the output depends solely on individual operating efficiency or speed. Clerical workers, while being studied, seldom perform their tasks on a normal basis. They are self-conscious and often resent being observed. Finally, studies of the worker have a damaging effect on morale. The feeling that their tasks are watched with a view to reduction of their responsibilities and elimination of their jobs persists long after the study has been completed and ultimately impairs the effectiveness of their work.

Control over manpower. To determine the minimum essential manpower requirements for office activities, it is usually necessary to prepare a comprehensive inventory of functions for each staff group or department. Each identifiable activity should be outlined as to description, purpose served, frequency of occurrence, elapsed time required per transmission, level of skill required to perform, and manpower required (equivalent people or man-days per year). As the inventory is being built, the essential functions should be tested to see whether they are being performed by the simplest, most efficient methods. Whenever such investigation shows improved methods can be adopted, manpower requirements can be recalculated. It is important to think of manpower complement in terms of the man-hours purchased to get certain work done, in the full realization that those man-hours will, in due course, be reflected in costs.

It is just as important for management to recognize that the control of manpower comes down to the conservation of man-hours. Most opportunities for reducing manpower rest upon simplifying the work, cutting the corners, and saving one man-hour per day here, two there, and three somewhere else, and then working out a way to combine or rearrange assignments so that the total essential work can be performed with one less person on the team.

Another very important need in establishing effective control over manpower relates to the functioning of the service departments. Laboratory, accounting, and office personnel often feel obligated to provide requested services without being in a position to question and challenge their money-making value. At the same time, the requesting departments, because they are seldom charged directly for the services, are not forced to take the responsibility for their cost. This cause of waste can be controlled with an easily administered work order system.

SPACE AND FACILITIES

A clerk cannot operate efficiently if his workspace is either too cramped or too spread out. Also, the equipment necessary for the clerks' functions must be conveniently located. Office workers respond to modern, bright surroundings; they work more efficiently and more accurately. Increased lighting levels can increase productivity from 4 to 8 percent.

The flow of paper from one clerical function to another is a key factor and is worthy of careful study. Since most documents are hand-carried from function to function by clerical personnel, the shorter the distance they must travel the greater is the efficiency. The traffic pattern is also very important. Traffic flow past clerks' desks should be kept to a minimum. As flow increases, clerical efficiency tends to decrease. The converse is also true and can be used to improve productivity.

Included under the broad heading of "clerical" are many key areas. Secretarial functions are one of them, and they require a careful screening. The question that arises at once is whether a secretary is really necessary to an individual or is just a status symbol. Some points to consider in determining the validity of the hiring are:

1. How much time will be spent in taking dictation?
2. Can a stenographic pool or machine service the need?
3. Is a secretary needed to handle a large volume of appointments and meetings?
4. What does the secretary do besides the two basic functions of taking dictation and typing?

SERVICE AND EQUIPMENT

Record keeping may be informal or deficient in many areas of a business, and as a result the operations auditor may not get much out of a search for data. In many companies, on the other hand, filing is an important consumer of clerical time; in fact, document storage and retrieval may account for more clerical time than any other single office function. The time so spent may be perfectly justified, or it may constitute a gross waste depending on the equipment, methods, and record retention philosophy of the company. The equipment and methods the company should use depend on the views on record retention that it holds. What is filed and how long it is kept depend primarily on the company's retention policies and knowledge or recognition of the importance of filing technology. How frequently material is retrieved, on the other hand, is a function of the kind of business.

There are three basic types of filing systems: centralized, decentralized, and a compromise between the two. The rules governing which method to use are often flexible and must be matched to the company. Elimination of a file produces significant savings; prevention of the file's coming into being in the first place produces even greater savings.

Whether the filing system should be kept together in one place, spread among a number of locations, or reproduced in more than one place is a sophisticated question.

1. Records used by more than one department should be kept in one place most convenient to all users. Duplication of files should be avoided unless it is forced by geographic restraints.

2. Records used exclusively by one person or department should be kept at the user's work station.

The auditor should also look at the type of file equipment. Five-drawer cabinets offer a 25 percent increase in storage capacity over four-drawer equipment without usurping any more of the expensive floor space. Open-shelf files are easier to use, occupy less floor space, and are sometimes less than half the cost of conventional cabinets.

Filing methods are to be critically examined also. If, for example, an operations auditor observes dissimilar methods of filing or assembly in different parts of a company, he may be in a position to recommend further investigation. An active file is always easier to retrieve from and more accurate to refile into when it is numeric. A key determinant here is customer service. Unless most inquiries can be reasonably expected to be made by number, the potential savings will be wiped out by maintenance of expensive cross files. An inherent characteristic of a numeric file is that greatest activity (all new in-filing and most inquiries) is concentrated at the high-order end of the sequence. When a numeric file is large enough, as in an insurance company, to require more than one clerk, the terminal-digit method of filing can equitably redistribute the workload with beneficial effect on employee morale and speed of customer service.

RECORD RETENTION

All file systems must have a definite policy on record retention and destruction. The most effective retention policy starts with the question: Should the record be filed in the first place? CPA Morris Kadin wrote:[1]

> The auditor who attempts to comply with legal requirements by consulting Appendix A of the Federal Register is faced with almost 900 regulations that mention record keeping. Many of these do not specify exactly the records to be kept nor the number of years they should be retained. Many state departments have issued regulations mentioning record keeping requirements, but terms are equally vague on what is to be kept for how long.

Retention schedules should be developed for each individual enterprise to meet specific policies, legal requirements, and operations and administrative needs. When the principles and techniques of records management may be applied generally, the length of time that business records should be kept is always subject to local, state, and federal requirements, as well as the special administrative needs of the company. Regulatory bodies such as the Federal Power Commission and the Interstate Commerce Commission have

127

piescribed routines and regulations for the preservation and destruction of records that pertain to their affairs.

William E. Mitchell attempts to overcome vagueness wherever it appears by stressing compliance with the intent of the law. The following is an example of his practical philosophy:[2]

> Some states stipulate that payroll records must be kept by the employer for six years. The mistake, then, is to assume that the state law applies to *all* payroll records. It does not. We have to go back to the intent of the law and we have to be specific. . . . Towards what social reform was this state law intended? In this example we will say that it concerns unemployment compensation. What then is specifically required to comply with the law?
>
> The law requires the name, address, age and income earned for specified periods of each employee. It does not require how many hours he worked each day; it is not concerned with overtime or piecework.
>
> Payroll summary records may summarize the information required by the state. So it isn't necessary to keep thousands and thousands of time cards for a period of six years simply because the state law stipulates "payroll records are to be kept six years." Do not read time cards, job labor tickets, labor distribution worksheets, etc. into the law.

The auditor's responsibility does not end with simply complying with the intent of the law, however; there are additional alternatives to be considered. In some situations it may pay to take a calculated risk by discarding a document before possible need for it is gone. For example, a company may make a large number of shipments that are of relatively small value. The cost of being unable to prove delivery for a few missing shipments may be far less than the cost of keeping all delivery receipts for the period required by the statute of limitations.

Similarly, there may be little risk in dumping records like payroll checks before the end of the period imposed by the statute of limitations. Companies that do so expect that claims for pay mistakes will be made either promptly or not at all. Based on past experience, it is necessary to compare the costs of storing documents with the losses that would be incurred in their absence. One large retailer studied the relation between the total costs of record retention for mail order shipments and the costs that might result from not retaining those records. They concluded that the savings from destroying all records of shipment (only inventory reduction and sales statistics data were retained— no record of the individual shipment) were many times greater than the loss that might result from an improper merchandise return of which they had no record.

On the other hand, the auditor should not lose sight of the possibility that there may be a good reason to keep some records even longer than legally required because of their historical interest to the company.

The problem of retention can be eased by limiting the number of documents generated, including copies. Bear in mind that although multicopy documents may greatly enhance day-to-day operating efficiency, only one copy should be kept for record retention purposes.

FORMS CONTROL

The volume of business forms supplied to offices now runs over $500 million annually. There are estimates that every dollar spent on forms creates at least $20 worth of clerical expense in using the form. Hidden expenses occur in the use of unauthorized forms that often are ineptly designed and duplicate existing documents. The solution is professional control and management of forms preceded by an analysis of forms currently used. Sizable savings can result from effective forms management. They include:

- ☐ Reduction of the variety of forms.
- ☐ Increase in speed of execution through redesign.
- ☐ Reduction of error through good design.
- ☐ Reduction of printing costs by elimination of spot-job rush orders.
- ☐ Elimination of storage costs by off-site stocking, with drop shipments for current needs only.

Forms department activities range from complete forms analysis, design, and control to controlling the stock of forms. Very few companies today employ their own forms designer as such. The forms salesman is usually called upon for forms design, though a systems analyst will often initiate conceptual designs. Quantities ordered and used should be scrutinized to balance overbuying and obsolescence due to an overly zealous salesman against the economies of volume buying. Organizational units wholly concerned with forms design, usage, and control are relatively new in view of the fact that someone in almost every company is involved in some phase of forms analysis.

THE PAPER EXPLOSION

There is little hope that government will diminish its demands for proof of operations or that business will grow less complex. Also, the rapid development of office copying machines has produced a spectacular rise in the number of business documents that are produced and filed in offices. It costs approximately $75 a file drawer annually to maintain current office files, including space, labor, and overhead. Since over 50 million file drawers are in use in the United States, that means a total yearly cost of about $4 billion for file maintenance. Methods for condensation of required records, such as microfilm, offer the best hope of relief for the increasing file storage space problems, but they must be applied carefully. A comparative cost study by one company showed that it was more economical to store records for 21 years than it was to microfilm them for retention during the same period.[3]

Information-handling systems adequate to cope with the paper explosion have made some truly significant technological advances. Almost any clerical task can be automated by the application of electronics, magnetics, pneumatics, electrostatics, and mechanics. Electronic character recognition, known as OCR and MICR, holds tremendous promise for time and cost reduction in office procedures. Electronic machines are available to read hand printing from documents and soon will accept handwriting. Other machines now in research will print directly from spoken words or even return a voice response.

Standardization of codes would permit instant direct communication from human to computer, and from computer to computer, thus making unnecessary the mailing of countless forms and reports. The application of these and other advanced techniques will enable management to obtain the timely information required for efficient production without becoming further submerged in the flood of paper. Soon, it can be expected that devices capable of automatic analysis and interpretation of data, as well as of its storage and retrieval, will be available. With these developments automatic abstracting and translation machines will be in fairly widespread use.

An EDP system of the near future will make few routine printed reports of entire records. Instead, data will be organized with appropriate programs to enable management at all levels to interrogate the file when desired. Often a television-like display or other visual or audible means will be better and faster than printing. Such displays over communications lines will serve branches and remote management points without any creation or mailing of forms. Only particular information, sorted and summarized, will be presented for action.

REFERENCES

1. Morris B. Kadin, *A Fast Guide to Record Retention* (Newark: New Jersey Society of Certified Public Accountants, 1967), p. 1.
2. William E. Mitchell, *Records Retention* (Evansville, Ind.: Ellsworth Publishing Company, 1959).
3. Martin M. Prague, "Records Management for the Accountant's Office," *The New York Certified Public Accountant,* September 1970, pp. 726–731.

13

MANUFACTURING

Every company makes its living by manufacturing something, rendering a service, or both. If the primary function of an organization is manufacturing, the main activity is subjecting the supply and flow of materials to the operations of labor and machines. If, on the other hand, the basic activity is service, the main activity consists in scheduling and dispatching labor and, as necessary, equipment and materials. This section has been written primarily for audits of a manufacturing operation.

Areas usually of special concern to production and, therefore, to the operations auditor, are

- ☐ Short-term and long-term forecasting.
- ☐ The scheduling of production.
- ☐ Determining economic lot sizes for manufacture.
- ☐ Planning and control of operations performed on all parts, subassemblies and assemblies.
- ☐ Machine loading and scheduling.
- ☐ Manpower planning and training.
- ☐ Equipment and facilities planning.
- ☐ Storage of raw materials.
- ☐ Warehousing and finished-stock control.

Several of these items, in certain conditions, are deserving of a separate audit. In this book they have been so considered and are therefore given a section of their own.

The manufacturing cycle begins with production planning, which should be predicated on the best sales forecast the sales department is able to provide. If customers' orders are filled from finished stock, production is often initiated automatically when established minimum inventory levels are reached. In such cases, the sales forecast is the basis for the inventory limits.

Production planning must accord with established inventory levels. In manufacturing companies the determination of inventory levels involves balancing inventory economics with production economics. That is, inventories should be kept as low as requirements permit while production enjoys the most economical runs possible.

Another match that must be achieved if production planning is to meet the needs of the business effectively is between production plans and the capabilities of men and machines. Achieving the match requires that the assumptions made by production planners be realistic. That requires ongoing feedback, serving the dual purpose of providing a basis of effective control and information for the production planner. Actual results should be compared with the plan regularly and significant deviations from the target should be reported immediately for management review and action.

Production control is critical in manufacturing operations. Regulating the flow from the issuance of raw materials through manufacturing to the warehousing of the finished product can involve considerable knowledge, experience, and skill. Production control offers to operations auditing a clear reflection of general conditions in manufacturing. Effective control naturally is difficult, but it is vital that it be achieved. Without it, manufacturing operations strangle on their own processes.

MACHINE UTILIZATION

Production performance as a totality cannot ordinarily come under direct review by the operations auditor. Nevertheless, the auditor can construct a basis for appraising general performance by reviewing the procedures by which the company assures itself that manufacturing operations are as efficient as possible. Therefore, the company should regularly measure machine and worker productivity.

Investment in production machinery is rising rapidly. The demand for more products at declining real costs creates a demand for faster, more versatile, more precise, and more fully automatic machines. The level of investment in production machines in most firms warrants periodic review of machine utilization on both the qualitative and quantitative levels.

What constitutes effective machine utilization varies considerably, and determining standards by which to measure utilization often is not simple. Essential guidelines to what is reasonable are supplied by the machine manufacturer on the basis of operations performed during factory tests. Those guidelines offer no more than a starting point; they usually must be modified to conform to conditions and operations unique to each plant.

MANPOWER UTILIZATION

One element of production the operations auditor is well equipped to measure is manpower utilization. Idle manpower may be attributable to weak foreman supervision, but it may also indicate the same underlying production control deficiencies as underutilization of machines. It is important, therefore, for the auditor to look into labor productivity, particularly in labor-intensive situations. The investigation must take into account the cost of fringe benefits.

Because efficient production is one of the prime objectives of any manufacturing enterprise, management must create conditions fostering least-cost production. There are four indispensible conditions for high worker productivity:

1. *Means.* Successful performance begins with providing the needed tools, materials, energy, and place.

2. *Understanding*. Each operator must know what is expected of him beyond any question or doubt.

3. *Knowledge*. Every man must have the knowledge he needs to do the job he is assigned.

4. *Goodwill*. The preceding conditions fail to result in satisfactory performance if the worker, in reaction to human relations failings in the enterprise, is unwilling to pull his weight and contribute to objectives.

Direct labor projections, adjusted for efficiency and down time or unbillable time, constitute a common managerial tool. Indirect labor is usually computed as a percentage of direct labor. For example, a crew of direct laborers is necessary to man an operation but, for each crew, a number of indirect laborers are usually assigned. Ideal production should, therefore, be reduced by observed or engineered estimates of inefficiency and down time.

The indirect-direct labor ratio is rarely proportional to direct labor. At different levels of production, different ratios usually apply. Usually the basis is annual statistics, which can be very misleading. A more dependable guide results from taking a number of work sampling studies. In the typical organization, a thorough study of indirect labor can lead to astonishing savings.

Only controllable factors should be used in the planning of manpower. Manufacturing foremen should be involved in developing the standards which will show how they and their supervisors are doing against a plan.

Another factor that affects manpower utilization is described by the learning curve. This is a fairly universal phenomenon which shows that workers' productivity increases in efficiency as they learn to handle new tasks. The significance of the learning curve for manpower utilization is that standards of performance in manufacturing operations should be adjusted for the changing productivity and the decreasing manpower needed as new jobs are mastered.

The auditor should also look into temporary hiring practices. It is often a fallacy to believe that savings will result from short-term hirings. Indoctrinating new employees is costly from the standpoints of initially low productivity and quality. Another disadvantage of seasonal hiring worthy of mention is the harm done to a company's image in the community. Such practices, in time, often lead to the most undesirable types of labor being attracted.

In the organization of manpower, managers should be conscious of balancing the need for efficiency, which is often defined as extreme specialization, with the feeling on the part of workers that they do not want to be regarded as robots but as individuals with special needs and skills. Wildcat strikes and the sabotage of production are two of the dramatic consequences resulting from management's insensitivity, or seeming insensitivity, to organizing work from the viewpoint of worker satisfaction. No amount of benefits, in the long run, can offset worker dissatisfaction with boring, seemingly unimportant work.

The operations auditor might consider whether the layout, workload, and job of workers have been considered in the light of these factors. Where a job cannot be enlarged or mechanized, it is sometimes helpful to fill the position with a person of limited skills and aspirations such as a retarded worker.

Overall manpower planning does not have the precision that is involved in machine loading, space usage, or even cash projections. What is required is a listing of the skills needed and available. The difficulty lies in the fact that the skills of human beings are dynamic, not static, and are subject to change in two directions: individuals can enlarge the scope of their skills by training and experience and can lose skills through disuse and obsolescence. Thus even the first task of listing present skills is a new concept for many companies. Integrated with the goals of a firm, which should include the skills needed in the future, an inventory of present skills can be a sound start for hiring and training. It is important that the inventory of skills be currently updated; certainly at least once a year will make good sense.

Symptoms of poor manpower utilization include the following:

Unplanned overtime.

Inventory produced beyond current needs as an insurance against possible bottlenecks.

Extra shifts suddenly called, unrelated to changes in orders or shipments—a consequence of poor manpower planning.

Compared to standards (developed by the company, the community, or the industry), excessive personnel turnover, indicating that supervision, salary level, or job satisfaction is lacking.

Below-standard productivity or excessive scrap, possibly indicating that workers are poorly chosen, trained, supervised, or paid.

No deliberate, conscious, continuous effort to update methods, procedures, and incentives, indicating that the company, if it has not already fallen behind its competition, will soon do so.

Within this context and the limits of labor laws and union contracts, the operations auditor should be conscious of the place of incentive plans as a means of improving the use of manpower. This is a large subject, and we will only mention that there is a wide range of incentive plans, the best ones being individually tailored to the worker or group.

14

MARKETING AND SALES

Getting products into the hands of people willing to pay more than it costs to make the goods or provide the services is, in one respect, the critical function in a business. No commercial enterprise that does not sell goods or services with profit can long survive. But selling with profit is not a simple matter; it is the end result of a complex set of activities that are included in the term "marketing." Modern marketing comprises these major activities:

1. Discovering customer requirements and getting them translated into product features. (Sales analysis, market research, engineering liaison.)

2. Contacting potential and actual customers and securing orders. (Sales promotion, sales training, selling.)

3. Seeing to it that the product arrives in customers' hands as promised. (Sales follow-up, expediting.)

4. Helping customers achieve the purposes for which they purchased the goods. (Product documentation, customer service, product training.)

5. Building images in the marketplace favorable to the company and its products. (Advertising, trade show participation, association membership.)

6. Keeping abreast of economic trends, customer patterns, and competitor activities. (Trade and industry research, motivation and buying pattern studies.)

7. Laying plans and developing mechanisms that foster effective utilization of marketing resources. (Sales management.)

Each of the seven activities is an element within the total marketing effort that offers a field for audit investigation.

Investigation can also be structured by the two broad categories of marketing activities: strategic, which focuses on planning, and tactical, which focuses on doing. Each has distinctive characteristics and informational requirements that can be studied separately. Such cognitive activities as sales analysis, sales forecasting, market research, and marketing planning are mainly strategic, and such creative activities as advertising, promotion, sales management, and customer service are mainly tactical. Engineering (product design), liaison, and sales training are both strategic and tactical; also, they are ongoing activities of equal importance to the near and the long-term future.

Areas of Analysis

INFORMATION

Like finance and R&D, marketing is information-dependent. It is probably fair to say that the effort put into moving goods or services into customers' hands can be no more effective than the information relating to it permits.

Marketing information offers the operations auditor a rich field of investigation. The field has two aspects: information stemming from and reflecting on current marketing activities and information yielding a basis for meeting trends, exploiting emerging opportunities, and sensing future conditions.

Sales analysis offers the best starting point. Each company, regardless of size or complexion, should know some specific things about what it has done to generate the sales it has made. For example, it should know:

- [ ] Salesmen's call rates.
- [ ] The ratio of sales calls to sales made.
- [ ] The ratio of selling costs to sales value. The cost of sales calls.
- [ ] The distribution of sales, geographically and by customer size.
- [ ] Who purchasers are, by class of trade and other characteristics.
- [ ] Profits by salesmen, territory, individual customer, and class of customer.
- [ ] Product mix analysis by customer.
- [ ] The variance of sales forecasts from actual byproduct mix, salesman, and so on.
- [ ] The effects on volume and profits of special promotions or price changes.

Such information, particularly when it is compared with the data for the preceding period, has many uses in the hands of top and sales management. Take the simple matter of the cost of sales calls. When most firms think of sales costs, they think of the annual cost of keeping a salesman on the road. Few bother to determine the cost of making a call. If they did, they might change their selling strategy. They would probably find, as McGraw-Hill research found, that the cost of sales calls is skyrocketing. In 1955 an average sales call cost a company selling to industry $17.29. In 1969 it cost $49.30; up 185%. In some industries it cost even more, in the neighborhood of $57. A company that knows the cost of making each sales call is far more likely to take care to control what goes on during each call than a company that does not know.

Other kinds of information must be available to the sales staff in order for them to be in a position to manage their own affairs better. The following are examples:

- [ ] Product specifications to facilitate proper sales representation and product usage.
- [ ] Price information on raw material, processing, shipping, and competition so prices can be set on a realistic basis.
- [ ] Sales compensation practices that insure the best basis of continued salesman motivation.
- [ ] Product acceptance information so that advertising promotion and product design changes can be made when necessary.
- [ ] Production backlog, inventory status, and delivery information so that delivery promises can be realistically made.

136

There is a natural tendency for companies to stick to ways that worked in the past. The forward-looking company, however, is aware of the dangers inherent in procedural fixity and seeks to introduce mechanisms capable of yielding better marketing information as a basis for developing new solutions and strategies. Many of these companies have turned to the computer in their search for more and better information.

Computer applications. About 90 percent of the country's largest companies are using the computer for marketing purposes. Sales analysis is, of course, the most common application, because almost every company has a good deal of sales-oriented data on hand, but more than 70 percent of the computer-using companies go beyond that. In addition to analyzing sales territories by product lines, major products, customers, sales representatives, and so forth, they analyze sales trends, gross margins by product, gross margins by customer size, and return on sales effort. Further, more than 40 percent of the companies are now doing computerized sales forecasting, a far more sophisticated and often more contributory application than historical sales analysis.

Other applications coming to the fore include physical distribution analysis, market strategy planning, share-of-market analysis, market research, survey and statistical analysis, advertising and promotion analysis, and budgeting. PERT, CPM, and related methods of investment scheduling are being used in about a fifth of the companies. Applications coming around the corner include product mix, price, warranty, and test market analysis and mathematical modeling to test proposed strategies.

Forecasting. A prime piece of marketing information the operations auditor should look for is a sales forecast. No company can afford not to have one; it serves as the foundation for production, manpower, financial, and marketing planning. To be maximally useful, forecasts should be made for both the long and short range. In addition, they should be multidimensional; that is, sales should be forecast at least by product group or brand, territory, and industry classification or end-use group. The number and kind of classifications will depend on the company involved and the tools, such as a computer, at its disposal.

Business forecasting is a difficult art. The complexity of factors involved often makes predicting the future, which is what forecasting essentially is, only slightly better than enlightened guesswork. Nonetheless, guides to market conditions in the near and distant future are mandatory if effective use is to be made of marketing resources. Business forecasts always include an element of judgment—for sound and necessary reasons—but there is no necessity for forecasts to be based on anything but relevant and accurate data. Without such data forecasting is little more than wool-gathering.

Effective forecasting therefore begins with the gathering of information. The kinds of information required are determined by the needs served by the forecast, the markets served, and the time period covered. The data needed by forecasters are not always readily available, and the difference between the average and the outstanding job of forecasting often lies in how well the forecaster fills the information gaps. He may do it gathering special data through customer surveys or similar studies. When he cannot gather information directly, he must fill the gaps with extensions or extrapolations based on informed judgment. Then the competent forecaster is miles ahead of the run-of-the-mill technician.

Forecasters often find it necessary or productive to use forecasts in sectors other than those in which they are immediately interested, such as the forecasts of the general economy or whole industries that are obtainable from government and financial sources. Also, a good many firms specialize in producing forecasts usable by company forecasters in determining the volume likely to stem from the execution of marketing plans.

Almost every forecast includes assumptions, and the assumptions must be both carefully made and explicit. When others' forecasts are used, the grounds of their assumptions must be known and their limitations understood. When he examines any forecast, the operations auditor will benefit by looking for the underlying assumptions and testing them for validity and relevance.

Forecasters use many methods to make the data they assemble yield useful information, but the following are the ones most commonly employed.

1. *Trend analysis,* or time series analysis, is applied to past figures to discover mathematical trends for use in making extrapolations. The method assumes that past behavior, motivations, and general demand characteristics will remain relatively constant during the period of projection; but because the business world actually is constantly changing, trend analysis may lose accuracy rapidly. It is least useful over short periods of time for the reason that most activities have substantial short-term variations.

2. *Correlation analysis* involves the establishment of a consistent relation between the factor of interest and one or more measures of aggregate economic activity. For example, there is probably a direct correlation between birth rates and the sale of baby clothes and foods.

3. *Construction of relatives* compares the present situation with past situations. Based on the business cycle, it compares the same elements in relation to their position on the business cycle curve.

Whatever the grounds for or elements in them, forecasts should always be presented in a range of probable accuracy, and not in absolute terms. The best of forecasts, valuable though they are to corporate planning, must always be treated as conditional instruments.

Marketing plans. Next, the operations auditor should review the marketing plans. The absence of formal or comprehensive plans should suggest many possibilities: lack of marketing representation in the firm's top planning councils; marketing on a reactive, exploitative basis rather than on a creative, controlled basis; and economies and advantages lost by failing to manage the marketing and sales effort on an integrated basis. When marketing plans do exist, the auditor should check to see that they are factually based, comprehensive, coupled with controls and performance review procedures, and fully communicated.

The last two points, because they are so seldom associated with marketing plans, deserve the auditor's special interest. Often, otherwise well-executed plans do not include controls or performance review procedures and are not communicated in the degree of detail needed by persons whose activities are relevant to the marketing effort. Every plan, marketing or otherwise, requires controlled implementation if it is to succeed. The feedback required to operate the controls ought also to be used in evaluating plan progress.

Finally, on the point of communication, the worth of a plan can be realized only when every person related to the plan has possession of its basic facts and understands the intents encompassed by it.

MARKET RESEARCH

Each business, regardless of size, has to have pertinent and reliable information that can guide the exploitation of its market opportunities. Market research fulfills that need. The five natural objectives of market research are information files on customers, prospects, competitors, products, and sales activities. Much of that information is often already in the house, but the data are apt to be disorganized and therefore unusable for most purposes. The starting place for market research is the organization of existing data. With that completed, the company can determine what data are missing and set about obtaining them.

Marketing guides that are of great value to a company and are quite easily attained are profiles of company markets, customers, and potential customers. One technique that can be used to create the guides is the following:[1]

List the name of every account on your books at the end of your most recent fiscal year. To this list add the names of all accounts that have become inactive in the past five years. Your list should show the following information for each account: (1) an industrial identification, preferably a Standard Industrial Classification (SIC) number; (2) the number of employees; (3) the customer's name; (4) sales for the current year; (5) sales in dollars for each of the previous years; (6) the difference between sales in the current year and those in the poorest of the previous years; and (7) the difference between sales in the current year and those in the best of the previous years.

A customer profile will reveal sales trends that are hidden from view in measures of total volumes. Investigating why some accounts have declined can lead to recovery of a lost market; determining the factors behind increases in growth accounts can lead to increased sales with other accounts in the same industries. A customer profile can serve as a basis for evaluating the strengths and weaknesses of current sales efforts and the effectiveness of the company's salesmen in penetrating their territories.

The operations auditor should look into the kinds of information used in market research, particularly to get some information on cost effectiveness. In that effort he should keep in view the fact that a good many data useful in market research are available free or for next to nothing. The federal government is a prime source, but state governments are also very active in gathering statistics. Many states publish directories of companies by industry and by SIC code numbers. Standard & Poor's, Moody's, and Dun & Bradstreet provide not only financial data but also information on other aspects of companies. Federal Reserve banks publish weekly and monthly reports on business and economic trends in their districts.

External data sources. Company finance departments frequently have financial information on firms in their markets. That will usually include banks, customers, suppliers, and competitors and perhaps even firms in related industries. Trade associations often gather and publish data, and some trade journals publish annual directories that contain industry statistics. Certain publishing firms maintain research departments and libraries.

The Conference Board publishes an economic almanac and other information on various subjects. The National Planning Association puts out long-range forecasts of the total economy. Enterprises such as the Research Institute of America publish long-range reports usable in marketing planning. The National Association of Purchasing Agents conducts a regular survey on business expectations among its members that has shown a high degree of accuracy over the short term.

Some other groups also provide useful data. The Survey Research Center of the University of Michigan, for example, provides survey data on many subjects, one of which is consumer buying expectations. Firms such as F. W. Dodge in the building industry specialize in gathering and providing data on specific industries. Other sources of market research information include the following:

☐ *Company records.* Depending upon the methods and degree of accuracy maintained, individual company records provide much information.

☐ *Annual report.* Some company annual reports contain helpful data; the New York Stock Exchange has a good library of such information.

☐ *Foreign trade missions.* Many embassies maintain trade missions in cities other than Washington.

☐ *Economic consultants.* People and firms that specialize in consultant work provide a range of service that is often useful.

Many forecasters employ data that, based on historical patterns, tend to lead, follow, or coincide with fluctuations in the general economy. Over a period of business cycles, the following data series seem to fit the three categories. They are listed with their sources:

Leading Series
    Average hours worked: Department of Labor
    Housing starts: Department of Commerce
    New business (net): Department of Commerce
    Common stock prices: Standard & Poor's
    Corporate profits: Department of Commerce
Coincident Series
    Retail sales: Department of Commerce
    Personal income: Department of Commerce
    Industrial production: Federal Reserve Board
    Unemployment rate: Department of Labor
Lagging Series
    Installment credit: Federal Reserve Bank
    Manufacturing inventories: Department of Commerce
    Bank rate on business loans: Federal Reserve Board

These are not all the series that fit the three categories, and it may well be that some other series would apply to a particular industry with a higher degree of accuracy than the ones cited. The crucial question is whether an attempt has been made to identify a high correlation with company history and to use that knowledge for intelligent forecasting.

PROMOTION AND ADVERTISING

Industry spends billions of dollars yearly on sales promotion and advertising. Probably the largest share of the expenditures is made without known objectives. It is certain that enormous sums are spent annually with mindless energy on one kind of promotion or other with no further justification than "it's the thing to do." There may well be no more costly class of mistakes in marketing than spending money on promotion and advertising that have no specific missions.

Gauging the effectiveness of efforts to maintain and increase market position through expansions of product exposure, buyer awareness, and product knowledge via communications media, as contrasted with personal selling, is one of the more difficult tasks operations auditing can be called upon to perform. Evaluation of such efforts entails, in some degree at least, measurement of the impact on actual and potential customers—a hard measurement to make in any circumstances. Accordingly, the operations auditor is limited to making certain tests that, by implication, yield some measure of the effectiveness of promotional advertising.

A good starting place for the operations auditor is to ask for such marketing objectives and plans, both trade and consumer, as exist. If they are not available, he should ask these questions.

☐ For whom is each product geared? What individual or group needs is it designed to satisfy?

☐ What are the indirect markets? Through wholesalers or retailers? Through users or specifiers?

☐ What are the direct markets? Who are the end-consumers or end-users?

☐ What are the subdivisions of both the direct and indirect markets—industries, geographic areas, educational or economic or ethnic groups?

☐ What priorities have been assigned to promotional efforts in each of the market subdivisions?

☐ What is the relation between budget allocations (total and per market) and current and to-be-accomplished results in sales, public impression, or whatever the end result is expected to be?

The next step is to gather all the material possible reflecting current and planned promotional campaigns, including mail, newspaper, radio, television, and trade show. Then by using marketing goals and priorities and the dollars assigned to accomplish them, the operations auditor should perform an analysis of the specific programs that will enable him to evaluate campaign effectiveness. The analysis should be subdivided by category of effort; that is, examples of media advertising to consumers or trade, direct mail, and sales promotion programs should be examined from these viewpoints:

1. Does the material highlight the product or service? Is the message clear?
2. Does the material convey specific information? Is the material informative?
3. Is the material consistent? Does it create similar ideas, impressions?

Next the operations auditor should see if the markets at which the material is aimed have been properly identified. It is amazing how much promotional effort, and advertising effort in particular, is made on the basis of carefully apportioned dollars but with little regard to the aim of the effort. Markets can be identified, of course, only in terms of the potential for sales the company can make. In many markets that are identified, the identifying company cannot sell a given product—as Ford realized after trying to sell its Edsel to a market that did not want a car with marked departures in styling.

After seeing whether the market has been properly identified, the auditor can see whether the medium has been determined on a rational basis. Several standards common to the advertising promotion field, such as cost per unit message, are applicable here. The auditor should also aim questions at uncovering the in-house methods being used to evaluate the effectiveness of the specific areas of the promotion program—coupons, coded response requests, order analysis, sales research, new customers opened, and so forth.

Finally, the auditor should examine the budgeting basis and methods. Analysis of the ad budget and program (schedule of media advertising, with name of publication, circulation, publication's demographics, and so forth) will give additional insight into the relationship between original marketing objectives, campaign effectiveness, and dollar application.

SALES MANAGEMENT

Naturally, the skill with which sales or marketing activities are managed and resources are used is of particular interest to the operations auditor and is usually much easier to assess than promotion and advertising. The effective sales manager is far more intellectual than is implied by existing stereotypes. He thinks reflectively and creatively about his salesmen, the buyer, competitors, and the strategies employed by his competitors. He takes pains to learn about those strategies and then applies his knowledge of them to change the complexity and thrust of his firm's sales effort.

The ineffective sales manager does not think that way. Though he might agree that marketing is a critical task, too seldom does he apply new thinking to it. When sales are trending downward, he will usually resort to the time-worn devices of extra calls, increasing the sales force, and cutting prices. Pursuing such strategies will sometimes win the gains he seeks, but he is bound to lose more often than the sales manager who selects his strategies cogently and is free of traditional constraints.

In reviewing the performance of a sales department, the operations auditor should look for qualities of modern management technology. He must ascertain whether the sales manager is using systems concepts, statistical and mathematical techniques, and computer technology to solve marketing problems. He can take it that innovation is a sign of health in the marketing effort and search for signs of new thinking and ways. Finding no such signs will give him a fairly good fix on the quality of the marketing effort and an indication of the scale of problems he should look for.

The activities embraced by sales management are many, but probably no single activity holds more portent for sales success than the training and directing of salesmen. Both depend heavily on the skill with which the salesman's qualifications are judged and his performance is gauged. The importance of a salesman's training and supervision cannot be overemphasized when we recognize that the free-world marketing system faces a serious challenge in the rising tide of individualism and the expanding economic opportunities, conditions that are reflected in the increased turnover of salesmen in many companies. A good salesman will not tolerate being badly managed; he will leave a poorly managed sales force to find a place in a well-run, forward-looking market organization. Butt says[2] that the marketing staffing problem can be defined in terms of:

1. Recruiting, hiring, and training salesmen.
2. Determining how many salesmen should be hired and where they should be located.
3. Selecting salesmen's territories in terms of number of accounts, profit potential, call frequency, and other logistics.
4. Deciding how much time each salesman should spend on soliciting customers, traveling, writing reports, and managing territories.
5. Determining how the salesman's effort should be applied by product. (For example, high-margin versus low-margin items.)
6. Calculating the quantitative relationship of sales effort and other competitive weapons to sales performance and marketing strategy.
7. Analyzing the performance of the salesman and the marketing system in order to change and improve the system.

To those seven signs might be added two others:

1. Determination and implementation of the compensation plan.
2. Providing the sales force with catalogs, prices, and discount schedules.

There are times when the performance of a salesman can be difficult to measure; it cannot be measured by sales volume or other direct achievements. For example, a salesman who succeeds someone who, over a long period of time, created hostility to the company and its products may not be able to reverse the buying pattern even though he himself is competent. Therefore, the operations auditor should, in evaluating the sales process, break it down into parts he can readily appraise:

☐ Job performance, subdivided into the major elements considered important to doing a successful job.
☐ Personal value, subdivided into sections for appraisal of the salesman's strong points, weak points, and capacity and readiness for promotion.
☐ Actual achievement, based on sales achievement for the period.

To evaluate actual achievement, five different criteria can be used:

1. Calls per day broken down to high, medium, and low rates of call.
2. Number of orders per 100 calls.
3. Number of orders per man-day.
4. Average order size, in units and dollars.
5. Sales volume per man-day, in units and dollars.

CUSTOMER SERVICE

The "complaint department" is anachronistic; it must give way to something positive: customer service. A properly handled complaint can result in a lasting friendship. Instead of a signal for both sides to set up defenses and act instinctively to win, a complaint should alert management to an exceptional opportunity to display the product and service as they are genuinely intended to be. The audience could not possibly be more attentive.

The operations auditor cannot quantify the probable effects of customer complaints on profits; he will have to content himself with analyses aimed at detecting patterns and isolating sources that can be the subjects of his further scrutiny. Service aspects that can be quantified include turnaround time between customer request and service and cost per unit for service by model or brand or class of customer. Cost control and evaluation cannot be exercised over a nonquantitative customer service policy.

Action on delayed deliveries must be handled carefully, since impulsive reaction might lead to ultraconservative practices that could be just as unprofitable as the missed promises they seek to prevent. The reason is that a service-minded sales management can request large inventories, extensive warehousing facilities, and long lead times, any of which could tie up working capital beyond the risks of a leaner service policy.

In one shipping company subject to severe competition, the vice-president of marketing kept track of all customer requests for adjustments. He found improvement necessary in deliveries, handling, billing, dunning, sales promises, and insurance coverages. Most important, he learned what might cause customers to stop using the company's services. Lost sales do not show as a line item in the financial statements.

Customer complaints, adjustments, and returns are a sensitive pulse of any company's relations with its market. They say a great deal about the quality of reception of the product or service by the customer, and it would behoove the company to listen carefully. Analysis of customer complaints can give a company great insight into its market research function. It is usually wise to have a senior officer responsible for the handling, review, and correction of any operational weaknesses revealed by the analysis of complaints and returns.

REFERENCES

1. James E. Gulick, "Profile Your Customers to Expand Industrial Sales," *Management Aid Bulletin* 192, Small Business Administration, 1968, p. 3.
2. Richard V. Butt, *Sales Effort and Marketing Strategy* (AMA, 1969). pp. 11, 12.

15

ENGINEERING

One of the more difficult functions of a company to audit is engineering, mainly because the results of engineering activity are not always directly measurable and often show up more meaningfully elsewhere.

In most companies engineering has a higher proportion of professionals than any other department except R&D. That, however, does not assure that the engineering department will be well run; in fact, it usually mitigates against efficient administration. Like scientists and physicians, engineers are interested primarily in the work involved in their own discipline and only secondarily—if at all—in management and procedures. Their education places a premium on technical knowledge and creates little appreciation of or competence in administration.

ENGINEERING CONTROL

Also like other professionals, engineers tend to be highly individualistic. They develop their own working style and, typically, do not care much for controls, formal procedures, or any other constraints on their professional freedom. On the other hand, because engineers are very good at offsetting procedures, engineering schedules often get out of hand. Then emergency action must be taken to bring things back under control. Unfortunately, the emergency measures are often laid on top of a control system that is already complex. When that is the case, the engineering administrative apparatus begins to collapse under its own weight. The frequent result is that the best engineers start to look for employment elsewhere and management is unhappy with the entire engineering effort.

From an operations auditing viewpoint, the basic facts are that it takes a long time and a large investment to build up a competent engineering effort, and the effort can be kept effective only through sound planning and control. Planning and control themselves constitute formidable problems; in engineering they involve psychological and organizational problems as well. Many engineering organizations pay only lip service to planning and control, with the net result that the environment of engineering work, though it exhibits an aura of rationality, is actually irrational. Engineers are assigned to work on system

145

components in the absence of system analysis; assignments have no defined outputs; projects are exploded into component parts and work on the parts is assigned without integrated completion dates. Even when the planning is adequate, it is not always backed up by appropriate controls. For example, there is often no feedback mechanism on which to base coordination when the original plans must be modified.

The fact that engineering is difficult to manage leads some people to structure the effort to a fare-thee-well. But that produces no better results. Too much differentiation, too many controls, too much reviewing only increase the volume of paperwork and add to the possibility that engineers and scientists will be distracted. Plans, controls, performance reviews, and related procedures should be tailored to the special needs of the unit and company.

Unfortunately for the operations auditor, standards by which to judge engineering performance are hard to come by. The activities subsumed under the title "engineering" vary greatly from one company to another and even from one corporate division to another. There are, for example, considerable differences between product engineering and facilities engineering and between in-house design engineering and field engineering. The problem of appraising engineering effectiveness is compounded by the current dynamism in engineering knowledge ("the half-life of an engineer is six years") and the resistance of engineers to the development of standards. Thus, evaluation of an engineering function must often be made on a qualitative rather than quantitative basis, such as how well the function serves particular needs or how well it fulfills the rubrics of sound business operations.

ADMINISTRATION

Some engineering managers tend to pay more attention to their engineering responsibilities than to their administrative ones. Such managers are apt to make fat cost estimates, be overoptimistic about completion dates, treat status and commitment reports lightly, and build empires of engineers, draftsmen, technicians, and designers.

Obviously, an engineering department will serve corporate needs best when it performs its assigned engineering and administrative tasks with equal skill. That performance is not easy. Two greatly differing sets of requirements are involved, and people skilled in one area seldom do well in the other. For that reason, engineering departments usually have two rather separate organizations—one oriented technically and the other administratively. In most cases, the key engineering personnel are involved in both organizations and deal with both kinds of work. On the other hand, there is a growing tendency toward separating the two by assigning specialists to handle engineering administrative work only. The administrative organization is concerned with such matters as:

☐ Providing work plans and project schedules.
☐ Developing work progress and cost controls.
☐ Providing adequate physical facilities and equipment.
☐ Developing information that can be used to estimate standard costs.
☐ Relating company goals and policies to engineering objectives.
☐ Providing a competent staff to achieve the objectives.
☐ Providing a program for training and upgrading the staff.

It may also be responsible for systems for numbering drawings and parts; systems for producing, storing, retrieving, and protecting drawings; provision and maintenance of test facilities; manpower and skill requirement analysis; and other activities necessary to support the engineering effort.

Today, the manager of engineering must embrace a body of knowledge such that technical administration is worthy of being called a profession by itself. It is so large and dynamic that dedicated effort is required just to stay abreast of it. The effort is well worthwhile, however, for only by keeping up with developments in his field will the manager be able to make the most of the engineering talents and skills under his direction.

Because planning is the heart of any administrative effort, planning as it affects engineering should receive the auditor's early and careful attention. Planning for engineering well into the future is of considerable importance if the firm is to have an adequately staffed and productive engineering effort three to five years from now. Only if management anticipates both technological and managerial needs well in advance will the company put itself within reach of the markets of the future.

Important though longer-range planning is, the auditor must not lose sight of the fact that engineering effectiveness depends heavily on current work being well planned and executed. Effective engineering groups are seldom built when work is ill defined and directed. The auditor should therefore closely examine the project definition, staffing, and scheduling. When current work is not being performed in accordance with specified intentions, it is unlikely that the right work is being finished in the right quality by the time it is needed.

CONTROLS

As attested by the plight of numerous engineering-intensive firms today, control over engineering timeliness and costs is among the thorniest problems corporations have. In many companies engineering projects are more often late than on time and the budget for engineering is often the worst constructed and managed item in the corporate budget. One reason is that engineers are so solution-oriented that they tend to forget total corporate needs. When costs reach budgeted amounts and the work is still incomplete, engineers usually press to increase the budget on the ground that sunk costs can be recovered only by further investment. When due dates are reached before the project is completed, they are usually silent or tend to focus on the inevitability of the delays rather than on measures for speeding up completion.

Engineers dislike working to detailed budgets; they prefer to have annual, lump-sum ones. When they do have them, they may write off to expenses sizable sums that should be capitalized or adopt loose practices that force other departments to remain overstaffed. To illustrate, the construction department may have to be larger than it should be or may be forced to maintain excessive inventories because it receives an excessive number of change orders from engineering or because engineering did not, in the interests of cost control, standardize sufficiently.

Engineering managers must be made aware of the actual costs of their operations. Further, they must be given the means to monitor and influence the cost of activities within their responsibility. Examples are project costs reported on a cumulative basis by time period and in total and actual versus budgeted costs by departmental function. The determination of the best cost system for a particular project may require collaboration of the estimating, systems services, and accounting departments.

The traditional elements used in preparing departmental budgets, such as salaries, purchased services, supplies, equipment purchases, travel and living expenses, and out-of-pocket training and education expenses, provide a minimum framework for measuring cost effectiveness. Far better is budgeting that facilitates measurement and reporting of expenses and time incurred versus costs and total time estimated for major projects. Such budgeting facilitates reporting that can be used as a basis for taking action.

Establishing controls depends on the measurements possible. Considerations relating to the two are given in the following paragraphs.

1. The measurement of engineering work usually has to be split between appraisal of short- and long-term efforts. The two require different frames of reference. Short-term effort can usually be measured against the specifics of the accomplishment assigned, and long-term effort against business objectives such as those touching on profitability and product plans.

2. Estimates carefully arrived at are fundamental to the purposes of control. They not only provide the administrators with up-to-date time, cost, and financial commitment data but also give the treasurer or controller an idea of cash needs. Sound estimating greatly facilitates anticipation of problems in time for remedial action to be taken.

3. Standards are an element of control. They may encompass many items—in-house and field labor, contract labor, materials, and services—and be generated out of many sources. For example, objective costs, such as cost per square foot of floor space constructed, may be used as a control.

4. There must be a continuous process of project evaluation to keep management apprised and forewarned. The estimating group's responsibility is not over until it reviews final project costs and, when necessary, modifies standards and calls attention to high-cost areas offering possibilities of cost reductions.

5. Visual methods are useful tools in the measurement of performance. Gantt charts, for example, are traditional. Also, PERT (program evaluation review technique) and PERT cost systems have been coming into use as more sophisticated and accurate guidelines for companies heavily involved in project programs.

6. Clearly established procedures should be instituted to designate who contacts whom about what. During a study of the engineering department in a construction company, a common complaint of the company's subcontractors was: "Every time they send a man around, it's a different one. Too many people get in on the act, and we get the feeling that everybody is looking at our contract from a different angle. We never know whom to get hold of when we have a problem, and orders get countermanded all the time."

PERSONNEL

The auditor should usually obtain personnel turnover figures as part of his effort to determine whether engineers are being well utilized and personnel practices are conducive to keeping top-grade people. In a recent study of a petroleum engineering department, for example, it was found that the turn-over rate in one section of engineering was five times greater than in another. The reason was boredom: engineers were underutilized. Calculations that could have been done by computer were being done manually; projects were being piecemealed into increments that held little intrinsic interest; new ideas were not being courted; and the concepts being employed were conservative and based on completely familiar knowledge. The study found that the super-visor was an excellent engineer but had negligible administrative and motivat-ing capacities. Apparently, he was unwilling or unable to discuss problems, listen to suggestions, and help his engineers upgrade their skills and knowledge. As a result, his best men quit to join a competitor who was more appreciative of the factors that stimulate an engineer.

Sustained underutilization must ultimately cause a good engineer to quit; it atrophies the only things he has to sell—his abilities and his knowledge. Thus, a major reason for taking positive steps to get full utilization out of engineers is that doing so will help keep them current. Engineering knowledge has a high rate of obsolescence, and considerable effort is needed to keep abreast of developments. Relieving engineers of mundane, underdemanding tasks is an absolute prerequisite to getting them on the road to new knowledge.

One way to effect a gain in engineer utilization is to employ engineering technicians. It has been claimed that engineers devote up to 70 percent of their time to nonengineering work. It is not possible for them to avoid such work entirely, but sincere effort can reduce it markedly. Such non-engineering activities as scheduling, administration, expediting, and graphics should be assigned to technicians or specialists.

One way to minimize engineer turnover is to build into engineering units definite and recognizable opportunities for advancement. Growth should not be narrowly constrained; it should be encouraged along either professional or managerial lines. Since both technical and administrative capabilities are acquired through training as well as hands-on experience, the auditor should look at personnel development activities. It is not at all rare for engineering budgets to contain not a red cent for them, with the result that skill-enlarging activities either do not take place or are deceptively reported.

Key consideration in personnel development work is that it is done in the presence of clear and relevant objectives and in accordance with empirically determined employee needs. Those considerations apply to engineering depart-ments as well as to any other.

ORGANIZATION

Job content and organizational relationships have a powerful influence on engi-neering effectiveness. Highly structured or complex organizational arrange-ments are hardly ever called for, but effectiveness is often handicapped by a lack of useful degrees of work definition and differentiation. For example, the authorities, responsibilities, and accountabilities of positions in engineering departments are apt to be less properly defined, assigned, and related than in other departments. Further, there is a tendency for companies to be casual about seeing to it that their engineering departments are properly situated and integrated in their overall organizations. On the other hand, oftentimes there are conditions poorly served by applying certain widely accepted principles of organization to the engineering function. Traditional or conventional views of organizational design often are unproductive when applied to fields of activity, such as engineering, that can be highly individualistic.

Although engineering organizations are often more sloppily structured than they should be, some wastage of engineering talent owing to excessive specialization will occasionally be met. Such engineering specialization as structural and electrical is, of course, almost impossible to avoid, but unnecessary specialization can fragment knowledge and create subunits that raise severe control and organizational problems. One company that manufactures power-generation equipment had so much specialization in its engineering department that eight levels were necessary to accommodate the differentiations in work. Moving toward generalization enabled the company to reduce them to four. As a result, less supervision was necessary and engineering productivity rose.

The tendency in engineering today is to organize flexibly, as evidenced by the grouping of engineering activities on a project basis. The alternative to assigning all the work related to a given project to one group is to pass work from one functional group to another. The alternative has severe disadvantages: no one is charged with the full responsibility of the entire project; no one is in a position to weigh priorities; the volume of communicating activity becomes burdensome; and technical conflicts often arise. Measuring progress or troubleshooting the project is difficult because no one can speak for the project as a whole. If engineering is not project-oriented, a change in organization may be desirable.

When engineering is involved in product development, engineering costs and effectiveness become of even greater interest to a firm. Engineering is then heavily involved in the creation of products sold to make a profit for the corporation. Almost all factors—the engineer's qualifications, utilization, supervision, support, and information—become more critical. From the organizational viewpoint, care must be taken that engineering has ready access to and remains in close touch with production, marketing, R&D, and other areas that may be important sources of input. Engineering must, for example, design products that production can manufacture most effectively and that sales can interest people in buying. If engineering units are run without regard for the concerns of other organization units, the penalties are constant design changes, a different parts-numbering system, designs frozen before adequate tests have been completed, and incomplete or late delivery of drawings to production.

Unfortunately, from the viewpoint of sound organization, the do-it-yourself temptation prevails with engineers, and engineering departments often try to be organizationally self-sufficient. For example, unless systems analysis and data processing help is pressed on it, the engineering department tends to undertake that work itself. (Many engineering departments have computers while usable capacity on the firm's general computer goes to waste.) That is uneconomical; engineering should not design procedural systems or fulfill other roles, such as purchasing, for which it is not qualified by knowledge or experience.

One way to greatly enhance compatibility of interests is to establish a reasonable flow of personnel into and out of engineering from adjacent departments. Another way, and one that avoids the attenuation of professional competence that rotation into nontechnical jobs entails, is to establish joint planning. Either way will prevent the parochialism expressed in such statements as: "We never really know what sales has sold. They never stop to ask if we can make an article at the price quoted and in the quality promised," and "There's nothing wrong with the engineering department except we can't produce what they design."

A consequence of organizational isolation is that illicit engineering functions tend to develop in the corners of other corporate units. For example, when engineering does not work closely with production, the latter is often moved to engage in some engineering on its own, and thereby create a potential for duplicated or contradictory effort. Production may find it expedient to undertake its own plant modification design work and perform maintenance engineering. Neither action is economically sound; production will tend to make decisions in both areas on a self-interest rather than an economic basis.

When there is a good deal of plant engineering and either production is allowed to do it or it is deliberately kept separate from the other engineering activities, associated problems such as confusion in respect to parts-numbering systems, plant design, major equipment modification requirements, heavy maintenance engineering, and even production are not uncommonly found. These problems, aside from their particular manifestations, are also organizational problems. Hence, it should be of interest to the operations auditor to see what efforts are made to offset or anticipate them, as by having regular and open meetings between engineering and other organizational units.

SERVICES AND FACILITIES

Engineering facilities are often poorly designed or overtaxed. Engineers are often forced to work in spaces originally designed for other functions, and such quarters are hardly ever adequate to the needs of engineering work. That is particularly unfortunate because inadequate facilities can significantly affect the quality of design engineering. If files are difficult to reach or badly organized, the engineer may find it more convenient to redesign than to employ or modify a standard. If reproduction facilities are inaccessible or bad, he may use an original drawing to the detriment of improving the company's designs. If secretarial services are overtaxed or poor, he may have to handle his own communications, and the result will be insufficient correspondence in the filing system for the guidance of others. If noise levels are excessive, the amount of time involved in the production of quality work is almost sure to rise sharply. All those factors are important and should not be ignored in an operations audit.

16

ELECTRONIC
DATA PROCESSING

This chapter will deal only with data processing that involves the use of computers. There are other forms of data processing (for example, those that involve noncomputer equipment such as electric accounting machines) that should be audited also.

Computers are considered by many people to be the most important invention of the twentieth century and one of the most significant in history. An effect is that operations auditors can expect to encounter computer operations more and more frequently and in an increasing variety of applications. Eventually, the typical auditor will probably spend at least as much time on electronic data processing (EDP) as on any other single audit element.

COMPUTER GROWTH: THE FIRST PHASE
So far, two phases have made their appearance since the onset of EDP. Generally speaking, the first phase lasted approximately two decades; the second phase has really just begun. The first phase was marked by rapid technological development but low productivity; the second phase is exhibiting a reduced rate of development but rapidly improving control of EDP functions.

The computer, like most great inventions, was the result of the coming together at a moment in time of three phenomena: (1) the maturing of a prerequisite technology, (2) the attainment of automation-supporting transactional volumes, and (3) a sharp escalation in the cost of doing business. The first two were absolute preconditions: until electronics made the production of large-scale calculative circuitry possible and commercial-industrial activities reached volumes capable of supporting automation, there was no possibility of or pressing need for EDP.

In the period following the technological breakthroughs and the attainment of corporate sizes that made the computer commercially feasible, most companies experienced significantly increased competitive pressure and rising costs. Many of them sought, by investing in EDP, to reduce or contain costs, improve customer service, and obtain better information for decision making and management control. Inevitably, the expenditures were sizable.

Nonetheless, EDP has taken hold with startling suddenness. Though the first electronic computer did not become available for business use before the early 1950s, the rush to computers was well under way by 1960. By 1970 the computer population reached an estimated 74,000 installations worth some $12 billion and annual expenditures reached about the same amount. The combined costs then represented more than 2 percent of the gross national product. By the mid-1970s, the number of computers will probably more than double. When that point is reached, computer systems will amount to something like 10 percent of the entire U.S. investment in business.

The rate of change in computer technology is having more impact on business than the rapid growth in the number of computers. The price of unit information is decreasing at least as fast as computers are increasing in number, primarily because a number of breakthroughs in computer design and manufacturing have made available smaller and less costly computers with capabilities equal those of earlier, larger versions. The principal benefit is that a typical application costing $1 for equipment in 1964 and 35 cents in 1971 will probably cost no more than 15 cents by 1973. A consequence is that half of today's installations are small-scale; that is, they rent for $3,000 a month or less. By 1980, it is estimated, the majority of installations will be small. With declining costs, improved capabilities, and rising developments in time-sharing and service bureau operations, the advantages of computer processing will soon extend to almost every business enterprise regardless of size.

Computer economics. The economics of properly used computers has been established beyond conjecture. Once the data bank is established and the program has been finalized, the computer is nearly one million times faster in performing a single operation than a mechanical calculator or human data handler. Provided the volume is sufficient to offset the extensive setup time, the computer can perform routine clerical operations a good deal cheaper than people can. For example, it costs a bank only one three-hundredths as much to post a check by computer as manually. Firms that took advantage of these and similar powers of the computer have been able to grow faster than the economy and competitors who did not learn at all or did not learn as fast.

Despite these facts and the great potential of EDP, results from using computers have been mixed. A small number of using companies have prospered; a far greater number have got little out of computerizing; and a small number have been disastrously affected. A relative handful of companies, notably in the power and insurance businesses, were ideally situated to benefit from EDP; they had sufficient and short enough transaction cycles to justify rapid systemization and the assembly of large staffs of computer specialists. But most companies were not so ideally situated, and although they had fair success in applying computers to accounting and other routine record-keeping functions, they did not really save money or secure other benefits in moving to EDP.

Worse, to some firms the costs of their mistakes were fatal or nearly so. For example, one large department store that not long ago went into bankruptcy may have been driven to the wall by computer problems; $2 million of the company's accounts receivable were locked in a computer that failed to print out bills for sums owed to the company. It took the concern six months to straighten out the system, but by then between $150,000 and $200,000 was uncollectable. In another case, one substantial retailing company in a period of more than a year failed to collect $6 million due it, mainly because of computer problems.

Though there have been many unhappy experiences and the risks are still considerable in making the move to EDP, it is now established beyond doubt that the company that learns to use a computer effectively can gain important advantages. The corollary is that the gaps in competitive capacities between companies will tend to widen as some companies succeed better than others in adapting EDP to major business functions.

COMPUTER GROWTH: THE SECOND PHASE

The first two decades of the computer were marked by fantastic growth, enormous fear of and reverence for the computer's capabilities, and the emergence of awesome problems. Expectations were seldom realized; costs often vastly exceeded budgets; and a handful of firms were broken because of system failures or unwise investments in EDP. However, a new phase in computer technology has emerged, as signified by a fairly quick shift from generally unrealistic attitudes and practices to general treatment of data processing as a normal business operation to be governed by sound business principles.

Several conditions caused the shift. The first was that the preponderance of installations proved disappointing: their costs were very high and they did not justify their costs. Second, the knowledge lag was largely overcome; many executives got to know how computers work, and began to learn how to control data processing operations. Third, the economic downturn in 1970 forced widespread reappraisal of EDP investments; thousands of companies for the first time had to apply brakes to EDP activities and treat EDP as a resource to be managed.

The fact that the computer industry felt the jolt of the recession and that installations are now being treated more like any other business resource does not augur a significant decline in the expansion of computer applications in business. Though the economic downturn forced management to come down to earth in respect to data processing, equipment sales will probably continue to grow between 15 and 18 percent a year. Top management will demand more proof of return on their EDP investments, but there are many reasons for thinking that developing circumstances will continue to force companies to turn to or make better use of EDP. In strong support of this view is that the growth rate of service bureau and time-sharing business is greater than that of equipment sales, which is 15 to 18 percent per year, and promises to be even greater in the future. It has, in fact, been helped by the recession, because the closer scrutiny now given proposed EDP investments often turns up a lack of economic justification for in-house installations when EDP is nonetheless needed. The answer, in many cases, is to have data processed outside or share a computer.

Business in the rest of this century will undoubtedly be even more complex than it became in the 1950s and 1960s, when it shifted to the next order of magnitude in complexity over the 1930s and 1940s. It seems fair to say, therefore, that EDP effectiveness has to come under much better control than it has to date if computers are to realize anything near their service potentials. It is likely that a third phase will be reached, one in which the enormous task of keeping concepts, procedures, and programs current will come under control the equal of that exercised in other business areas while a tremendous expansion in application virtuosity takes place. Phase three will be the coming of age of EDP, and its arrival will be signaled by the first of many profound changes in man's work and living styles.

CONDUCTING THE AUDIT

Systems in general are becoming so large, complex, and costly that corporate interests demand they be audited, and EDP is of such economic and procedural importance that probably no system other than the financial one should be more heavily audited. Though control of EDP activities has improved considerably in recent years, in many firms it still has a long way to go before it reaches the effectiveness common to other corporate functions. It is not too extreme to assume that there lies in almost every installation a potential either of great dollar savings, great improvement in productivity, or some of both.

So dependent on EDP activities have some firms become that a number of authorities think the larger EDP systems should be audited continuously from inception. Without arguing the point, it is certain the EDP operations auditing is mandatory at least in geographically dispersed, computerized companies and in companies where the resources committed to EDP are a significant portion of the company's total resources. The potential for operations auditing to contribute to the understanding and the work of improving the effectiveness of EDP activities increases as computerized systems expand and become more integrated and complex, decision making becomes more computer-dependent, data processing for diversified and geographically dispersed activities becomes more centralized, and the need for computer-oriented organizational arrangements intensifies.

On the surface, it would appear that asking an operations auditor to audit so highly technical a field as EDP would place him at a disadvantage. On the contrary, his being technically limited does not of itself disqualify him from determining how well EDP is fulfilling its obligations to the firm. In fact, his lack of expertise in the field can actually contribute to the quality of an EDP audit. For example, he is least likely, assuming he has been well trained as an auditor, to be swayed by the argot or the dissembling of EDP personnel.

Some understanding of the field is, of course, required, but it should be based much more on knowledge of business fundamentals and the objectives set for EDP by its users than on close familiarity with the ways machines are programmed and do their work. Unfortunately, the auditor has more control over one form of knowledge than the other. Knowledge of business fundamentals is universally available, but knowledge of EDP objectives is not. The provision of clear and realistic objectives for EDP is rare.

Audit guidelines. In the absence of sound and clearly stated objectives

155

and extensive knowledge of the technicalities of EDP, upon what can the operations auditor build his confidence that the results of his audit will be dependable and useful? The answer is his possession of the general principles of business enterprise and management, his knowledge of and skill in performing operations audits, and his knowledge that the same kinds of results should be expected of EDP as of any other corporate function or department. Elements of such expectations have a reasonable basis when (1) EDP is a cost-justifying service to the corporation at large, (2) EDP contributes to the effectiveness of other departments, (3) spending for systems development is carefully controlled, and (4) there is maximum utilization of equipment and manpower. Each of these elements constitutes an auditable aspect of an EDP function.

If it is granted that the four elements specified in the preceding paragraph can be audited by a nontechnician, then it follows that the operations auditor can play a useful role in obtaining realistic appraisals of the company's EDP function. He can help gain understanding of the quality of performance by making appraisals from at least five perspectives:

- [ ] The cost effectiveness of the total EDP effort.
- [ ] The quality of overall systems planning and implementation.
- [ ] The degree of satisfaction with and utilization of EDP output.
- [ ] The coverage of risks entailed in computer processing.
- [ ] The degree to which potential and higher-decision-serving applications have been computerized.

None of these appraisals are simple, and each has many aspects. Yet, as the term "perspective" implies, they force the auditor to look at the EDP effort from different angles—itself of major benefit.

From the viewpoint of audit effectiveness, perhaps nothing is more important for the auditor to keep in mind than the necessity to be conservative in his approach to the EDP function. Because the EDP field is so relatively new and its demands on rationality are so great, it is well-nigh impossible to find an installation that cannot be criticized. EDP is still poorly understood and controlled in most companies. Inefficiencies in EDP are often tolerated in such companies to a degree that would cause waves of horror elsewhere. The operations auditor can enter almost any company with the assurance that, in the EDP area, he is likely to discover problems—in spades.

That likelihood being confirmed should not, however, occasion the auditor's tearing a strip off the function. The auditor should never lose sight of the fact that the computer still arouses fear, still causes a good deal of apprehension. Even after twenty years of EDP many executives feel that the computer will somehow reduce the company's need for them. That the computer can have exactly the opposite effect escapes them. In most companies, as a result, EDP has not yet been made to produce anywhere near its full potential, and insensitive criticism is likely to make many people, including top management, feel under the spotlight.

Projections versus achievements. A more fundamental reason why the auditor must be careful to weigh the problems he encounters is that far more has been written about optimum data processing systems than has been achieved. Therefore, he should not fault a system for deficiencies that cannot be solved by existing technology and available skills or that are natural to any developing system. He should fault it for things that should have been anticipated or are being performed without regard for existing standards and the firm's goals. In other words, the discovery of opportunities for improvement does not necessarily signify deficiencies in management and control; it may only signify immaturity in an effort that is being effectively directed toward major accomplishments. The only deficiencies that can be assumed noteworthy from the appraisal viewpoint are the problems or opportunities for improvement that stem from laxity in determining feasibility or intention to do something about the failures that ensue.

Since EDP everywhere is full of problems, the operations auditor's job will not simply be to find and identify EDP problems. His principal job will be to develop clear and accurate descriptions of the problems and establish relative importance as aids in deciding priorities and committing resources to deal with the problems.

In reviewing EDP activities, the operations auditor will meet defenses of exceptional sophistication and power. He must be prepared to circumvent them, and his best chance of doing so lies in aiming his investigative efforts at selected targets. He must be acutely aware of the need to ask the right people the right questions and to verify that he is not getting stock or evasive answers. His first task, therefore, is to structure his approach. That has been anticipated for the auditor inexperienced in EDP by the provision in this volume of a questionnaire of some length. Auditors familiar with EDP will probably want to redesign the questionnaire and divide the work differently.

The auditor should expect to encounter and distinguish between two kinds of problems: those unique to EDP and those common to other business functions. Unique to EDP are problems related to system analysis, programming, data input, and file protection. Problems common to other business functions are that system plans are fragmentary or improperly detailed, operations are poorly budgeted, performance is gauged subjectively, terminology is defensively used, and the rate of technological change is used to justify control deficiencies.

To do his work properly, the operations auditor should become aware of certain facts relating to EDP:

The average life of present EDP installations is something less than four years.

Companies in the most experienced user group (large corporations) are spending from 1 to 3 percent of revenues on computer installations, and the percentage is rising.

Recent surveys indicate that from 35 to 50 percent of computer installations cost more than they save over manual operations.

Operating and related costs have been averaging about 200 percent of rental costs. As machines get less expensive and people get more expensive, those costs are coming closer to 300 percent of rental costs.

The costs of handling bread-and-butter functions on an automated basis are usually at least equal to handling them manually.

Making effective use of computers normally requires their use also in the major functions of the business, such as finance, marketing, production, and distribution. However, most companies have not succeeded in putting their computers productively to work in these areas.

The number of organizational levels between presidents and EDP is declining; it averages one level between the two. Top-level executives now supervise the function in 30 percent of the companies.

Increasing numbers of EDP managers are reporting to nonfinancial executives. In 1960, approximately 75 percent of computer executives reported to controllers, vice-presidents of finance, and so on. By 1968 that percentage had dropped almost to 50 percent, and the evidence shows the trend to be continuing.

The importance of measuring the effectiveness of computers by such concrete measures as costs, budgets, and savings is gaining widespread recognition, and an increasing number of companies are implementing such evaluative and control systems.

The bulk of EDP installations are still without effective operational and cost controls. The three major problems that affect EDP quality seem to be lack of experienced or qualified personnel, lack of management involvement, and hardware and software failures.

One of the chief misunderstandings about data processing is that aggregates of hardware form systems. Such aggregates are, in fact, no more than a vital link in an information system.

The number of companies that use or plan to use time-sharing or generalized file systems is getting quite large and is increasing rapidly.

Data communications expense—that is, the cost of communicating data either into the computer directly or for batching—amounted to only 1 percent of the total computer expense in 1960. By 1968 that had grown to 13 percent of the total, and evidence points to continued growth in communications expense.

The preceding facts are closely related to the reasons why the promise that management can get better and more timely information for decision making with a computer has not often been realized. Amplification of several of the foregoing points follows.

In the matter of costs as a percent of revenue, the authors in 1969 conducted a study in which the following question was asked: "If you process data on a punched card or computer system, what percent of sales does it cost (including salaries)?" The responses of 36 small companies (up to $50 million in sales) and 54 large companies (over $50 million) are given in Table 4. The results show, almost certainly, that data processing, as a percent of sales, tends to cost more in small than in large companies. Only a third of the small companies, as compared with more than two-thirds of the large companies, spend less than 1 percent of their sales for data processing. The results generally confirm those obtained in other EDP studies.

Control of computer effectiveness. The rental or depreciation cost of computers and peripheral equipment dropped from 55 percent of the total cost of operating an EDP system in 1960 to 41 percent in 1968. The change largely resulted from two factors: the declining costs of hardware on a per computation basis and constantly increasing costs of software development. There is no evidence that a reversal of these trends will take place.

Table 4   Costs of data processing.

DATA PROCESSING AS PERCENT OF SALES	SMALL COMPANIES		LARGE COMPANIES	
	NUMBER	PERCENT	NUMBER	PERCENT
Less than 1	12	34	39	71
1	10	27	6	12
1 to 2	6	16	6	12
2 to 3	4	11	3	5
5	2	6	—	—
Over 5	2	6	—	—
	36	100	54	100

In regard to the growing recognition of the importance of measuring and controlling computer effectiveness, the auditor should be familiar with the key factors that underlie successful computer system programs. Studies reveal that in companies with effective programs:

□   Top management views the computer as a major economic resource, not just a supertypewriter or an advanced accounting tool.

□   Management has set clear objectives to insure that the EDP program serves the primary interest of the business.

□   Top management realizes that the main problems in getting computer payoff is managerial and organizational rather than technical.

□   Top management and operating management participate actively in each step of systems development.

The substance of the lesson of the past decade or two is that, when management plays its essential role, important consequences follow: broad-scale use, significant tangible benefits, and high return on investment. It is also clear that application of the management techniques that have made industrial enterprise what it is today is among the requirements for raising data processing effectiveness to satisfactory and higher levels.

Though it is being increasingly recognized that the computer can begin to realize its full potential only when it has been brought to bear on the key functions of the business, little has actually been accomplished toward that end. Strangely enough, the rapid growth in computer capacities has been the major deterrent. The speed of succession of computer generations, following the change from unit record equipment, has been such that conversion from one generation to another has been a preoccupation of most EDP staffs.

According to one survey, more than half the companies that have had EDP more than five years have completely reprogrammed their applications to meet the specifications of the latest generation of computers. The short cycle does not favor EDP productivity. Conversion is so time-consuming a task that bread-and-butter functions, such as payroll, inventory, and accounting, are given precedence over more potentially profitable applications such as

159

production control, machine loading, stock replenishment, and investment modeling.

The example of payroll illustrates the point perfectly. Payroll was one of the earliest, common unit record applications; companies with several hundred or more employees found it economically sound to use tab equipment for payroll and associated reports in place of clerks. When the first computer arrived, it was natural to convert payroll to the new equipment. And at just about the time when that and similar programs were working smoothly and the staff was in a position to get to work on new applications, the next computer was on board and conversion began all over again. Thus, established applications have preempted the attention of most EDP staffs in the first two decades of the computer era.

The real potential of computers lies not so much in the capacity to perform routine clerical operations as in the ability to do rather complex problem solving in the logical sense. Payroll, for example, is an essential service, but it also is and always will be an expense item. No matter how sophisticated the payroll program becomes, it adds little to the profit potential of the company. In effect, although payroll transactions are performed more expeditiously—and hopefully at lower cost—on a computer, the processing does not increase the sum of decision-making information available in the company. If equal time and effort had been expended in computerizing sales analysis, production control, cash flow analysis, or financial modeling, the chances are that the profit potential of the firm would be considerably enhanced.

It is of interest that certain mathematical formulas developed in the seventeenth and eighteenth centuries by Pascal, Leibniz, Newton, and Gauss, for example, regression analysis and method of least squares, are now easily handled by any computer but are rarely utilized in computer programs. By failing to use the computer in calculative, as against purely arithmetic, operations, a firm loses the computer service that has the most important economic consequences.

ELEMENTS OF THE AUDIT

When he conducts an EDP audit, the auditor will do well to segregate the two major aspects of an EDP function: the physical (equipment configuration, programs, and output) and operations (the running and development of it). The questionnaire for data processing printed in Part 3 does not distinguish between those aspects, but the auditor must. For example, he should not chalk it against configuration that system development is not what it should be. That an IBM 360 is running in series 1400 emulation mode does not necessarily point either to feasibility study failure or deficient operations.

Scope of the operations audit of EDP covers at least the following elements:

- ☐ Systems design effectiveness.
- ☐ Organization and staffing.
- ☐ System performance in terms of quality and cost.
- ☐ Clerical support procedures.
- ☐ Input preparation methods.
- ☐ Efficiency of machine utilization.
- ☐ Output formats and effectiveness.

- ☐ User satisfaction.
- ☐ Identification of improvement opportunities.
- ☐ Policies and practices.
- ☐ Installation security.
- ☐ Staff and user training.
- ☐ Operating planning and controls.
- ☐ Documentation.
- ☐ Project progress and reporting procedures.
- ☐ Library maintenance and security.
- ☐ Physical facility arrangement.
- ☐ Programming and processing specifications.

When he audits the data processing department, the operations auditor should first determine whether the department has a charter and, if it has one, what it is. He should then determine whether it is reasonable and inclusive. Having gained an understanding of the objectives and powers of the department, the auditor can then work to become familiar with the installation. In that phase he should first pull together general information about the department with the help of the forms reproduced in the Appendix. If basic information pertaining to department organization, staffing, equipment utilization, allocation of resources, standard operating procedures, and costs is not readily available to the auditor, it can be fairly assumed that the department is out of control. There is no need for the auditor to go any further in his analysis before issuing an audit memo to the department on the status of its controls.

Though it was said earlier that this chapter deals with electronic data processing only, the operations auditor should not restrict his EDP fact finding to interviews with EDP personnel. He should also interview persons in operating units, such as production and sales, and specialty units, such as the systems and procedures or internal auditing staffs (when OA is a separate function).

There are two reasons for the broader investigation. One is that the operations auditor should be concerned with the effectiveness of electronic data processing in meeting overall management and corporate objectives. The second is that auditing an EDP installation per se is a grossly deficient activity. Data processing is best audited as a *totality*, which means that data processing should be audited at every stage in the process and in whatever form it takes place. In other words, the most profitable audit of data processing will range from examination of dp activities from pencil stubs to electronic gear.

Each EDP system is only as good as its data input is accurate and its output is usable. Accordingly, the operations auditor must take a "systems approach" to the audit of data processing. He should explore many facets outside the EDP function itself that may have bearing on the function, including company policies and practices, procedures, clerical workload, time delay factors, and utilization of reports. That is especially true when a third party must rely on computer output data in the performance of his job. Sales reports, for example, may serve as a basis for marketing decisions. The source of much of the sales data is the invoicing procedure, often the functional responsibility of the financial department. Yet the invoicing function is a byproduct of the order-processing activity, which in turn is dependent upon the sales organization. Thus, the operations auditor must in certain applications consider the entire work flow, including communications between the company and its customers and vendors.

For that reason, a visit to each department that either supplies data to or receives data from the EDP department is likely to provide information useful in gauging EDP effectiveness. It is important for the auditor to keep in mind that the service rendered can best be judged by the end product and that control of product quality is more worthy of investigation than the techniques resulting in the output.

Probably no other index of EDP effectiveness offers a quicker and more precise measure than the computer output. The auditor should, early in the audit, request that he be provided a sample of each regularly run report, and he should refer to the samples when he talks to the departments that receive them.

One of the principal sources of EDP problems is that data processing departments more often serve their own needs than those of operating managers. Most operating managers are mystified by what goes on in a computer installation, and they are thereby led into making one or both of two major errors: (1) They put what they assume are, or have been led to believe are, machine requirements ahead of their own information requirements. (2) They ask the machine to pour out far more information than they can use. However, when management states its information requirements in terms of its own needs and limits its interpretation of needs to what is usable, the resulting reports are usually superior to those designed solely by EDP specialists.

Unfortunately, however, when laymen specify both the format and the content of reports, the results show that they do not know a great deal about either the machine or their own requirements. Not only are the reports generally so voluminous that they cannot be effectively used but they are frequently so poorly designed that they do not highlight emerging or potential problems. A computer can turn out far more information than a manager can use. If it is allowed to spew out reams of useless information that simply burns up time in evaluation and interpretation, data processing equipment can be more a hindrance than a time-saver. Under those conditions information can become an end product rather than a means to an end.

One reason why computer output so often overwhelms the user is that most managers continue to think in traditional terms and require that computer reports summarize data as accounting reports do, because that is the manner most familiar to them. Of even greater importance, managers tend to resist exception reporting, which is the key to effective utilization of computer equipment.

Another source of information flooding is the subject of the following statement by Bernard J. O'Keefe:[1]

Specialists surrounded by computers make forecasts, amass data, construct information packages and generally set the environment for management decisions. Then if the specialists decide business will go one way or another, top management must go along. In other words, top management is at the mercy of its specialists.

After making that statement, the writer goes on to raise a warning:

Until management stops believing everything it sees in the printouts, the myth of the omniscience of electronic data processing will remain.

The operations auditor should keep those points in mind when he reviews computer output.

PLANNING AND CONTROLLING

Though it borders on oversimplification to say so, EDP performance, including systems analysis, design, and programming as well as computer operations, can be no better than the associated plans and controls. Since planning and controlling of data processing activities have generally been weak in the past, it follows that EDP functions have generally not been effective in the past.

There have been two reasons for the weakness of EDP planning and control: (1) most computer technicians are unacquainted with corporate needs and (2) top management does not know what is required to make EDP productive. Because EDP technicians are without experience in business operations and needs, they are unable or unwilling to devise computer systems that effectively serve the firm's interests. However, a good share of the fault lies with top management. The fundamentals of good management have not often enough in the past been seriously applied to corporate data processing. Though managers were quick to recognize EDP as a tool offering tremendous benefits to users, they did not recognize that computerization can easily produce a disaster when it is poorly planned or controlled by top management.

Sound management of the data processing function involves elements that differ little from those applicable in other business areas. For example, the scheduling techniques used in data processing do not differ in principle from those used in production planning, nor do cost controls and budget techniques that can be advantageously used in the data processing department differ fundamentally from those used successfully in managing engineering activities. A standard list of elements essential to EDP planning and controlling includes at least these:

Top management participation.
Operating management consultation.
Planning for the future.
Budgeting and performance management.
Internal scheduling.
Job acceptance controls.
Processing controls.
Project management and evaluation.

Top management participation. It is now perfectly clear that productive computer operations can result only from significant top management involvement and direction; only managers with the broadest possible purview of the company's role and aims for the future can direct EDP in the best interests of the company. That responsibility cannot safely be abdicated in favor of computer technicians or anyone else. Successful results accrue only as top management develops overall objectives and accomplishment priorities, establishes proper organizational environment, assigns clear-cut responsibilities and authorities, and insists on comprehensive and detailed plans.

Equally important is follow-through to see that planned results are achieved. Top management must see to it that all activities, including data processing, dovetail within the framework of corporate objectives and strategies. Top management involvement in coordinating the complex interrelationships of EDP service with other branches of the corporation is vital to the company's future. When top management delegates responsibility for such coordination to EDP or staff services, the chances of failure are vastly increased.

Operating management consultation. It is absolutely necessary to have the participation of operating management if EDP is to be successful in its primary aim of helping to solve corporate problems. If computer reports are to be useful, the people who design and prepare them must know the use to which the information will be put. Otherwise, EDP is left to operate in a virtual vacuum. If that is so, computer people will busy themselves with tasks that have little bearing on the objectives of the enterprise.

Coordination of EDP and operating people cannot be left to chance. It is necessary to go into the various departments of the company, study the potential applications, prepare a long-range plan, and submit the plan for review and approval by top management.

Planning for the future. EDP planning should encompass three time frames related to the major classes of EDP activities:

1. Short term, in response to the existing needs of the enterprise. Planning in this time frame deals primarily with operations and current problems. Typical matters of concern are improvements in scheduling, computer utilization, cost of supplies, report format, and program efficiency.

2. Intermediate, in response to the changes needed and/or possible during the life of the installation. This planning is usually for a two- to four-year period and involves changes throughout the company. Sometimes called tactical planning, it basically seeks to improve effectiveness by improving the processing of information along existing lines.

3. Long range, in response to the changes needed beyond existing subsystems. This planning is conceptual and broadly defined to make possible changes in company organization and product emphasis.

In keeping with good planning sense, all plans should be written and distributed to appropriate levels of management. Periodic review should be performed to measure progress and bring into focus the needs for changes in management objectives. That is not a large task; only a little information is needed as a warning of impending failure to achieve goals. The company with a sound EDP facility has given proper attention to developing measurable performance criteria. Accordingly, the operations auditor will do well to look for evidence of the effectiveness of preplanning.

When management does not know what it wants until the computer system is installed—the usual case—the cost of creating the eventual output always is far in excess of what it could have been. Not many data processing departments have a five- to seven-year plan that indicates the goals they are trying to reach within that time. The operations auditor would do well to find out to what extent long-range plans do exist. Long-range plans cannot be properly laid until the following have been considered:

1. Opening of new areas of the company to automation of data handling.

2. The characteristics of the information systems that will meet corporate financial and operational control objectives, improve sales and customer service, reduce or stabilize administrative costs, and improve information for management decision making.

3. The characteristics of the equipment and methods to be employed, corporate policies and practices needed, and the required organization and staff.

4. The order of magnitude of costs and benefits of the potential systems improvements.

5. The time, financial, personnel, and management resources required to effect the plan.

6. Areas that offer more immediate opportunities for improvement and that should be considered for early implementation.

7. Specialized talents required to achieve the long-range goals.

Budgeting and performance management. Well-known tools that they are to any successful business venture, budgeting and performance management must be applied to EDP. The data processing department should operate only as a service department; its expenses should be billed entirely to user departments. By putting the department on a cost center basis, user departments can be made more conscious of the costs of system changes. That concept has worked successfully for many companies with diversified operations; they have been able to evaluate the effectiveness of various parts of the business. However, some corporate officers have found it necessary to provide an EDP research and development budget to fund data processing work for departments that otherwise could not afford to advance to a level commensurate with that of other departments in the organization.

Efficiently produced system changes are vital to EDP department productivity, yet research and development projects are rarely managed toward that end. The means for project controls are readily available. In addition to the long-established methods associated with the control of projects and cost in other areas, new aids to effective project management are resource allocation, critical path, and PERT methods.

The performance level of the EDP function cannot possibly be known unless the costs are known. Accordingly, the auditor needs to find out to what extent costs of system design and programming are accumulated and analyzed. Further, he should find out how systematically costs are gathered. A sound cost control system enables management to know the costs of developing a specific application and the costs of program maintenance. Further, it gives concrete information against which management can evaluate whether the system is doing the job within an appropriate cost parameter.

The computer can help. There are now a number of operating systems that let the computer accumulate much of the internal data required to do adequate cost accounting. For example, an IBM program known as POWER II, or its equivalent, records during the processing of each job the time during which the various components of the computer were used.

Areas of Analysis

Internal scheduling. Only if there is proper scheduling within the data processing facility can there be assurance that user departments will receive their reports as prescribed and on a least-cost basis. When the equipment costs more than $30 an hour, it is essential that its maximum utilization be achieved; the cost of wasted time can build up at an astonishing rate. In a large, well-staffed data processing operation the operations auditor should see signs of an employee spending half if not all his time in the scheduling function to achieve the proper balance between the requested delivery time from the user department and the computer time available to perform that function.

The so-called third-generation computers are equipped with a device termed "operating systems" that is designed to resolve some of these problems. The system supervises the execution work by queuing input jobs by priorities assigned. As system resources such as the computer itself, core memory, and printer become available, the jobs are taken from the queue in priority order and processed. The system offers advantages beyond direct equipment control. For example, it can accumulate data on job running time and resource usage, information that is most useful in assigning priorities to jobs entered into the system.

The review of internal scheduling must include the factor of input as well. Unless data coming into the data processing facility are on an equally firm scheduled basis, it will be found that the resulting reports become erratic in meeting delivery commitments.

Processing control. There is some possible misunderstanding over the operations auditor's responsibility concerning processing controls, as the following excerpt indicates:[2]

> He should . . . understand flow diagrams of computer programs to insure that control requirements are incorporated and that any risks in terms of accuracy, reliability, promptness, or completeness of computer data processing are reasonable. The auditor should understand enough about programming to be able to test-check computer programs to insure that the programs accomplish the results desired. He should also check that audit safeguards (external to computer processing) are established to insure reliability and accuracy of data processing. He should review the computer installation after it has been operating for a reasonable period of time to determine its effectiveness as measured against the original goals.

The expertise needed to implement that standard is not a common possession of the operations auditor, especially the parts that have to do with the computer programming itself. Audits that are conducted in that depth require the assistance of generalized audit packages, which are computer programs that help to dissect operational programs for examination and review. (They include Audassist, Audex, and Audipak.) The operations auditor is interested only to the extent that the audit techniques exist and can be utilized if the situation should warrant their use. However, he does conduct an audit that is technically termed "around the computer," which means that the accuracy and effectiveness of the computer program used in every operation can be most easily measured by the recipients of the output.

A case in point might be the computerized payroll. Recipients of the payroll checks probably represent a stronger audit position than can be reached by any one person examining the detailed program logic. Like an experienced driver, the operations auditor can achieve his goal without knowing the intricacies of the machine. He must be able to recognize a malfunction, but he need not know how to repair it.

Job acceptance control. In EDP, job acceptance control is often equated with quality control in any efficient production facility, but it actually differs in technique and impact. The defective EDP end product cannot be detected by inspection of a random sample alone. Since most EDP reports become the basis for higher-level management action, one incorrect report can proliferate into a number of costly decision errors that can have wide implications throughout the company.

For that reason, a well-organized data processing center must include an internal control function that has responsibility accounting independence and authority. Through that control function should flow both the completed computer reports and the console printouts so that determination can be made not only that the correct input was used but that the proper magnetic files (that is, tape-disk) were updated and the security and audit trails of the system were maintained. Too frequently the control function bears the stamp of a clerical force that removes carbon from reports, bursts and binds the reports, and serves as the mail room of the EDP center. Those housekeeping functions are essential, but they must not adulterate the prime function of complete control of acceptable data delivery.

Project management and evaluation. In the EDP area, perhaps the single most costly aspect of the enterprise, and therefore the one that should receive the closest scrutiny, is project management and evaluation. All EDP operations are constantly receiving requests for new reports and also revisions of existing ones. Too frequently those requests, carrying the weight of high-level management, are merely routed to the nearest available programmer for immediate action. That results in a backlog of programming effort and frequently a patchwork of changes upon changes until the original job is hardly recognizable.

Well-run EDP organizations have found that, in the area of new applications, a team effort is needed. A project leader determines *in advance* what effort is required by a systems analyst and then by programmers to achieve the desired result. The time and costs of the project schedule are reviewed to determine acceptability by management before the project is started. Once the project is authorized, the project leader's responsibility is to report daily on progress made versus the original plan to insure completion on the scheduled date and within the approved cost parameters.

Continuous and complete communication with the department requesting the new service insures that the need for later revisions is reduced to a minimum. Minor changes to existing reports are generally handled by a so-called maintenance programmer, but they too are scheduled and controlled to insure both cost and accuracy control.

ORGANIZATIONAL EFFECTS
The location of an EDP department can tell a good deal about the unit's influence and role. Most companies persist in making EDP a satellite of the

financial function, and then EDP serves primarily financial purposes and is rather well shielded from employment by the operating branches of the firm. That is unfortunate. It is imperative that the availability of data processing services be limited only by technical and economic considerations, and if EDP reports to a function with highly specialized interests such as finance, it can hardly operate that way.

One reason for the frequently expressed view that EDP should report at the top executive level is that undue influence by any one of the users of the data can be reduced by keeping control at a high level. That is far from a proven thesis, but it is known that, to operate effectively, EDP departments must be freed from parochial interests, including their own. On the latter score, many an EDP department amounts to a company within a company, so loosely is the work performed tied in with the firm's interests. Such a department has self-contained R&D, engineering, and marketing and production resources and is subject to little in the way of outside guidance, audit, or criticism.

An inescapable feature of the move to computers is that it carries with it organizational change, although the pattern that emerges is not always predictable or consistent. Computerization is certain, however, to require new skills and knowledge, and to properly control, coordinate, and integrate the new with the existing skills and knowledge requires reorganization in some degree. For that reason, examination of organization as it relates to EDP is bound to be a revealing exercise for the operations auditor.

In the early phases of the computer revolution, no predictions of the computer's effects were more specific or certain than those having to do with organization and work. In the case of organization, the predictions have not materialized. But in the case of work, particularly work content and distribution, the effects have been marked. Evidence is the entirely new and major class of workers that has arisen. The number of Americans who spend the bulk of their time and ingenuity working in EDP will soon reach the half-million mark.

As to the effects of computers on organization structure, fairly extensive research has not turned up consistent patterns, even among the companies most sophisticated in the new information technology. That computers do have some kind of organizational effects cannot be doubted, in view of the computer's enormous appetite for work. Computers have displaced great numbers of people from direct work in order processing, invoicing, credit management, inventory control, purchasing, production scheduling, project control, and resource allocation. Nonetheless, the "shape" of the computer's organizational impact is, after nearly two decades, still unclear, and the operations auditor has no standard model for comparison. Hence, organizational changes, in and by themselves, do not offer direct measures of EDP performance.

Common organizational influences are not readily discernible for the probable reasons that no company has yet fully tapped the capabilities of the equipment on hand and the route to EDP efficiency is still largely chosen on the basis of opinion. But that patternless state is not likely to last much longer. It must be remembered that automation of information processing—even in the largest and most sophisticated companies of our day—is still in its infancy so far as understanding and application go. It is reasonable to conclude, therefore, that as computers and modern communication equipment continue to alter the dimensions of corporate life, they are likely to cause organizational drift, if not in one direction, in directions capable of yielding common results, among them significant improvements in efficiency, flexibility, and freedom of action.

To date, the computer's effects on manning are little clearer than those on organization structure. Obviously, the balances between clerical and managerial forces have been affected in some companies. Managers supervising the activities now commonly computerized (payroll, order entry, inventory management, shipping, and invoicing) have fewer people handling the same volume and have a different mix of tasks to perform. But the effects on manpower disposition vary from company to company depending on the state of the company at the time of computerization, the products produced, the markets served, and so on. About the only valid generalization that can be offered is that the nature of work has been profoundly affected when computers have been effectively employed but marked reductions in force have not taken place. In fact, it is almost axiomatic that large-scale reductions in personnel do not follow in the wake of computerization. A well-employed computer generates enough additional work to keep busy the hands it displaces.

Any survey of EDP installations will bring out the following points with regard to organization and staffing:

1. EDP units continue to reside in most companies within the accounting-controller-finance department.
2. Moves to get EDP out of the finance department are slowly taking effect; increasing numbers of companies are organizing management information departments at the corporate level.
3. Computer operations considered superior are usually managed by men who are well experienced in the company's general operations and are knowledgeable about what is required (from EDP also) to make the business profitable.
4. The principal staffing limitation in EDP lies not nearly so much in shortages of technical as in shortages of business-oriented personnel.
5. The independent attitude of computer professionals is a leading source of low EDP productivity.

STAFFING

Probably no staffing appointment holds more import for EDP than that of the manager. That can, of course, be said of any important corporate function; but because of the newness of EDP and because EDP effectiveness shows up in the results of other units, it is "more true" there than elsewhere. If that is so, what kind of person should management look for to run its EDP function? First and foremost, he must be a good businessman, conscious of the relationships between costs and the purposes of the enterprise. Few things can be more burdensome to a company than an EDP manager who has never been out of the computer room.

The EDP executive must be a businessman as well as a technician. He must, so to speak, be bilingual—a translator of computer languages into business languages, and vice versa. He must also be a good manager, capable of helping establish and of working within budgets and controlling systems so development investments in EDP have the earliest payout. He must be able to communicate not only with his subordinates and his superiors but, equally important, with managers of other departments at his own level.

The EDP function should have the same type of formalized training and personnel-upgrading programs that have been running for years in plants and offices. That means teaching EDP personnel as much about business operations as about the technical side of data processing.

Another facet of EDP training involves educating users and potential users within the company. Their participation in the development and implementation stages is a vital step toward a successful computer system. The EDP manager must understand the strengths and weaknesses of the user group. Although any information system must be fully planned and the scope of the system must be fully defined, the manager is obligated to develop an implementation plan that the user group can accept without total disruption. He must understand their needs and abilities to cope with automation and the pace at which they can digest automation. They are the people who require the most intensive training, particularly on how the system will support them in performing their jobs. There is also the element of retraining, because the computer will no doubt effect changes in their departmental schedules, procedures, and controls.

The distribution of authority vis-à-vis systems development should receive close attention in the audit. Confusion about who has the authority to initiate a change in the way data are processed or the information is produced causes immense problems. As an illustration, the computerization of accounts receivable may be possible and advisable. The credit manager has for years been utilizing a system of open items posted to a ledger card for each account. The EDP manager might see how to incorporate credit clearance as a by-product of his existing invoicing program and suggest that the best approach is to develop a balance forward system.

If the EDP manager is the dominant of the two, the situation in which the computer dictates the policies of the corporation may arise. However, if the credit manager is the dominant of the two, the computer may not be used at all for credit work or, if used, may be made to emulate a system that was not designed for a computer. In the latter case, the costs of emulation may offset whatever clerical savings were originally contemplated. On the other hand, if both managers are equally powerful or authority is ambiguous, a compromise that is expensive to install and unwieldy in practice may be reached.

Modern personnel techniques are available to the data processing manager, yet few companies have established EDP job performance standards. The work measurement techniques that are frequently used in the plant to set standards and measure operations are almost totally absent in EDP operations.

Because different languages are necessary to run an effective EDP function, the standards question is frequently passed over by personnel managers who are afraid to talk about it in a "foreign language." Programmers themselves usually talk the language of the machines they work with better than they can communicate with people. Therefore, the programmer needs a systems analyst, who can both understand the programmer's language and talk to the operating departments within the company.

SECURITY AND DOCUMENTATION

An EDP installation is an immensely useful tool, but it can also constitute a firm's most important vulnerability. Breakdown of the computer system or loss of data can, unless protected against, cause serious disruptions in a firm's business operation or profitability. Thus the matter of EDP security is a vital one that involves not only protection of equipment and facilities but also protection of the data, a much more precious asset.

A great deal of care is usually taken at the time EDP equipment is installed to insure its protection from disasters such as fire, flood, and environmental fluctuations. Far less care has been taken to insure against a much more common source of installation impairment: the human factor.

EDP staffs are not noted for low turnover or longevity and there is a knowledge loss each time a person leaves unless precaution against that loss has been taken. Unfortunately, too, there is growing evidence of frauds infiltrating computer-based operations. They have taken the form of defalcation in the case of a bank, theft of a customer master mailing list in the case of a publishing house, and file destruction by disgruntled employees.

All threats to EDP security, whatever their kind, warrant that the operations auditor pay particular attention to the documentation inventory. Complete documentation of any EDP operation can be classified into 20 categories. Not many EDP operations will have all 20 in current condition, but the larger and more effective installations will have most of them.

Table of organization. The structure of the EDP department will vary with the size of the installation, and the table of organization will establish the functional responsibilities of the staff. Large installations will have specialists assigned to certain activities as volume dictates, but regardless of size, each activity must be covered by someone. Every EDP function must have a control group or person and a file library function, in addition to operational, systems, programming, and clerical functions.

Frequently included in the table is an inventory of skills or background of the individuals for developmental purposes and specifications of position qualifications in terms of formal education, job training, and experience. The table should identify replacement sources for key jobs and contain plans for key job coverage as protection of jobs left suddenly vacant.

Position descriptions. The skills required by and the responsibilities and limits of the job should be written, and in great detail. The job description should also clearly spell out the chain of command for the position—upward, downward, and laterally. The responsibility for current operating budgets and future developmental budgets should be indicated. If the position has control over hiring, firing, and reviewing personnel, the specific policies to be followed must be identified. A plan for training and promotion (either in-house or outside seminar) should be identified.

Operational index. Every operation, report, and service performed in EDP should appear in the operational index; the list should contain all vital data concerning the function. That would include a numerical code for the operation, a code to identify operation frequency, a structured three-word title for every job, a time factor or cost for each function (annualized for consistency), a delivery date for each function, a program or library code number, a departmental code for the receiving department charged for that function, a code that indicates the bursting and binding specifications for the report, an indication of the number of copies required, a cross reference to the report or operation that precedes it, and the code number of the next operation to provide an audit trail for that report's relevance to other services. Some companies maintain the operation index in tab card format so that it is easier to update and can be run in different sequences for analysis; that is, by period of production, department charged, production number, or whatever.

Report manual. The report manual is a large binder that generally contains a representative sample of each report indexed to the corresponding report number in the operational index.

Operating procedures. Step-by-step instructions on how to perform every task not carried out on the computer itself are given in the operating procedures. Included are the control steps for each process, any clerical or manual functions (including bursting and binding of reports), and keying operations.

Computer run books. All of the operator instructions, identification of the required files, any special settings, all programmed halts, and the specific action to be taken when a halt is encountered are contained in the computer run book. There must be a book for every computer operation.

Machine utilization records. All of the data with reference to machine usage, run time, down time, rerun time, and any other category as may apply are kept in machine utilization records. In some installations they may be an elaborate report run on the computer, in others, a hand-drawn report.

Record documentation. A complete explanation (both verbal and graphic) of all disk, tape, card, and record layouts and their contents should be made in a separate file but may also be part of the program documentation or computer run books.

Volume and time reports. A log enumerating jobs processed, how many and how long versus standard. It should contain information on all quantifiable data flowing through the EDP section.

Program documentation. For each program a file folder should contain logic flow charts, coding sheets, controls, assembly listings, decision tables, program maintenance records, location of object and source decks, input and output layouts, halt listings (and action to be taken), description and approvals of all changes and modifications to the program.

System flow charts. A schematic flow chart, usually drawn with a symbol template, should show how every operation relates to every other one in the entire EDP system. It should also clearly indicate the entry and exist points of data to and from non-EDP departments.

Code definitions. The structure and definition of each and every code used in the system should be listed. Each possible program-acceptable code should be identified and classified as to what it means within each subsystem.

Report schedules. The current status of reports, showing the scheduled due date, date actually delivered, and revised due date for any report past due, should be included in the report schedules.

Forms and supplies control. There should be a record of every printed form layout, together with samples of current and prior versions. A current inventory of all forms and supplies and a schedule showing when the inventory will be checked are also necessary. Reorder points, copies of bids, current costs, and pertinent correspondence should be maintained.

Equipment control. A complete table of computer equipment and any and all peripheral equipment, together with manufacturer code numbers, company code numbers (if applicable), specifications, costs, and either a copy of or the location of the actual purchase-rental contract or agreement constitutes equipment control.

Cost center analysis. A record of the cost of each operation chargeable to the appropriate cost center is necessary for cost center analysis. A list of the titles of executives responsible for each cost center should be part of the record. Cost center analysis will vary from manual records to sophisticated computer-drawn reports.

Record retention schedule. A detailed record of all disk, tape, card, and paper files with specific instructions as to disposition should be maintained. It should include dates as well as the method of disposition. The schedule should include instructions for maintaining an up-to-date record of all programs and necessary files (in a location other than the data center) to assure recovery from any disaster, natural or man-made.

Program library. Security and retention of both utility and custom computer programs are the usual responsibility of the librarian, and a precise procedure for that function should be in evidence.

Reference library. A structured orderly library of all computer and machine manuals and program language manuals should be maintained and used by the EDP staff.

Systems-programming log. A record of the current status versus scheduled completion dates of all projects, along with the names of people responsible for each project, should be entered in the systems-programming log.

THE FEASIBILITY STUDY

The current state of EDP is such that no installation of any size can settle down to routines and equipment it can expect to use for a long period. In larger installations, analysis and study of some major change are almost always going on.

In performing audits of EDP, the operations auditor will frequently encounter the feasibility study, a decision tool peculiar to the EDP field. In the first phase of the EDP revolution the main focus of feasibility studies was on whether computerization was possible; practicality, for the time being, had to take a back seat. Because the potential of the tool was so great and exciting, management made many emotional or intuitive decisions regarding its application. Since then it has become evident that feasibility studies, which are usually initiated to explore areas of high systems potential or cost more safely, are as needed in the EDP area as machines are. Sound, long-range system planning cannot be done without them.

Nonetheless, considerable confusion about what constitutes a feasibility study exists today even among EDP experts. Since the influence of computers upon business will keep growing, a feasibility study must go beyond the traditional questions such as: Should we go the computer route? What is the right equipment for us? Should we purchase or rent the equipment? What will operating costs be? Typical of the new questions are: What should a computer do for us? How will it affect the company's organization? To whom should data processing report? What controls must be built into the system? Getting dependable answers to questions like those is not easy; it

173

requires careful, intensive study. And if the answers are to be obtained at reasonable cost, the study will probably involve the best brains in the company and some outside assistance as well.

There are many reasons why the feasibility study is demanding, and most of them have to do with cost. Other factors include service to the customer and increased capacity. Whether a first or a new computer is the best answer to a company's needs is a critical cost question, as is how to employ the equipment selected to achieve the lowered cost of unit information that was one of the prime reasons for computerizing in the first place. The latter is a far more sophisticated question than the former, and the answer to it often rules out an early move from manual to computerized methods or from one computer to another.

Too often, computer feasibility is measured against present manual or automated systems instead of the improved systems they are capable of being. When feasibility is measured against revised present systems, the result often is that unit information costs rise instead of decline following the arrival of a new or replacement computer. The implication is clear: the contribution to be made by a new system cannot be realistically measured until it is known whether the existing system can be upgraded and, if so, what the costs, both in time and dollars, of upgrading will be. The feasibility study answers such questions as the following:

1. What are the requirements of the current system, whether manual or automated, and what are the problems of the system? (Why are we considering a new automated system?)

2. What are the functional and information requirements of the proposed system?

3. What are the major alternative approaches that may be preferred? Why?

4. What is the technical feasibility of the proposed solution?

5. What is the operational feasibility of the proposed solution?

6. What is the economic feasibility of the proposed solution?

7. What is the relationship of the proposed system to existing and other planned systems and procedures?

8. What qualitative and quantitative benefits can be expected? When?

9. What is the implementation plan, including statement of resources and requirements, division of project into logical stages, and identification of checkpoints for management review.

Feasibility studies should cover many subjects traditionally ignored on the ground that they are imponderable; examples are training and reorganization. Any major change in data processing entails a training cost if other costs are to be kept to the minimum; therefore, computer orientation training programs for all personnel must be considered. Managers of the business and all personnel who may be responsible for input or use of output, as well as EDP personnel, must be trained. Moreover, training content must be carefully scrutinized, since training can drive management and the machine farther apart rather than closer together.

Computer training usually teaches executives how the machines work and how to program them, knowledge that is irrelevant at best and misleading at worst. EDP training for executives should be concerned with imparting knowledge of what the machine can do and what goals should be set for it. That relates to the fact that, though at times the equipment is at fault, most cases of poor computer performance are due to managerial ignorance. Management tends to rely excessively on technicians to determine what jobs the computer should do.

EDP training for the people responsible for input and use of output, as well as data processing, must concentrate on the need for accurate and *controlled* input and throughput to assure complete understanding and follow-through with the prescribed procedures.

SELECTING A MACHINE

Selecting a machine is often made much more difficult than it should be because of the nature of the interests in the selection. For that reason the decision should not be made without consulting persons who are both knowledgeable and independent, a decision process that is itself not very efficient. Dependence on computer salesmen or vendor representatives should not be allowed because vendor employees cannot, after all, give objective opinions. Aside from in-house non-EDP personnel with computer experience, there are two sources: outside consultants whose work is likely to keep them abreast of daily changes in computer technology and other firms with similar EDP needs.

More than one equipment manufacturer should be dealt with; at least three competitive bids should be procured. The bids should be accompanied by proposals that consider first cost, future expansibility, cost of installation, software (programs and applications already written and available for use), support (how much experienced manpower the vendor will supply for programming and for installation assistance), backup (comparable equipment available in the area in case of emergency), education and training facilities, and cost and quality maintenance. Each of these has a value that may vary from company to company.

Once the equipment decision is made, there are further specific steps. Whether to lease or buy is an important question beset by major hindrances: company practices and policies and dynamism of the computer field. As a result, the decision to lease or buy a computer is more often settled on the basis of intuition than on fact. That is not surprising, considering the state of the technology. But an error in a lease-buy judgment can be very damaging; it can cause the loss of several hundred thousand dollars or more and restrict future options in data handling.

There are facts on which to base a lease-buy decision, and the calculations should cover the following items: obsolescence, decreases in the basic lease price per throughput for the facility job mix, level of net conversion costs, maintenance costs, forecast of future utilization requirements, a segment of the hardware configuration such as the main frame, tax considerations, and forecasted future developments.

Development of a management information system to encompass major areas of a company generally entails a long-range plan with various implementation stages spread over a period of years. A plan of that kind bears vitally on the lease-buy question because it can show what the operating life might be; it may show, for example, that it would be economical to buy because the payoff will be approximately four years, which works out to be cheaper on a purchase than a lease basis. But it is a risky business at best. Purchase of main frame only is a middle-of-the-road approach that hedges against unpredictable technological changes in peripheral gear such as printers and tapes. In many cases, a company first entering the EDP field would probably be better off renting equipment because of the state of flux it will enter until its management has the required understanding and know-how.

What is needed is a diversification of skill usually not present within the organization. That skill can be provided on a temporary basis by one of the companies offering consulting services. Success is enhanced if top management defines what is to be done and engages the proper consultant to make the recommendations and implement the recommendations.

Before a feasibility study is undertaken, there are certain questions that must be answered. They are listed in Table 5. If the answers indicate com-

Table 5   **Questions on which to base a feasibility study.**

QUESTION	INDICATES FEASIBILITY STUDY DESIRABLE	INDICATES ALTERNATIVE INVESTIGATION
Are you experiencing increased work volume?	Yes_____	No_____
Are you planning acquisitions or other growth?	Yes_____	No_____
Are you getting the *summary* information you need to manage effectively?	No_____	Yes_____
Are you getting summary information early enough to take corrective action?	No_____	Yes_____
Is the same information being recompiled by different people in different ways?	Yes_____	No_____
Do you bill more than _____ line items per month?	Yes_____	No_____
Do you pay more than _____ invoices per month?	Yes_____	No_____
Do you employ more than _____ people, or is your payroll a complex system?	Yes_____	No_____
Is a large volume of calculating being done by clerks?	Yes_____	No_____
Is there information you would like to have that cannot be generated by your present people and/or systems?	Yes_____	No_____
Are there recurring bottlenecks and delays in meeting your present information and closing schedules?	Yes_____	No_____
Do you consolidate information from many different sources?	Yes_____	No_____

puterization, then the company can proceed. To get the answers accurately, a committee should be established to study the specific areas in which the computer is to be used. It should include the highest level of management, representatives of the affected areas, and an experienced computer specialist, either from within the company or a consultant. (If the computer specialist is a company employee, an outside consultant should be called upon to confirm his decisions.) The committee should study very carefully what effect computerizing its members' individual areas will have on each other and all the other areas of the company. It should hold meetings with all the other department heads to discover all possible contingencies. *Time and money spent in advance of actual computerization will be returned many times over in the form of smooth and orderly transition and lowest operating cost.*

When the committee has a broad implementation outline and feels it has satisfactorily answered the initial questions, the company can proceed to the next step, a detailed study, with documentation, for each application to be computerized. After that has been completed and reviewed by the committee, the process of staffing the installation and getting the equipment can be undertaken. Care must be exercised not to deviate from the plan unless the committee approves the deviation. Changes can be made, but they must be made with care.

Too frequently, EDP implementations have been technical achievements and financial or operational disasters. Many companies have had reasonable success in implementing computer systems in administrative and accounting functions—areas that have had a fair degree of structure to them prior to the introduction of computer methods. The advent of advanced technology represented by third- and fourth-generation computer capabilities, the push for computer application in the more complex areas of the business such as manufacturing planning and scheduling, concurrent developments in the management sciences, and an extreme shortage of qualified technicians and business managers have led to a rash of major disasters. Many of them have been highly publicized. Untold numbers of top managers have been affected by the fiascos. A number of companies have folded.

This is as good a place as any to caution both the experienced and inexperienced auditor about one major point: Although both the narrative and the questionnaire are aimed at the going general installation, the auditor must keep in mind that data processing departments differ widely from one another in configuration and scope. In fact, the only thing they may have in common is that they are generally in a state of constant flux. Feasibility study in that environment is never-ending. That lends a feeling of ambiguity to the questionnaire that is in part justified. Keep in mind the fluidity of EDP and the control that must be exercised over it.

REFERENCES

1. Comment on George J. Berkwitt, "The New Myths of Management," *Dun's Review* (September 1970), p. 26.
2. Francis C. Dykeman, in *The Contributions of Management Auditing and Financial Reporting* (Englewood Cliffs, N.J.: Prentice-Hall, Inc., 1970), p. 176.

17

COSTING AND PRICING

Costs have powerful influences on the fortunes of a business and affect almost every aspect of the firm. As reflected in the prices asked for the products they enter into, they are critical to the salability of those products; as elements in arriving at prices objectively, they are indispensable. Nevertheless, many managers operate with the thinnest knowledge of costs, and prices are more often than not set on the basis of subjective appraisals rather than factual cost information. Pricing can be effective only when cost information is sound.

Developing sound cost information, as auditors, especially, know, is far from a simple task. Even when manufacturing processes remain static and material costs are a small percentage of the cost of goods, costs may be difficult to construct or can change for many reasons. Industrial prices ordinarily rise in step with unit labor costs. Manufacturers participating in the *Fortune* quarterly inventory survey reported that their costs rose close to 3 percent in 1968. Since then, according to both BLS indexes and purchasing agents' reports, they have been going up even faster.

Every aspect of a business has cost characteristics that, if not maintained in some proper relation to sales dollars, can erode profits. Apart from manufacturing or production costing, information on costs is significant for decision making in warehousing and materials handling, quality control, sales strategy, purchasing, and distribution.

COSTING SYSTEMS
There are three basic costing systems: the job cost system, the process cost system, and the standard cost system. The job cost system is used when product costs can reliably be identified, as in the production of tailored or customized products. All labor and material costs are charged directly to the product, and indirect costs are allocated by a predetermined overhead rate.

A process cost system is used when products are manufactured in large batches or by mass production. Costs incurred in a department are averaged over the units produced. Products still in process at the end of a period are recomputed into equivalent finished products. The total cost charged to a department is divided by total computed production of the department. That gives an average cost per unit for the period.

Standard costs are the planned costs of a product under current or anticipated operating conditions. They are based on normal or attainable conditions of efficiency and volume. It is not possible to discuss standard costs in detail in this chapter—whole textbooks are devoted to the subject. It is sufficient to say that soundly established standards are the gauges for checking costs of production and other functional areas. A variance above or below the standard is the gain or loss contributed by the function. The following example was published by the Small Business Administration in one of its bulletins.[1]

Suppose you use a certain liquid in your process. Over the last few years you've paid an average of 52 cents per gallon. So you take that as the "standard" cost. Then you get a chance to pick up 1,000 gallons at 49 cents per gallon.

When you come to work out the effects of that purchase you make a distinction. You still figure each gallon of liquid going into your product at the standard 52 cents. *But* you chalk up a profit of $30 ($0.03 per gallon saving on 1,000 gallons) for your purchasing operation. You'd keep right on using 52 cents as the basic cost per gallon of liquid when you put a price on the finished item.

Later, you might have to pay 55 cents for another 1,000 gallons of liquid. You would then account for the variation from standard by showing a $30 loss due to purchasing inefficiency. You would figure that for pricing purposes each item you made still cost the standard amount, 52 cents.

Having variances isolated in this way makes it easier to see where a good or poor job is being done. A bad break in buying should not be charged off as an added manufacturing cost.

The establishment of a range within which variances will be deemed acceptable paves the way to management by exception—calling attention to the exceptional as distinguished from the routine. Through such a costing system, an attempt can be made to keep track of and control actual costs by comparing them with estimates or standards.

ABSORPTION COSTING

Two contemporary standard costing methods are absorption costing and direct costing. Under conventional absorption costing, accounts are labeled according to the expense—materials, wages, taxes, and so on—and there is no separation of fixed and variable costs. Manufacturing costs, both fixed and variable, are allocated to the products sold during the period to determine gross margin. Costs of unsold products are deferred in inventory until the products are sold. One disadvantage of absorption costing is the difficulty of apportioning overhead expenses to the constantly changing levels of production. Changes in production volumes inversely affect cost per unit, since fixed overhead must be absorbed by greater or fewer total units produced.

DIRECT COSTING

In direct costing a distinction is made between costs that fluctuate directly with production volume (variable costs) and those that are relatively insensitive to changes in volume (fixed costs). Direct labor and material costs, for example, usually vary in total with the level of operating activity; their unit costs are fairly constant. Items like rent and depreciation tend to remain constant in total, which causes their unit costs to vary with volume. Under direct costing, the product is charged with only the variable costs of production. Since no fixed costs are charged to the product, cost per unit is not materially affected by changes in production volumes.

Separation of fixed and variable costs permits a truer determination of product marginal income or profit contribution. The use of direct costing simplifies the analysis of results and thus clarifies and expedites decision making in all areas of executive management.[2] Other benefits that accrue from variable and fixed cost separation include the following.

☐ Facilitates analysis of the profit implications of selective price and cost changes (profit planning) or other strategies that might be employed to meet a competitive threat.

☐ Presents costs on the basis of supervisory responsibility without the distortion of fixed overhead allocation not incurred by the manager in charge.

☐ Expedites assignment of responsibility for fixed costs by not hiding them in the product cost pot.

☐ Helps produce more accurate make-or-buy decisions, since a decision to buy will usually not reduce the company's fixed expenses.

☐ Facilitates clearer determination of profit contribution by product, customer, salesman, and so forth.

At the time this book was written neither the Internal Revenue Service nor the American Institute of Certified Public Accountants recognized direct costing as being among "generally accepted accounting principles." However, both were reexamining their positions. To obtain the obvious advantages of direct costing for internal financial reporting, it is usually necessary to make a year-end inventory adjustment for reporting to the public tax authorities. That is not difficult; it consists in adding back to inventory and deducting from expenses the fixed expenses per unit, based on the actual production level for the year, that would have been allocated to inventory value under the traditional absorption costing method.

BREAKEVEN ANALYSIS

The breakeven point is the level of sales at which profits begin. A good cost system will give management a breakeven figure from which to work, and ascertaining that figure should be one of the operations auditor's most important functions.

The separation of fixed and variable costs is essential to breakeven point determination. The most commonly utilized tool is a simple breakeven chart on which cost elements and sales are plotted as in Figure 2. The chart also serves to illustrate the basic principles involved.

Figure 2 **Breakeven chart.**

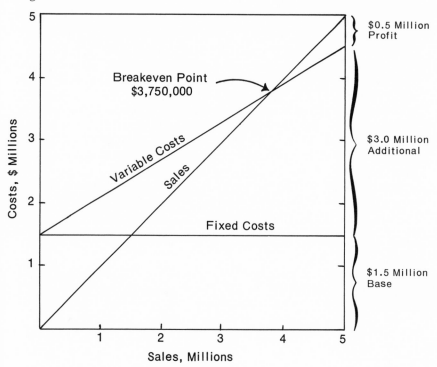

Assume the following situation:

	AMOUNT	PERCENT OF SALES
Sales: 5 million units at $1	$5,000,000	100
Variable costs	3,000,000	60
Gross margin	$2,000,000	40
Fixed costs	1,500,000	30
Profit before taxes	$ 500,000	10

The sales are represented on the chart by a line from zero to $5 million. Fixed costs are then entered as a horizontal line at their total level, $1.5 million. Variable costs of $3 million are plotted from zero sales at the fixed-costs line to $5 million sales. Since they are precisely proportioned to units produced, the line is straight. The point at which the variable-cost line crosses the sales line is the breakeven point. In this example profits do not begin until sales pass $3.75 million.

It is important to note that the generally accepted absorption costing interpretation would imply in this case a unit cost of 90 cents ($3 million variable costs plus $1.5 million fixed costs ÷ 5 million units) and a unit profit of 10 cents. By separating fixed from variable costs (the direct costing approach) the true facts are revealed: the first 3¾ million units earned a zero profit per unit and the remaining 1¼ million units earned a 40-cent profit per unit.

At times determining whether a specific cost is fixed or variable can be confusing. Maynard's *Handbook of Business Administration* states:[3]

> Direct labor is usually considered to be a variable cost, but many times it is fixed. Whether or not a cost is fixed or variable depends on company policy and whether the element of cost is controlled by management to be fixed or variable. For example, assume in the case of direct-labor employees that the policy is to lay off such employees when work is slack. If the number of employees is maintained proportional to the amount of work, then the cost is variable. However, suppose the company is afraid of losing these workers to a competitor if they are laid off, and decides to keep them on the payroll even when work is not there for them to do. Now the direct-labor cost is fixed.

> The test of whether a cost or component of cost is variable is to ask the question, Would this element of cost be reduced if the level of sales temporarily dropped a modest amount, say 20 percent? For example, in the case where there are five clerks in an accounting department and sales drop off in a given month, would the number of clerks be reduced? Usually, the answer would be negative, so the element of expense is not variable, but fixed.

PRICING

Correct pricing makes the essential difference between success and failure in business; it is based on the ability to respond quickly and sensitively to changes in demand, competition, and supply in the marketplace. Maynard describes the objectives of pricing as follows:[4]

> The ultimate goal in pricing is to establish a selling price for an order or product that produces a desired return on the specific capital invested in that order. Such a selling price is a "target selling price" representing both the seller's specific investment levels and his concept of what a fair return should be. Because this target is an expression of a specific figure and a desire for return, a target price is no guarantee of market acceptance—as is no other formula price. . . . The target selling price provides a yardstick which tells management the trend of its pricing in relation to desired return on capital.

Beyond costs and market advantages, as implicit in patent protection or transportation preferences, there are only a handful of strategies on which to base pricing:

Strategy of meeting competitors' prices. Many smaller companies are not in a position to materially affect the level of prices in their particular industry because of either superior prices or marketing. They are forced, therefore, to adopt a follow-the-leader pricing policy. If intelligently administered and coupled with effective control over manufacturing costs, that can be an advantage to a smaller concern because it frees the company from extensive record keeping and data analysis.

Pricing below competitors' prices. A policy of lower-than-average prices is often chosen as the alternative to sales promotions. A manufacturer may reason that the elasticity of demand for his product is such that lower prices will result in greater volume, which, in turn, will result in lower unit cost and higher profits (see Absorption Costing). However, if he has miscalculated and the elasticity of demand for his product is small, underpricing may invite retaliation and a price level at which no one can make profits. Underpricing may be accomplished indirectly with services, free deals, special discounts, freight absorption, premiums, product warrants, and other techniques.

Pricing above competitors' prices. Quality assurance, responsibility of the seller and service, and other nonprice considerations may support pricing above the market. The strategy often connotes a higher standard of quality and craftsmanship, but the firm employing it must be in effective competition with other concerns handling similar products. In the long run, the firm that uses the higher-price strategy must produce a superior product. Under these circumstances the strategy may yield exceptional profits.

Pricing to deter emergence of competition. Protection through patents or copyrights or the development and maintenance of significant product advantages can often deter the emergence of competition. But when a company does not have the capability of developing entirely new products or so improving old ones that they become recognizably superior to others, it may have to price its products to make it disadvantageous for other firms to enter its markets.

No company that seeks to place its profitability on the best basis employs any one of the pricing strategies for long. Sooner or later, all companies except those destined to dissipate their assets must price their product or services on a sound cost basis. Joel Dean states that in describing what he thinks is meant by a pricing policy in saying:[5]

1. Prices should aim at maximizing profits for the entire product line, that is, they should stimulate profitable combination sales.

2. Prices should be set to promote the long-range welfare of the firm, for example, to discourage competition from entering the field.

3. Prices should be adapted and individualized to fit the diverse competitive situations encouraged by different products.

4. Pricing policies should be flexible enough to meet changes in economic conditions of the various customer industries.

5. A predetermined and systematic method of pricing new products should be provided.

6. Replacement parts prices should be determined from an organized classification of parts by type and manufacture.

COST-PLUS PRICING

The most extensively employed practice in setting prices is to add a fair profit margin to costs, which may include distributed or allocated costs and overhead expenses. Fair profit is usually defined as the excess over calculated costs permitted by competition.

The popularity of cost-plus pricing in its various forms does not mean that it is the only pricing policy or the best one. Usually it is simple and easily rationalized on the premise that it accepts historic volumes and competitive reaction, and it usually guides allocations of costs without taking into account probable effects on volume, market share, and incremental costs of changes.

Cost-plus pricing has become fairly common in recent years. It is useful when the product is complex or when a number of products for different customers are being produced simultaneously and associated costs are not readily segregated or worth segregating. The apportionment of the elements of cost is negotiated by the parties involved, and a percentage of total cost is added for profits. There are several methods for arriving at cost-plus prices:

Full cost pricing. Selling prices are computed by adding to the total factory cost an allowance to cover selling and administrative expenses and profit.

Marginal cost pricing. The marginal costs are those incurred only if the product is actually produced (see Direct Costing). They include raw materials, direct labor, and variable administrative and selling expenses (for example, salesmen's commissions).

Return-on-investment pricing. About return-on-investment pricing, one book states:[6]

> Most business firms measure the profitability of their products or product lines in terms of the margin of sales. This is sufficient for concerns in which the amount and turnover of capital invested in the various products are approximately equal. However, where different magnitudes of investment in working capital and facilities are required, the use of margin of sales can lead to erroneous conclusions as to the real profitability of the product lines. In the final analysis, return on investment is the ultimate gauge of business efficiency.

Flexible cost pricing. A combination of the preceding three costing methods is called flexible cost pricing. As different competitive and internal conditions occur, a pricing executive can select the costs and other quantitative criteria most relevant to the situation. Ordinarily, cost simply indicates the lowest practical limit of price if profit is to be realized, and pricing policies must be reevaluated frequently in response to changes in demand, competition, and supply.

In addition to marketing strategies, the legal elements of pricing must be considered. No attempt will be made here to review the Robinson-Patman Act or other laws that affect pricing. Legal uncertainty should not be used to reject economically sound pricing policies, but it should be brought to the attention of the company's legal advisor.

PRICE CHANGES

Any exception to a company's normal price policy, such as extending unreasonably long credit terms or allowing unrealistic discount on related items, is not a price policy, but a strategy. It can be costly and painful. This is the gray area of pricing in which competition often forces hasty decisions, pushes for adjustment, or invites other deviations from stated policy. It is the area in which creative pricing is born or destroyed, because it is there that management can detour, undermine, or compromise the principles of creative pricing that it has already formally accepted. As Phelps points out:[7]

> All pricing is basically experimental, but some companies experiment more freely than others and some have a sounder basis from which to proceed. Price changes should be governed by policies carefully formulated and clearly stated.

The importance of maintaining flexibility in pricing policies is borne out by the fact that those who set and stick to prices rigidly often cut themselves off from worthwhile profit opportunities. Pricing uniformity has many advantages, but pricing flexibility, if sensibly and realistically employed, can create profit opportunities ruled out by fixed prices. Pricing decisions must, of course, be weighed against customers' and competitors' reactions, and possible long-term effects must be carefully considered. But opportunities to create sales through price adjustments should not be discarded except for good reasons.

When a company's sales order backlog is below that needed for operation at full or profitable capacity, corrective marketing action is warranted. That action can involve price reductions, special discounts and allowances (as for advertising), more liberal credit terms, special drives, and so forth.

KNOWING THE MARKET

The auditor must keep in mind the necessity for the pricers to know the marketplace. He must try to get management to define as accurately as possible what it thinks its market is and then relate that to its method of doing business. For example, if the product is not unique and price is the only determinant, what is the company doing to reduce its costs? Conversely, what is being done to make the product or company unique? Does management constantly ask itself why people should buy its product? For example, is prompt delivery generally assured, thereby allowing the customer to keep a lower inventory? The direction that the company takes will be dependent upon its evaluation of the marketplace.

Management's major efforts to increase profitability can be focused on one of two targets: increasing the profit margin or increasing the sales volume. The target selected will depend on the economics of the business.

All businesses can be divided into two groups: those with little value added to the product (distributors, jobbers, assemblers) and those with high value added (professional services, technical manufacturing, high research risks). Generally, the gross margin—the difference between selling price and manufacturing or purchase cost less *all* variable costs—will be in proportion to the value added. For example, a cigarette wholesaler has a smaller margin per unit than an electronics manufacturer because the wholesaler adds relatively little to the product as compared with the manufacturer.

The low-margin business should put its major effort on decreasing costs or increasing the selling price, in other words, on enlarging the spread between revenue and cost to increase the marginal profitability. That effort will generally be more remunerative than increasing volume.

On the other hand, a high-gross-profit business will benefit disproportionately greater from an increase in sales volume than from an increase in its gross margin rate. Note the example in which A is a low-value-added firm (for example, a distributor) and B is a high-value-added one (for example, an electronics manufacturer). In situation 2 a 50 percent increase in sales volume

	(1)		(2)		(3)	
	A	B	A	B	A	B
Sales	100	100	150	150	100	100
Variable cost of sales	80	60	120	90	75	55
Variable gross margin	20	40	30	60	25	45

is significantly more important to B than to A because of the higher rate of gross margin. In situation 3 a 5 percent reduction in cost increases A's gross margin by 25 percent and B's by only 12½ percent. That may explain why increased volume can be an illusion and an unwise diversion of management energy when margins are small. The effort should be devoted to cost cutting and price increases.

The operations auditor can determine in which of the two types of marginal income the company (or unit) he is auditing fits. From that determination he may have a lead to further investigations of management plans and controls.

CONCLUSION
Understanding costs and the factors that affect them and that create both favorable and unfavorable variances is probably the most useful aspect of managing a business. Costs pervade every aspect of management and must be understood and controlled if long-range maximization of profits is to be achieved.

"Cost for pricing" implies that the cost accounting system will provide costs of production to guide management in deciding upon pricing policy and prices. Before auditing· the methods of costing and pricing, it is important to remember that cost is a fact, whereas pricing results from policy. The operations auditor is not in a position to make concrete pricing proposals, but he can find out whether the company is pricing its products and services with good and sufficient knowledge or with assumptions likely to endanger profit maximization.

REFERENCES

1. *Pricing Arithmetic for Small Business Managers* (Washington, D.C.: U.S. Government Printing Office, 1959), p. 2.
2. H. B. Maynard (ed.), *Handbook of Business Administration* (New York: McGraw-Hill Book Company, 1967), pp. 10–36.
3. Ibid., pp. 10–56.
4. Ibid., pp. 8–80.
5. Joel Dean, *Managerial Economics* (Englewood Cliffs, N.J.: Prentice-Hall, Inc., 1951), p. 401.
6. Elizabeth Marting (ed.), *Creative Pricing* (AMA, 1968), p. 63.
7. D. M. Phelps, *Sales Management: Policies and Procedures* (Homewood, Ill.: Richard D. Irwin, Inc., 1953), pp. 284, 285.

18

PURCHASING

From one point of view, business operations can be thought of as beginning with the procurement of materials, supplies, and services needed to produce and sell a product, so purchasing can be critical to profitability. The influence of purchasing on a business depends on the percent of value added to the finished product and to a considerable extent on the profitability of the business.

Material cost quite often exceeds 50 percent of the selling price of the product; in only a few businesses is it less than 20 percent. For example, in the tire-recapping business 80 percent of the value of a tire coming off the line is in the casing and new rubber—both purchased items. Therefore, each percentage of improvement in material cost is worth around four times the same improvement in labor cost.

The importance of the purchasing function can be seen by a comparison with the sales function. When a salesman sells $100 worth of merchandise, assuming 10 percent profit margin, he carries about $10 into the profits. However, when a purchasing agent saves $10, he carries all of it into the profits. Therefore, a capable purchasing agent can make as much profit for his company via a $10 saving as a salesman can via a $100 sale. Skilled purchasing becomes even more important when competition is increasing and profit margins are falling. Each purchasing transaction costs between $10 and $40 for requisitioning, bidding, abstracting, analyzing, placement, expediting, receiving, and collating.

ORGANIZATION

That the importance of purchasing is generally recognized is reflected by the fact that procurement in many successful companies is either centralized or centrally controlled and that in most companies the head of purchasing reports at the top executive level. But that recognition does not always result in purchasing's adopting or being forced to hold suitable organizational and procedural perspectives. For example, centralization of purchasing in some companies has fostered a sense of self-importance sufficient to slow activity to a crawl, and in other companies it has led to excessive or dead inventories because it has not been accompanied by the establishment of adequate purchasing standards and controls.

The operations auditor should retain awareness that the main justification for formalizing purchasing activities is economic and that effective purchasing does not necessarily stem from extensive proceduralization or from consolidating the function organizationally. Purchasing authority in some cases must be granted widely, if not always substantially, in order that the best acquisition costs may be enjoyed; and the key to evaluating how well purchasing is accomplished is to check purchasing costs rather than whether procedures or organizational formats are orthodox.

In a company or unit with limited needs, purchasing may not be specifically assigned or may be handled by no more than a purchasing agent and a clerical assistant. As the dollar volume of purchases rises, purchasing units and differentiation within the units tend to appear. In the largest organizations the buying staff is made up of specialists in the procurement of particular types of commodities.

Dollar volumes do not offer much as measures of purchasing effectiveness. In companies with large sales, purchasing departments may be small or may have several hundred employees, depending on the nature of the company products or operations. Further, there is no correlation between the dollar volume of purchases and the size of a purchasing staff. Enormous numbers of items may add up to relatively small dollar amounts; a few items may add up to a sizable percentage of a company's sales volume. Purchasing effectiveness relates far more to the service consciousness and intellectual vigor of the purchasing staff, the policies bearing on procurement, and the currency of purchasing procedures than it does to staff size and sales or buying volumes.

Inasmuch as the acquisition of materials, supplies, and services is stimulated by many different needs and uses and most large firms are multilocation enterprises, few companies have totally centralized purchasing authority. Many companies find it advantageous to centralize the purchasing only of high-ticket items such as steel or chemicals and leave the purchasing of other items to nonpurchasing personnel. The degree of centralization relates to the economics involved, which in turn relates to such factors as storekeeping, traffic management, and materials control requirements.

Though most companies have distributed purchasing authorities on an economic basis, attitudes with respect to purchasing seldom exhibit the same balance. Purchasing personnel are prone to have centralist attitudes, and nonpurchasing personnel tend to think they have a good deal to say about procurement. Neither attitude creates the cooperation and integration that purchasing must have if it is to be a paying effort.

Purchasing responsibilities. A convenient place to start the audit of the purchasing function is to obtain a definition of procurement responsibilities, but the auditor must remember that responsibilities for acquisition seldom cover everything a company buys. It is therefore important to identify the items whose procurement is solely the responsibility of the purchasing executive or department as opposed to the items purchased directly by the using departments. That insures clear delineation of monetary responsibility and eliminates duplication.

The one-man purchasing department, obviously, presents no problem of internal organization. But as the number of people in the department rises, organization becomes increasingly relevant to efficient operation. In large purchasing departments the chief purchasing officer is greatly concerned with administrative and executive duties. His participation in negotiations and buying is usually limited to contracts and items that involve substantial sums.

However much or little he is engaged in actual buying, the effective manager sees to it that his department systematically undertakes supportive activities such as finding new supply sources, searching for substitute materials that cost less or afford savings in assembly or manufacture, analysis of order status and cost trends, economic research to determine optimal order points and quantities, and providing consultative services to other corporate units such as engineering and manufacturing. He also sees to it that the essential services of record keeping, filing, order typing, invoice checking, catalog library, and so on are provided in the quality needed.

Larger buying staffs usually have item-by-item assignments, and each buyer has responsibility for an item or commodity classification that is regularly purchased. In the largest departments, assignments are usually made to commodity-buying sections each of which is headed by a senior buyer with one or more buyers and assistant buyers under his direction. There may also be separate sections for follow-up and expediting, traffic, and disposal of surplus materials.

As to the division of responsibilities and authorities, final decision on the type and quality of materials to be purchased rests with design or using departments, but selection of source is a prerogative of purchasing. In making requests, using departments are responsible for providing complete information on specifications and standards of quality. It is then the responsibility of the purchasing department to procure the required materials from reliable sources at the lowest possible total cost.

Those relationships should not be slavish, however. The purchasing department should have the privilege of questioning a requisition whenever it feels improved buying can result. It should also have some voice in the preparation of specifications to avoid (1) unessential details that would restrict purchasing sources or (2) deviations from commercial standards and tolerances that would raise acquisition and/or inventory costs.

Contacts with suppliers should primarily be in the domain of the purchasing department. Negotiating and buying effectiveness can be seriously impaired by commitments or preferences expressed or implied to vendors by other personnel. There are, of course, times when it is important to bring sellers' representatives and plant personnel together for discussion of technical details and exchange of useful information. It should, however, be made clear, and be enforced, that all vendor contacts are to be made through the purchasing department.

The computer has had a major impact on purchasing. It is not entirely accurate to say that it has been causing decentralization of purchasing activities, although it certainly has had some effect in that direction. It is not yet clear whether it has had other necessary organizational effects, but it certainly is causing many significant changes in purchasing procedures. For example, the procurement function is being integrated with the decision processes on an increasing front of activities such as product design, production planning, and marketing planning, and the integration is giving rise to new disciplines such as value analysis. It is also intensifying the interface between purchasing and the vendor community. By using a computer, purchasing can increase the universe of suppliers with whom it deals and do a much better job of analyzing and controlling vendor performance.

The following are the typical activities performed by purchasing departments to achieve their objectives:

Information

1. Maintains purchase records, price records, and the records of maximum and minimum stock and normal consumption together with economic order quantity.

2. Maintains vendor records and the records of transport companies and the various freight rates.

3. Maintains specification files and catalog files.

4. Maintains records of surplus materials.

Procurement

1. Checks requisitions. That includes not only the routine checking of specifications, quantity, and delivery time but also the authority and the possibility of using similar materials already in stock.

2. Secures quotations. Sometimes a source of supply may be indicated by the using department. However, to secure benefits of competition and to determine alternate sources for maintaining stable supply, it is always necessary to invite more than one quotation.

3. Analyzes quotations not only for prices but also from the viewpoints of other related costs, the terms of credits, the delivery time, and so on.

4. Selects the vendors. A suitable vendor-rating system may be developed depending upon the size of the company, the nature of the business, and also the availability of data processing service. Vendor reliability (that is, financial condition and past performance), price history, delivery record, technical competence, and research facilities are some of the important factors that are always included in a good vendor-rating system.

5. Chooses between long-term contract or open-market purchase. Certain items that form lower dollar volume (sometimes called C items in ABC analysis) are generally handled through long-term contracts to retain the discount benefit and still avoid the excessive costs of frequent small orders or unnecessarily tied-up capital.

6. Interviews salesmen and collects information on new materials and products.

7. Negotiates contracts and checks the legal conditions.

8. Schedules purchases and deliveries.

9. Issues purchase orders.

10. Follows up for delivery and checks receipt of materials.

11. Verifies invoices.

12. Corresponds with vendors and makes adjustments with them for rejected or defective materials.

Research

1. Performs market and material studies for the purpose of finding material or component substitutes as well as for helping R&D in the development of new products or activities.

2. Conducts cost analyses to serve as a basis for decision making on many fronts, including the determination of engineering changes that affect costs, price, and make-or-buy decisions.

3. Investigates supply sources and inspects suppliers' plants.

4. Helps develop and maintain on a current basis standards and specifications for new as well as established products and capital items as well as items for resale.

Miscellaneous

1. Disposes of scrap, obsolete, and surplus materials.

2. Handles reciprocal trade relations.

AUDITABLE ELEMENTS

Purchasing efficiency is not, of course, simply a matter of organization. Of the many factors involved, the most important are cost and time. Few companies fail to acquire what they need to get the product out, but most companies pay more than they should for goods or services or do not have them at the most economic point of application.

Purchasing can be defined as obtaining the right thing in the right quantity and quality at the right prices for delivery to the right place at the right time. Correct as that statement is, it constitutes an oversimplification because rightness, in that association, can be evaluated only by determining the profitability of the items manufactured and by comparing acquisition costs with such industry standards as exist, a considerable task of itself. The difficulty in performing those steps will vary from company to company, but purchasing effectiveness cannot be realistically appraised any other way. Therefore, one of the first considerations of the auditor should be to see whether it is feasible to set up a collecting program for the information needed to perform the necessary kind of analysis.

A fruitful point of investigation for the operations auditor is an examination of the documentation that stimulates buying action. Requests to purchase seldom originate in the purchasing department; each purchase must be authorized by a requisition that originates in another department. For example, when the minimum stock quantity established by inventory policy has been reached, a bill of materials for a given factory work order must be issued or there must be some other authorization. Even in companies that have computer programs similar to IBM's IMPACT, purchase requests usually originate outside the department.

Therefore, something specific has to happen before the purchasing department can act. The operations auditor should track down the triggering elements. Investigation of them will often show that the documentation is informationally inadequate, is based on outmoded standards, or receives little attention beyond being processed—is not subject to analyses or examinations adding to knowledge of trends, contributing to value analysis, or leading to procedural improvement.

The system for informing the purchasing department to act is the next step the auditor should review. To do so he will have to make a flow chart of the chain of events leading up to the issuance of a requisition. Following that he can investigate purchase procedures themselves. Check elements for the auditor lie in the activities common to purchasing departments, which are:

1. Receiving requests to purchase.
2. Securing or verifying authorization to purchase.
3. Receiving and interviewing vendor representatives.
4. Selecting the vendor(s).
5. Negotiating prices and issuing purchase orders.
6. Specifying shipping conditions and routing.
7. Securing evidence of receipt of materials and services.
8. Following up delivery.
9. Negotiating adjustments with vendors.
10. Acting as information source to engineering and production.

Other responsibilities frequently found in purchasing departments are:

1. Operation of material and supply warehouses.
2. Sale of scrap.
3. Purchases for employees' use.
4. Checking invoices.
5. Maintaining files of vendors' invoices.

Investigation of each of these activities, whether they are responsibilities of purchasing or not, will produce information of value in the appraising of purchasing effectiveness.

The purchasing function is likely to be most productive if certain basic principles are followed. The auditor will learn a good deal by checking the degree to which each of the following principles is being observed:

Innovation. The purchasing department should have an innovative role and should be involved in the work of systematically searching for new ways of doing things. Purchasing agents are often the first to hear of new ideas, and they should be motivated to communicate what they find to likely users. For example, one alert purchasing agent, on seeing a picture of a new type of vehicle developed for moving logs, sent a picture of the vehicle to his yard foreman. That in itself was not so exceptional, but what was exceptional was the innovative role. The purchasing agent was employed by an auto-wrecking yard, and the log-moving vehicle proved to be the answer to a problem.

In one case a somnolent purchasing department processed requisitions for aluminum sections specified by engineering for over a year without questioning their suitability and competitive comparability. A young, new assistant purchasing agent finally raised the questions. His investigations revealed that the company's products had the most expensive aluminum in its industry because of overengineering and ignorance. Savings of 20 percent were realized in aluminum purchases, equal to 8 percent of sales.

Knowledge center. Purchasing agents should act as knowledge centers to all branches of a business and supply, as needed, information about products of which they have special knowledge. A hallmark of an effectively run purchasing department is a high state of organization and completeness of its information file. An effective purchasing function *always* has current and comprehensive information at its fingertips.

Value analysis. Purchasing departments should be practicing some kind of value analysis at all times. The purchasing agent should be motivated to know a great deal about the processes and products used in the company and solicit the efforts of visiting salesmen to come up with better ways and better products. Since salesmen are rich sources of information, new supply sources and new salesmen should be constantly invited in.

Price comparison. Prices of purchased items should be regularly compared with prices from competitive sources or for competitive materials. Even when an item is purchased through competitive bids, the cost is not necessarily reasonable. The evaluation should be made by purchasing personnel, and the findings should be left in auditable form. For example, some companies have approved-vendor lists that are coded as to primary and secondary sources. Every time a bid is sought, form letters are sent to the same firms. The replies are then entered next to the respective names and the lowest bidder gets the job.

Alternate sources. Purchasing departments should be constantly searching for alternate sources to safeguard production and assure maintenance of vendor competitiveness. Evaluation of make-or-buy decisions is related to that activity.

Related charges. Purchasing should not be simply first-cost-oriented; the purchasing agent should know not only the basic cost of the material but a good deal about related charges as well. For example, a manufacturing company used large quantities of sheet steel that was received in 10,000-pound palletized lots. The company's crane at the receiving dock was not capable of lifting a 10,000-pound pallet; therefore, each pallet had to be divided by hand before it could be unloaded. The result was that unloading of the railroad cars took far more time than the railroad allowed, and significant demurrage charges were incurred.

Additional services. Purchasing should be concerned with getting vendors to provide services that can reduce the cost of goods when used even though the first cost may be higher. For example, storage can add substantially to the cost of materials or parts applied to or used on the production line. Purchasing should therefore seek suppliers who warehouse blanket orders and ship on an as-needed basis. In a steel fabricating firm, a persistent purchasing agent was able to eliminate his company's marking identifying data on steel pieces by having the steel supplier do the marking at no additional cost.

Computer use. If the company owns or has access to a computer (time sharing is ideal here), the computer should not be utilized only as a superclerk to maintain detailed files, process accounts payable, and perform similar routine chores. It should be more productively used, as it will be in performing such tasks as:

1. Forecasting future demands for existing and new products.

2. Constantly monitoring economic order quantities and points, especially for items for which the demands, availability, or carrying costs have a history of varying from period to period.

3. Determining most economical price breaks. A lower price must be weighted by possible effects upon costs of ordering, receiving, warehousing, and tied-up capital.

4. Calculating inventory levels to best utilize available storage space.

Areas of Analysis

If investigation shows the purchasing department to be following the principles discussed in the preceding paragraphs, the auditor can be reasonably satisfied that the department is fulfilling some of its responsibilities well. That does not mean that it is operating as efficiently as it can. It means only that it is doing some of its work as it should.

Kickbacks represent the most sensitive problem area in purchasing. Because of competitive pressures, some vendors offer direct or indirect payments to purchasing agents to influence them to buy their products. The operations auditor is not a detective and is not responsible for seeking out situations where kickbacks are being used. However, his investigations of purchasing procedures may lead him to suspicious conditions.

The ethical and legal implications of kickbacks are obvious. Their economic consequences are significant—purchasing is not conducted on a firm-oriented basis but for the personal gain of a purchasing official. The operations auditor should look for failure to obtain *valid* competitive bids. Even though three bids are obtained in accordance with an established procedure, so that files appear proper, two might be from sources which are unrealistic and were chosen because of a reputation for high prices. The auditor should make sure bids are current and truly competitive.

What is needed is compliance with a widely disseminated policy forbidding purchasing agents from accepting any gifts from vendors, including Christmas presents. The policy might include a statement that the offering of gifts and their acceptance will result in immediate termination of relations with the vendor and employment of the purchasing employee.

Many purchasing functions lend themselves to routinization, and in becoming routine they also become lethargic and unimaginative. Therefore, cost savings and contribution to company profits are important indices in judging the efficiency of the purchasing department.

The operations auditor can and should measure purchasing efficiency by taking a random sample of purchase requisitions and orders and classifying them by dollar value, levels of authorization, and number of authorizations required. The analysis is usually most revealing and sometimes even startling. It may show that purchasing volume and value are wholly out of agreement. In other words, because a department processes a high volume of purchase orders does not necessarily mean it is well run. The opposite can be true; the department may be paper-oriented rather than action-oriented. More than one large purchasing department operates more or less as a switching station for paper. In such situations, operating executives are often forced to spend hours signing purchasing documents. It is not unusual for such documents to bear six to eight signatures of men who should be doing far better things.

The purchasing department's effectiveness can be measured by comparing the costs of the audited company with those of similar companies and by examining trends in the ratios of purchased elements to selling prices, acquisition costs to cost of money and wage index, and purchasing to production volume. If those trends are negative or no better than stable, there is good reason to take a harder look at purchasing effectiveness.

The simplest measure of a purchasing department's effectiveness is, of course, the cost to spend a dollar—the ratio of purchasing expenses to dollar volume of purchases. It should be similar for companies of equal size in the same industry. Generally, as the size of the organization increases, the ratio decreases. The decrease is often the result of larger companies being able to use computers in buying or requisitioning, system contracting, and similar purchasing techniques.

The difficulty with the ratio is that any reduction in dollar volume of purchases causes the ratio to increase, which is not necessarily a sign of loss of purchasing effectiveness. For example, if hard-nosed negotiations result in significant savings, or the company increases its proportion of manufactured to purchased items, the ratio will increase. However, it is unlikely that that can happen very often in these days of unbroken inflation. It can happen once in a while—and once for a given product—but not so often as to invalidate the index.

It is vital not to be misled by theoretical or fictional savings offered as justification for the size and effectiveness of a purchasing department. Real savings result from such factors as the successful substitution of cheaper or more effective materials into the manufacturing process. The fundamental objectives of purchasing for a manufacturing industry may be summarized as follows:[1]

1. To maintain continuity of supply to support the production schedule.

2. To do so with the minimum investment in materials inventory consistent with safety and economic advantage.

3. To maintain standards of quality in materials, based on suitability of use.

4. To procure materials at the lowest cost consistent with the quality and service required.

5. To implement such programs as value analysis and cost analysis to reduce cost of purchases.

6. To keep top management and other levels of management informed of materials developments which could affect company profit or performance.

But those objectives are not easily reached. Their attainment requires a skillful team of buyers directed by a competent manager who understands and will employ what is known as dynamic purchasing function. It emphasizes cost improvements by the following four ways:[2]

1. Negotiation—the proper assembling of facts and statistics and the knowledge of how to use them for successful negotiation.

2. Vendor change—by developing an appropriate vendor rating system new or additional vendors may be developed, resulting in cost savings.

3. Specification change—by value engineering or value analysis, determining substitute materials or economic specification change.

4. Internal improvements—by regrouping personnel and collecting information which shows what area to concentrate on for maximum savings (for example, the ABC's of inventory turnover).

In other words, depending on the size of the company and the nature of the business, a separate department with competent people who have the necessary authority and accountability to fit into the organizational structure and who are impelled to follow the principles of dynamic purchasing is required to achieve the fundamental objectives of purchasing efficiently and effectively.

REFERENCES

1. Victor H. Pooler, Jr., *The Purchasing Man and His Job* (AMA, 1964), pp. 22, 23.
2. Stuart F. Heinritz and Paul V. Farrell, *Purchasing: Principles and Application* (Englewood Cliffs, N.J.: Prentice-Hall, Inc., 1965).

19

MATERIALS HANDLING

In an era that has seen systems engineering emerge as a full-blown discipline, materials handling has received a good deal of attention. The concepts of integrated materials handling are now well formed. Adoption of the system viewpoint is almost a necessity if a company is to achieve least costs in the production cycle. Materials handling is intrinsic to almost every manufacturing and service function; therefore, it is a cost-adding element even though it does not change the product or service.

Materials handling as construed in this chapter includes all materials movement and all materials rests; raw materials, semifinished goods, subassemblies, and finished items; and receiving, storing, moving through production, packing, and shipping. It can be broken down into three major divisions:

1. *Plant movements.* The movement of materials from place to place within a plant with nothing done to them in transit.

2. *Processing.* The movement of materials from place to place simultaneously with the performance of manufacturing processes such as heat-treating, painting, drying, and baking.

3. *Storing.* A handling action that stops material at a point to await further finishing or puts it in storage to facilitate ready recovery for return to the process cycle.

Depending on the nature of the business, materials handling can be a major or a trivial cost factor. In the first case, the efficiency with which materials are handled will have a definite influence on profitability; in the second, the value of materials handling efficiency will not deserve a great deal of attention. Unfortunately, it seems to be more characteristic than not to pay inadequate attention to materials handling even when it is a significant activity. A sound starting place in an operations audit of the materials handling function is to ascertain the scope of the physical activity and the amount and kind of effort aimed at optimizing it.

Two aspects of importance in determining the effectiveness of materials handling are the way materials are moved and the reasons for moving them. The first involves equipment and methods; the second involves scheduling and communications. The operations auditor can use that separation to his advantage in performing his evaluation. It facilitates breaking the audit field down into increments that can conveniently be the subjects of different methods of investigation and measurement.

PLANS AND INFORMATION

It should be recognized that materials do not flow naturally, but move from place to place according to instructions. In a manufacturing operation they can be moved from one machine or department to the next as planned or as needed or by some combination of planning and need. Whichever basis or combination is used, methods and routing of materials must be planned if economical utilization of manpower and facilities is to be achieved.

Planning on both levels—timing and methods of routing—offers good investigative starting points to the auditor. For example, how well a company's need for proper timing is being met can be tested by observing what takes place at the receiving-shipping dock. The degree to which trucks are waiting to be unloaded or men are waiting to unload something are clear indicators of the scale of the planning problem that exists.

Costs are another aspect at which the operations auditor can look profitably. Materials handling costs are often hard to accumulate, because in the typical company materials handling involves nearly everyone in the plant and is seldom the full-time work of many people. Thus, normal methods of direct costing are inapplicable. Sampling or time study methods are a good deal more applicable, but few companies have the talent to perform or the interest in such studies. The lack of interest often stems from the fact that materials handling is almost ubiquitous in most plants and is therefore virtually unseen.

The following are the various aspects of the materials handling cycle: (1) receiving, (2) intraplant handling, (3) packing and shipping, (4) inventory storage and handling, and (5) communication. Each of these aspects should be checked into by the auditor and should receive as much attention as is required to obtain a clear understanding of how well it is being dealt with.

With respect to planning, the operations auditor should be aware that the best results in materials handling are sometimes facilitated by bringing all materials handling under the control of a materials handling department or engineer, depending on the size and character of the plant. Industrial truck equipment in a large plant, for example, is controlled and operated most efficiently under one central authority. Without centralization, each production department has a tendency to accumulate and restrict the use of its own trucks.

FACILITIES AND EQUIPMENT

The trend in the processing of goods is heavily toward automation, and that has many implications for materials handling. There is, for example, a need for better scheduling so costly machines are not idle. Thus, materials handling is becoming an even more significant factor in production. The following are some specific effects stemming from technological improvements in the production area:

1. Disruptions of material flow have become significant production bottlenecks.

2. The potentials for cost reductions in the movement and storage of materials have increased appreciably.
3. The quality and cost of final products are becoming increasingly affected by handling, packaging, and shipping methods.

As a result, seeking to improve the flow and costs of handling materials has in many plants become a serious enterprise. In the plant with large-scale materials handling activities, consideration of flows, methods, and equipment is virtually a continuous effort.

The number of materials handling devices is legion, but all can be placed in one of five categories:

1. Facilities, for example, the amounts and layout of the spaces in which handling takes place.
2. Endless conveyors, for example, gravity roller, portable belt, bucket elevator, and overhead rail.
3. Single lift devices, for example, cranes, hoists, and grabs.
4. Vehicles, for example, hand-lift, power-operated forklift, and tractor-trailer.
5. Associated devices, for example, positioning and transferring equipment.

Materials handling equipment is designed to move materials; therefore, efficiency is high when it is so employed. Stated in another way, greater economy is obtained as the ratio of equipment investment to units of material handled is reduced. The auditor should keep in mind the relative cost of each type of materials handling device. For example, in a tractor-trailer combination, the tractor usually costs seven or eight times as much as the trailer portion. From that it can be seen that it is not usually economical to have the power unit and the cargo permanently combined. To have them combined increases the ratio of capital investment to carrying capacity needed, because the power unit and its operator must wait each time the trailer is being loaded or unloaded.

Economy in handling begins with taking steps to insure that materials are handled the least number of times. The relatively new method of handling trailer loads of goods evolved from applying methods used for material shipped to a foreign country. Formerly the material had to be loaded at the shipper's plant, unloaded at the dock, loaded on a ship, unloaded at the receiving port, loaded onto another trailer for delivery to the user's plant, and, finally, unloaded at the user's plant. Now, the shipper can load the trailer at the warehouse, load the entire trailer on the ship, unload the entire trailer at the destination, and haul it to the user's plant. The same principle applies to shipments by rail, and piggyback service has evolved.

One of the most important principles of materials handling is standardization. A mixture of methods or equipment is not usually as economical as standard methods and equipment. Nor do the economics of standardization relate necessarily to one aspect of cost such as first cost. Take pallets as an example. The true objective of standardizing them is to reduce not the cost of the pallets, but the costs of handling and storage. Obviously, there are limits to how far standardization can go. As a rule of thumb, however, standard equipment should represent 90 percent of the dollar value of the average company's equipment inventory.

Standardization of equipment entails standardization of handling methods, which in turn relates to the process and space involved. Taking space alone, it is a fact that not too many plants have been designed with a systematic approach to manufacturing in mind. Older plants, particularly, are often deficient in adequate unloading areas, aisles, reserve-storage locations, and similar facilities and can be made efficient from the materials handling viewpoint only with great difficulty. Nevertheless, the idea of optimizing materials handling is relevant in every circumstance, and no company should fail to minimize its plant's deficiencies.

Standardization must not be attempted with too limited a view of the elements involved. Economy in materials handling is obtained by the use of equipment and methods that are capable of serving as flexibly as possible. Therefore, all equipment and methods should be designed to permit economical operation under changing conditions.

Certain objectives should be set up in planning for improved materials handling:

Carry, whenever possible, pieces, parts, or materials in containers rather than in individual packages.

Control the weights of containers to minimize the requirements for handling equipment.

Eliminate odd-sized containers to the extent possible to improve utilization of the conveyance or assembly-plant handling equipment.

Reduce as much as possible the unit cost of material received through accommodation on the part of the supplier. For example, receipt of materials on pallets instead of in packages will allow both vendor and receiver savings.

Use shuttle rack packaging. For example, having the assembly plant furnish the supplier with racks for in-house use will save handling or packaging costs on the part of both supplier and customer.

Select shipping modes not only to take advantage of a better freight rate but also in consideration of correlative costs, such as the costs of the protective measures required.

When purchase contracts are negotiated, obtain package quantities and specifications that are based on production usage and so will aid in controlling materials.

Keep the weights of fork trucks, trailers, pallets, and so forth as low as possible to minimize their bulk and complexity and the cost of energy to move them.

Keep the ratio of the dead weight of the equipment low compared with the weights of loads handled.

Aim to improve equipment productivity by providing automatic couplers, nonfriction bearings, rubber tires, and other equipment features suited to conditions.

Move material in a straight line whenever possible; the ideal is to have the subassemblies or raw materials enter the building at one end and leave as finished products at the other with the least amount of cross- and backhauls in between.

Reductions in crosshauls and lengths of hauls have many benefits; among them the most important is reduction of congestion in critical spaces. Also, the pace of material movement within the plant can be slowed down and interference with manufacturing operations can be reduced.

When possible, materials should be moved by gravity. The principle is not important in one-level plants, but in multilevel structures, it is applicable, and the operations auditor should check to see how well it is being observed. On the other hand, a number of applications are independent of plant structure. Receiving and shipping operations, for example, usually lend themselves to the use of gravity equipment in the form of wheel conveyors.

PRODUCT ANALYSIS

Achieving optimal materials handling conditions involves considerations beyond handling operations. On occasion, changes in product design (such as the eye in the head of an internal-combustion engine that serves no purpose to the engine itself) can be made with beneficial influence on materials handling costs. For that reason, the cost implications of proposed design changes to packaging and shipping should always be subject to analysis and review. Periodic review of existing designs from the materials handling viewpoint is also advisable.

If a penalty or a saving is to be incurred in materials handling costs because of design changes, the assembly plant should be notified well in advance so it can alter its handling equipment and methods or facilities to accommodate the change. The operations auditor should look for evidence of this kind of cooperation.

INVENTORY CONTROL

Another area that has an effect on materials handling operations is inventory planning. Changes in inventory have direct effects on materials handling. Overinventory requires an excessive amount of storage area and often causes crowding of materials handling space. Underinventory often causes transportation over longer distances, back-and-forth motion, and disruption of lines of flow. Poor inventory control also means penalties in the form of premium transportation, handling, rented storage area, demurrage, follow-up, and so forth.

The operations auditor should, as part of his appraisal of materials handling activities, develop a clear understanding of the inventory control system in effect. With that input he will be in a position to complete his evaulation of the effectiveness of materials handling.

20

MAINTENANCE

For the purposes of operations auditing, maintenance can be thought of as activities relating to the inspection, servicing, and repair of existing tools of production, including buildings, utilities, and manufacturing equipment. Minor construction is considered to be maintenance when it has the objective of improving the performance of operations, but not when it is related to the installation of added or different facilities.

Maintenance traditionally has received little attention as a cost element in business. Consequently, in many locations it is an ad hoc operation that offers many opportunities for improvement, particularly when the value added by machinery is high.

The field of maintenance did not, generally speaking, receive systematic treatment until after World War II. Before the 1940s, maintenance did not often comprise a significant portion of overall product costs. After World War II, increasing automation and capital equipment costs focused more attention on maintenance. The investment in plant, equipment, and facilities is rising at an unprecedented rate, and maintenace costs as a percent of total production value are at least keeping pace.

The maintenance factor can be very important to a company today. American industry currently pays out about $20 billion a year for maintenance, and costs are climbing at an estimated 3 to 5 percent a year. For most companies, maintenance, including construction and repair costs, is averaging 5 percent of sales. But for some industries, such as steel, the figure goes as high as 12 percent. It is not unusual to find more maintenance workers than production workers. The facts indicate why most companies should periodically take a good look at maintenance costs.

The remarkable thing about maintenance is that it often receives short shrift from management even though it is widely recognized that the cost of maintenance can vitally affect profit performance. Maintenance workforce productivity, as defined by hands-on work or tool in hand, in major companies has been found to be as low as 18 percent. Studies of plants with significant maintenance workloads show that nearly a third have no maintenance program at all, nearly 40 percent lack maintenance controls, and approximately 80 percent have no work order systems or only defective ones.

Maintenance traditionally has been left in the hands of craftsmen or crafts supervisors, and the cost has usually been thought of as fixed rather than variable. The prevalence of those ideas is slowly declining, as attested to by the rise of the maintenance engineering position and function. But the operations auditor can expect, nonetheless, to meet many instances in which maintenance offers rich opportunities for cost reclamation.

INFORMATION

The main ingredients of best-cost maintenance (lowest cost to achieve production objectives) are:

Properly determined maintenance levels.
Properly determined maintenance practices.
Properly selected tools and materials.
Properly trained men.
Properly established controls.

The operational terms in the preceding items are the verbs "determined," "selected," "trained," and "established." They imply overt action and a basis for taking the action. In all cases, the basis includes a heavy element of information.

Information in the form of factual reports on conditions and needs and guides to action is fundamental to good maintenance. Schedules, standard procedures, and policies can go a long way toward providing assurance that plant and equipment are being properly maintained so as to minimize down time and cost while yielding the desired production quality.

The operations auditor will not often encounter good information. Maintenance has mostly been thought of as a hammer-and-wrench activity, and few people have ever thought of it as an information activity as well. The result is that maintenance data banks are usually quite empty. A good case can be made for the argument that the quality of maintenance cannot exceed the quality of the information it works with.

The following information is needed as a basis for effective decisions with respect to facilities and equipment maintenance cycles, maintenance force levels, replacement policies, contract versus in-house maintenance work, crew sizes and composition, maintenance schedules, preventive maintenance versus repair policies, equipment down time, parts replacement versus reconstitution, parts inventory, and so on.

☐ Historical information: data on the work previously done on items requiring maintenance.

☐ Technical information: specifications for operating, maintaining, and repairing machinery and facilities.

☐ Policy information: experience-based statements for guidance of maintenance operations.

☐ Organization information: documentary descriptions of the functions and responsibilities of maintenance, responsibilities of operations with respect to maintenance people, and desired relationships between the two.

Areas of Analysis

The need for historical information is too obvious to require elaboration, but the need to collect, update, and use specifications for operating, maintaining, and repairing facilities and equipment is not so obvious. Few companies have systematized the collection, retention, and application of technical information, with the result that maintenance practices seldom square with maintenance needs.

The last two kinds of information—policy and organization—usually are even more deficient than technical information. The need for maintenance policies is very great, since the policies touch on capital investment. Sound financial management ultimately causes firms to determine what maintenance—and therefore replacement—policies shall be. At the extremes, policy can call for either the use of items to destruction or maintenance of items for the longest life. Neither extreme is usual, and normally something in between is called for. In part, the compromise is predicated on maintenance cost experience, which also serves as a basis for new machinery procurement policy. Thus, the operations auditor should carefully investigate formal maintenance policy and unwritten practice. Do they appear sound and consistent? Are they understood and being adhered to?

Organizational information is next to be looked for. The responsibilities and authorities of maintenance staffs are seldom thought out and reduced to writing, and the result is that communications and cooperation between maintenance and operating staffs are often badly handicapped. When the maintenance function is not accorded organizational status, it cannot possibly fulfill its responsibilities. Then maintenance considerations are unlikely to be taken into account in plant and operation planning decisions, at labor negotiations, and in training programs.

PLANNING AND SCHEDULING

In recent years it has not been uncommon for programs aimed at upgrading maintenance to yield immediate improvements of 30 percent or more. That dramatic effect usually stems in large part from putting maintenance on a planned, scheduled basis.

Planning is fundamental for determining maintenance levels and workforce size and composition, provisions for emergency work, and the inventory levels of parts and supplies. Planning includes the maintenance requirements of facilities and equipment; the time, skill, and tool requirements of maintenance actions; and the resources available for maintenance. It encompasses a large number of elements, such as identifying job requirements and priorities, organizing the maintenance jobs, estimating job costs, determining job duration, and measuring the effectiveness of maintenance work. Fortunately, the task is not as formidable as it sounds. Unlike much other planning, maintenance is not beset by many imponderables. Most of the necessary information is available.

Work order system. The key to good maintenance performance lies in having a formal work order system and more maintenance work on hand than can be performed in the immediate future. Having a sound backlog makes it possible to establish priorities ranging from immediate to when it can be done. All necessary maintenance work should be authorized by some responsible supervisor.

A well-designed work order system is necessary if any measurement is to be applied to maintenance work. There are two general types of work orders: (1) blanket or open work orders, which are used to cover ongoing work done in any area such as routine oiling of machinery, and (2) job orders, which are used to cover individual maintenance projects.

There are two dangers associated with the first type of work order: that they will be used too freely and that they will be used without a realistic measure of the work entailed. Failure to control those dangers leads to slackness and the charging of idle time to routine jobs. On the other hand blanket work orders help simplify the scheduling task and minimize paperwork when they are properly used.

Work orders of the second type, job orders, will govern most of the work, and it is imperative that they contain the following minimum information:

1. Date.
2. Location of the work to be done.
3. Statement of what is wrong.
4. The best indication of what is required.
5. Priority, that is, emergency, as soon as possible, when convenient, or correlated with production schedule.
6. Name of person requesting the work.
7. Signature of the supervising foreman.

When the job order is also used as a closing document to signify job completion, it must include starting time, completion time, and attestation by a responsible person of the successful completion of the work.

CONTROLS

Controls are required over (1) methods and work execution and (2) the requisitioning, procuring, storing, and handling of raw materials. Labor control involves time-and-methods studies and standards development; materials control involves determinations of economic order quantities, order cycles, and stock storage and issuing practices.

Control of tools and materials. Among other things, the control system employed should insure that maintenance materials issued from the storehouse are charged to the proper work order and that supplies not used are, when economically justified, returned to the storeroom and credited to the work order. Unless there is adequate control over unused material, caches are likely to be built up in the plant and charges to maintenance jobs will be distorted.

Maintenance inventory, stores purchasing, scrap and rework control, and tool control are other areas that commonly have deficiencies. Tool control, for example, usually falls well short of its objective to provide the craftsman with the tools appropriate to a given situation. In some companies, such as airframe manufacturing, tool control is considered sufficiently important to warrant the creation of a distinct organizational segment within the manufacturing or engineering department.

Jobs that take only the standard tool kit items offer no difficulty. But many jobs require at least one special tool or piece of equipment, and that's where the tool problem starts. Almost all special tools that have to be controlled because of their tendency to disappear are expensive. Because they are expensive, they are usually controlled tightly. As a consequence, there is a lot of walking back and forth—itself costly. That serves to illustrate the scale of the tool problem and to indicate that the problem is amenable to treatment at a fairly sophisticated level.

The intelligent application of controls is predicated upon standards against which to measure performance and costs. Standards must be reviewed and updated, and they must be comprehensive.

It is increasingly common to regard maintenance as a contractual relationship with operations, but in any case maintenance expenses must be charged to the appropriate equipment user or cost center. Only then can valid costs to produce or costs to operate be obtained. Those costs should include not only labor and materials but also heavy equipment usage (or rental) and transportation. The operations auditor will do well to spend all the time necessary to become familiar with accounting data on maintenance activity, because that information offers the best basis for comparative analysis with a view to saving material and manpower costs. Maintenance controls include preventive maintenance checklists and schedules, comprehensive work order forms and their verification, job analysis and estimating procedures, deviation analysis, and job inspection procedures.

ORGANIZATION AND PERSONNEL

The prime organizational factor relating to maintenance is that the department must be set up as a service department that exists for the benefit of all other departments. The auditor will occasionally find that maintenance is the responsibility of the production manager. That arrangement entails conflict of interests. Machines should be inspected, lubricated, and serviced in accordance with manufacturer's recommendations, but the desire for optimum production often causes independent and sometimes harmful maintenance practices to be established.

The prime ingredient of best-cost maintenance is a well-organized and trained workforce that is competently supervised and motivated. Is the organization structure designed to encourage initiative or to frustrate it by unnecessary controls, levels of supervision, unclear lines of authority, or confused areas of responsibility? Does the organization permit supervisors to supervise, or are they obliged to be paper shufflers, clerks, dispatchers? Are foremen given training in technical safety as well as in supervisory methods?

Information, planning, and controls notwithstanding, the ultimate success of the maintenance function rests entirely upon the men charged with carrying it out. Are the functions and responsibilities of maintenance understood by operations? Is the interdependability of both recognized? Is there a clearly understood means of communication and cooperation between the two? Are maintenance considerations taken into account in plant and operation-planning decisions, at labor negotiations, and in training programs?

Effective planning needs the services of specialists who report to top-level supervision in the maintenance department. By assigning the responsibility to specialists, schedules that permit the best utilization of manpower and materials will be developed. Emergencies can be so handled as to minimize the disruption of schedules.

21

ACCOUNTING

Accounting is the voice of the common language of business transactions—money. It offers an opportunity to examine the financial controls, procedures, and reporting of the enterprise. Basic areas of concern to the operations auditor include an overview of the efficiency, timeliness, and accuracy of recording transactions; the uses to which data are put; the decision-making aids provided; and the control of assets. They also include the accounting principles observed. Outside, independent public accountants provide the major check in that regard, but it is management's responsibility to observe proper accounting principles. All in all, accounting is a good place to start the operations audit.

FUNCTIONS OF ACCOUNTING

In total, the accounting system should serve the reporting and decision-making needs of the company in an efficient and economic way. There should be no need for "little black book" sources of information by operating personnel. Through the reporting of actual results, the system should provide the data needed by managers at all levels to plan and control their operations.

It is the accounting department's responsibility to see that proper accounting principles are followed and that management gets the information it needs. The accounting department does not produce profits; it only serves the needs of the company and its outside stockholders and creditors and the interested regulatory agencies.

To be fully useful, the reports turned out by the accounting department must be accurate, timely, impartial, and consistent. If those attributes are not present, operating personnel, rather than act on the facts presented, will start to question the basis of the reports. It is not easy to develop a report that has each desired attribute, and particularly that of dependability. One thing that will help is the accountant's knowledge of the business. The system used in reporting and accounting must be individualized. It is true that each company within the same industry will have certain common accounts, but the detail and the reporting system should meet the needs of the people who will use the system.

Areas of Analysis

Accounting can be both historical (its most common use) and forward-looking (its most productive use). When it is not wholly historical, it comes under the term "managerial accounting." Among the techniques the accounting function should employ is responsibility accounting, which correlates organizational and operational authority (and, possibly, rewards) with accountability. Since organizational clarity and job descriptions tie in with functional responsibility, managerial accounting, when properly applied, has positive and wide-reaching effects.

Budgets, forecasts, cash projections, and management by exception are other techniques with which to apply accounting data to future operations and to tie together plans and controls. They make it easier to measure plans and actual performance. Further, the accounting department is responsible for setting up the internal control and the system of balances and checks that are necessary to maintain the security of the company. Although almost all companies use independent auditors to review their financial statements, they cannot depend on the outside auditor to discover a defalcation. That is the responsibility of internal management. In larger companies, the internal audit department is the agent for the function.

The operations auditor should survey the accounting department to see that it is servicing all echelons of management. To get the maximum usefulness out of accounting as a tool for management, it is generally most economical to have the best man available manage the department. The operations auditor should check to see that the independent public accountant has been asked, in the course of his regular audit of the financial statements, to evaluate the accounting system and its internal controls and to write a comment or management letter after the conclusion of every audit on findings and observations relating to the system, the reporting procedures, and any internal control deficiencies.

Accounting should be both general, by providing overall economic information on the enterprise, and specific, by supplying analyses of products, territories, salesmen, markets, and other useful segments of the company. Distribution accounting, for example, is a multifaceted tool that offers data for decision making on the different levels and in the different functions involved in moving the product to the consumer. Contribution reporting shows how profits are contributed by sources of income, and analyses by divisional, product, and geographic breakdowns are useful. Only direct, controllable costs are applied to the sources of income; no allocation of general costs is made.

Approaches to performance. The overall financial standard of performance, return on investment (ROI) or return on assets managed (ROAM), should be kept in mind. ROI is generally computed by dividing net income by net worth; ROAM substitutes controllable assets for net worth. Both ratios offer probably the best comparison of managerial performance over a long period.

Some basic company goals cannot be achieved in a short period, and efforts to rate them will have a lowering effect on ROI. Examples are the hiring of inexperienced workmen, the costs of whose acquisition and training will lower profits until the men are either weeded out or start producing; the research and development of new products; the move to more efficient quarters; a broad training program to upgrade key skills; and an advertising and promotion campaign in one accounting period that will increase the share of the market in subsequent periods. In other words, ROI and ROAM should be used only over a long period for managerial evaluation.

The other side of that coin is the misuse of ROI by failing to note that long-term growth can be sacrificed to immediate profits. ROI will look good in a year when all training stops, no maintenance is performed, research is out, and top personnel leave. Again, ROI is an additional, and not the only, measure.

A new and promising approach to accounting for the human resources of an organization is worthy of an auditor's attention.[1] Investments in people are constantly required and are constantly changing—hiring, training, coordinating, and losing people all have effects on the economic strength of a company. In its early stages, as far as measurement of the value of the human organization is concerned, human resource accounting tends to bridge the gap between short-term ROI and the human contribution to the factors of profitability and survival.

Measurement of the replacement value and outlay costs for the human organization will probably not become objective enough to be used in publicly distributed financial statements. For internal management, they can provide relevant information on the hiring, retention, development, and use of the firm's people, probably its most precious resource.

A useful application of ROI and ROAM is in comparing alternative proposals for investment. Standard costs are developed to measure the estimated profitability of different products based on objective engineering studies. Tied in with the marginal income developed from territories, salesmen, and product lines, standard costs offer a measure of profitability. Finally, if variances in pricing and quantities produced as compared with the standards are developed, a good control of manufacturing costs can result.

As the effects of inflation have become significant in recent years, many companies have prepared supplementary statements to show market or replacement values and the effect of changing price levels on their operations and financial position. For companies with a particularly large proportion of fixed costs and liabilities those supplementary statements may be relevant.

Finally, the motivational effects of the use of accounting data have recently been subjected to research. Participative programs in which second-guessing and wrist-slapping are replaced by jointly set goals, evaluations, and a game-like environment tend to be more successful.

REFERENCE

1. R. Lee Brummet, "Accounting for Human Resources," *The CPA Journal,* July 1970, p. 547.

3

QUESTIONNAIRES

Instructions
in the Use of Questionnaires

Raising a good question is often the key to uncovering a hidden problem or revealing a sound solution. As has been made abundantly clear, the operations auditor, in the authors' view, is primarily a question man and not an answer man. Accordingly, questionnaires similar to those in the following pages are the tools with which the audit will be most efficiently pursued, but it must never be forgotten that questionnaires are no more than tools.

VALUE OF QUESTIONNAIRES

The main value of a questionnaire lies in the conversation and information it produces, not in the questionnaire itself. For example, the questionnaire does not have objective value; the responses cannot be toted up to give some kind of quantitative measure. The effectiveness of a company's activities can no more be evaluated by adding up the yeses and nos of a questionnaire than the soundness of an apple can be measured with a pair of calipers.

Although the questionnaires reproduced here are models only, their items seem to the authors to have meaning in appraising organizational or functional effectiveness. The questionnaires, like all OA questionnaires, are not final products and undoubtedly have many flaws. Each can easily be improved in the process of tailoring to fit corporate needs.

SCOPE OF QUESTIONNAIRES

Inspection of the questionnaires will reveal that not every question capable of being asked is asked. That would be wasteful for several reasons. To begin with, OA is not a study in the sense of a management review performed in detail. It is more in the nature of an evaluation based on sampling techniques. Second, the main point of an operations audit

Sample layout for questionnaire.

Y	N	N/A	Administration and Management
			1.
			2.
			3.
			4.
			5.
			6.
			7.
			8.
			9.
			10.
			11.
			12.

NOTES

is to discover opportunities for making major improvements. Therefore, only questions that further those aims should be included in OA questionnaires.

As shown in the sample layout, the questions are answerable in four ways: yes, no, not applicable, or not answerable. The last two forms of answer, which are entered in the same column but with different marks, cover situations in which either the question is not germane or no answer can be obtained, perhaps because the information is simply not available.

Many questions, of course, cannot be satisfactorily answered in any one of the three ways. For that reason a space is set aside either at the end of the question or at the bottom of each page. In a number of cases, subsidiary questions follow those thought likely to yield substantive information such as quantities, ratios, and trend information. Each question or instruction is numbered so that easy reference to the notes is possible.

Instructions in the Use of Questionnaires

It will be found that the same or similar questions often appear in more than one questionnaire. If the practice is controlled, that is all to the good for two reasons: (1) Limited redundancy increases the assurance that opportunities for improvement have not been overlooked. (2) Most functions or activities in business have numerous aspects and therefore different kinds of influences. As an example, audits of corporate information and communication have as much interest in the quality of reports produced as do audits of EDP. Therefore, a number of questions will be applicable to both.

The individual answering questions must be guided by common sense. He should answer yes or no only when the evidence is powerful one way or the other. N/A when checked will mean that the question is not applicable and when circled that it is applicable but is not answerable, as when the information requested cannot, for one reason or another, be obtained.

APPLICATION OF QUESTIONNAIRES

As has been noted elsewhere, the questionnaire is only one part of an audit. Accordingly, it has space for two kinds of entries: checks against specific questions and notes stemming from or adding to the questions asked. Whether the questionnaires are general or detailed, they must be kept up to date. That may be done by incorporating notes so that attention is called to needed revisions when the papers are reviewed before the next audit. At that time the questionnaires can be updated.

The auditor must, in working with the questionnaires, always keep before him the fact that the answers to questions are not his own but those of operations people. He will often be tempted to answer the questions himself, but he must, except in the case of a question calling for the insertion of factual data, resist that temptation. Another problem he will be faced with is the natural desire to interpret or second-guess. Some of the information he will get will not be true, but there are safeguards against that. To the extent possible, the questions have been so phrased that a no indicates a problem. It has not, in every instance, been possible to arrange the questions in that fashion but, generally speaking, the answer no can be taken as a signal to look at something more intently.

The questionnaires included in this part of the book are designed to parallel the text of Part 2 as much as possible. As mentioned earlier, the classifications are arbitrary and may overlap. The section or personnel and staffing, for example, covers some aspects of personnel development, as does research and renewal. That is to be expected, and no undue effort was exercised to attain rigid separation.

In conclusion, it probably should be observed that questionnaire development has size-related limitations; only large-scale OA activities, such as may be found in a large company or professional firm, justify it. It is doubtful that a small firm could afford to shape questionnaires such as those that are provided in this book to the infrequent audit of a particular unit or function.

The Basic Description Sheet should be a part of the work papers of each audit.

Basic Description Sheet

Name of company _____

Type of business or service _____

Name of organizational unit or function under audit _____

_____

Basic activity or function of unit _____

_____

Number of employees in unit _____

Current sales volume or budget allocation _____

Date of organization of unit _____

Names and titles of key executives _____

_____

_____

_____

_____

_____

Date of audit _____

Audit supervisor _____

Names of auditors _____

Preliminary conference held?   Yes _____   No _____

Audit memos issued?   Yes _____   No _____

Exit interview held?   Yes _____   No _____

Report written by _____

Report approved by _____

Report issued to _____

_____

_____

_____

ADMINISTRATION AND MANAGEMENT

1. Is there a clear statement in writing telling where the company is going or what its immediate objectives are?
2. If yes, has the company made its objectives known to its people; that is, has it distributed copies to executives at all levels?
3. Are these goals and objectives understood and accepted by the corporate officers as shown in conversations with them?
4. Do these goals and objectives appear to be generally known and favored by the body of employees at large?
5. If the company has clear notions of where it wants to go or what it wants to make of itself, does it also appear to know what methods it will use to realize its aims as shown by the allocation of monetary, physical, and similar resources?
6. If the company has established clear and unambiguous objectives, has it also seen to it that each department and unit of the business has its share of the overall objectives spelled out for it; that is, has each organizational unit an objective that integrates with the overall objective?
7. Are the main business decisions of the company generally made on the basis of demonstrated needs of the business, that is, in the presence of objective information?
8. Is management of the business primarily market-, customer-, and productivity-oriented and not guided by lesser interests, such as proprietary notions or highly individualistic business or management views?
9. Do the company's financial statements provide enough information and are they readily understandable?
10. Is financial information given to all managers who need it in fulfilling their obligations?
11. Does the company have in the hands of each decision maker a body of clearly stated and written policies covering at least the most important repetitive events the decision maker is concerned with?
12. Has activity analysis ever been performed in the company? Has systematic study of what is required to "get the product out the door" ever been made and used as the basis of job design?
13. If yes, within the last three years for any position or department?
14. Do the executives of the company appear to have a strong sense of their general responsibilities; that is, do they seem to understand the responsibilities common to all managers and to be free of "that's his job, not mine" attitudes?
15. Do the executives of the company also appear, as evidenced in interviews, to have a clear and precise understanding of their particular responsibilities and authorities?
16. Does top management refrain from making the decisions that should be made at lower levels, as evidenced by the fact that persons charged with specific responsibilities generally feel they have been given and are allowed to exercise the authorities needed to fulfill those responsibilities?

17. Are systems and procedures generally documented?
18. Are systems and procedures documentations usually placed in the hands of users?
19. Is responsibility for the production, distribution, and maintenance of S&P documentation formally assigned and implemented?
20. Are the company's "how-to-do" documents (policies, procedures, rules, regulations) brought together in an easily usable manual?
21. Have standards been adopted for form and content of such manuals?
22. Are there controls to insure that the manuals are kept up to date?
23. Are all topics dated as to issue and review?
24. Does the company have a systematic, rational compensation plan with clearly stated principles as the basis for reviewing and changing compensation?
25. Is compensation standardized, by grades, classifications, and so forth, so that salary adjustments can be made without lowering morale and creating undue discussion?
26. Has the company added any new services successfully and discontinued others within the last five years?
27. If yes, within the last two years?
28. If no, has there been a consistent effort to improve services in these years?
29. Has the company built a good public reputation, in the opinion of its employees, based on its dealings with the community and its customers, suppliers, and competitors?
30. Has the company built a favorable image with its stockholders and employees?
31. Is there an adequate blend of central control with delegation of decision-making authority to the lowest feasible level?
32. Has the work of managers generally been devised on the basis of careful analysis so that the managers spend their time in the activities most valuable to the business?
33. Has the work of executives, generally, been similarly allocated?
34. Are the managers at all levels chosen and retained on the basis of integrity, ability, and industry?
35. Is the management atmosphere in the company one of openness and sharing of views, information, and power, and is it free of covertness and withholding of understanding and information?
36. Has top management created a climate so balanced between authority and self-discipline that both teamwork and individual initiative can exist together?
37. Does the company exhibit interest in developing breadth and flexibility in its executives by changing their assignments from time to time?
38. Is the age distribution and state of development of executives such that the company is assured of adequate succession in critical areas of activity?

39. As far as you can see, are personnel treated as being basically intelligent, capable, and willing?
40. Are mistakes tolerated within reason and used as a basis for helping the maker learn and develop new skills?
41. Does the management style apparent to you seem to value fresh creative actions more than conformity?
42. Does an appropriate amount of executive skill or knowledge redundancy exist so that the loss of any one executive will not severely affect the company's affairs; for example, is there someone in a position to function in the office of the president, controller, or production manager?
43. Is there some form or medium of free exchange of views between executives, such as scheduled conferences, impromptu meetings, or ready accessibility?
44. Does the company measure and rate the performance of its managers? If yes, check which of the following factors are used:

Profits over a period of time versus budget
Production over a period of time versus plan
Personnel turnover
Use of resources
Personal observation
Other (specify in notes)

45. Are budgets developed by people responsible for meeting them?
46. Are budgets not arbitrarily verified by higher authority?
47. Are budgets genuinely attainable?
48. Are budgets constructed from planned estimates rather than guesses on the basis of prior performance?
49. Are budgets the direct result of genuine planning?
50. Does the company know what its investment return (net income $\div$ net worth = _____ percent) is? If no, compute the ratio for significant parts of the company.
51. Does the company know what the return on its gross assets is? If no, compute the ratio of the preceding question for significant parts of the company.
52. If ROI is inadequate compared with the prime rate (a minimum standard), has management specific plans to improve ROI? If yes, describe plans in notes.
53. Does the company monitor its ratio of administrative managers (and cost) to total personnel? If no, compute the ratio.
54. Does the latest ratio indicate a relatively lean executive suite?
55. Are repetitive decisions quickly made candidates for standard procedures?
56. Does management appear to devote its major efforts to problem prevention rather than fire fighting?
57. Are problems evaluated for their profit effect and tackled in that order of priority?

PLANS AND PLANNING

The Process

1. Has the company a formal planning activity; that is, have responsibilities for the planning function been assigned to individuals in writing, and have time and facilities for planning been set aside?
2. Does it appear that the people involved are prepared to take reasonable risks on their own responsibility to accomplish the goals?
3. Is planning done on a scheduled basis rather than when personnel have time for it?
4. Does the company seek the active participation of all levels of management in formulating its plans?
5. Are production or clerical workers consulted about all plans affecting the work they do?
6. Is there a clearly defined avenue or apparatus by which planning-related information can be channeled to the planning officer or center and the individuals involved?
7. After plans are made are they reviewed by an impartial authority, that is, a person knowledgeable in but outside the area being planned?
8. Does the company venture to plan in areas new to it?
9. Are plans periodically reviewed during implementation by control reports?
10. If yes, when evidence shows the plans to be not working or unworkable, are they modified or formally terminated?
11. Does the company employ outside help when it cannot develop viable plans with the resources at hand?
12. Have priorities been attached to all approved plans?
13. Are plans laid only after rigorous search and evaluation of the company's main problems and opportunities have been made?
14. Does the planning process include a search for alternatives before plans are finalized?
15. Have matching controls been established for each plan to check progress?

Long-range (Strategic) Plans

16. Does the company have in writing well-defined current goals and objectives for several years ahead? (Specify three, five, or ten years.)
17. Have the objectives been discussed with and approved by everyone who had a part in the discussions before they were finalized?
18. Is this needed? (The number of people you ask does not raise the quality of the decision and may have the opposite effect.)
19. Are the objectives and goals challenging as well as realistic; that is, do you have real evidence that goals are challenging enough to the company's personnel to be motivating?

20. Has responsibility for the attainment of the goals been clearly and individually assigned to those directly involved in that attainment?

Short-range (Tactical) Plans

21. Have subobjectives been set for each organizational unit of the company?
22. Are the short-range goals and objectives compatible with the long-range ones?
23. Have the goals and objectives been communicated in writing to each unit and each responsible person?
24. Has the work involved in implementing each plan been estimated?
25. Have detailed plans and time schedules been set for attaining the objectives?
26. Has each group participated in formulating the plans and time schedules?
27. Have starting and completion dates for each work project been established?
28. Has everyone likely to be affected by the schedules been notified?
29. Does the company project expenses and income for one, two, and five years ahead?
30. Do cash flow projections provide proper guides to action in handling capital structure and liquid resources?

Budgets

31. Has someone questioned whether the cost of developing the budget is equal to its projected value?
32. Are budgets formed only after opportunities for cost improvement are reviewed?
33. Is the cost picture of the recommended plans and feasible alternatives known?
34. Have written budgets for plans been prepared, taking into account manpower needs, equipment, spare operating expenses, and profit expected?
35. Are budgets the result of challenged calculations as opposed to figures developed without analysis from prior experience?
36. Are budgets prepared by people responsible for meeting them?
37. Are budgets used (or considered to be used) as oppressive supervisory tools?
38. Are budgets revised without consultation and agreement with people responsible for meeting revised budgets?
39. Is there staff available to *assist* all management levels in the development of budgets?
40. Are budgets so detailed that the control becomes meaningless?
41. Are budgets subject to revision so that failure to attain budget goals might be covered?
42. Do budgets include cushions or fat that would dilute the effectiveness of the control device?

43. Are explanations of budget variances genuine as opposed to defensive excuses?
44. Does management rely on the budget as opposed to making hidden adjustment to compensate for inherent errors?
45. Are working budgets developed by major departments on at least an annual basis and then kept current one year in advance at all times?
46. Have careful projections been made of what plans or alternatives will achieve for the company?
47. Have written budgets for laid plans been prepared, taking into account your manpower needs, equipment, operating expenses, and profit expected?

General

48. Is responsibility for executing plans assigned?
49. Are proper, mutually agreed upon incentives associated with plans?
50. Is responsibility accepted, with incentives?
51. Is performance measured against plan and rewarded accordingly?
52. Do the company's plans deal with substantive matters that will result in change in the organization?

CONTROLS AND CONTROLLING

1. Does a list of active controls exist? If yes, obtain it and append it to this questionnaire.
2. If no, can the controls be identified? If yes, make a list and append it to this questionnaire.
3. If controls cannot be identified, can at least persons with control responsibilities be identified? Start a list and append it to the notes.
4. Does formation of controls follow the formulation of plans?
5. Does each control identified have a controller, that is, one person who is acting on or directing action on exceptions?
6. Are exception parameters set so that each control does not work too often?
7. Are controls established with feedback features; that is, is it understood that controls perform on the basis of variances in the activity controlled?
8. Is any control over five years old; that is, has any control been established five years or more without change in the original design?
9. If yes, is the control viable; that is, is it still active and needed?
10. If no, are any controls over two years old?
11. If yes, are they still viable and active? List inactive controls in notes.

12. Have existing controls been documented in procedures, descriptions, flow charts, or any other form?
13. If no, have good reasons been extended for not doing so?
14. Are plans under way for doing so?
15. Have controls been costed?
16. Have controls been subjected to value analysis; that is, have their costs been evaluated against the asset protection given?
17. Has responsibility for formal, periodic review of controls been assigned to anyone?
18. Is there a formal procedure for establishing, altering, or terminating a control?
19. If no, is there any recognition of the necessity for such an arrangement?
20. In reviewing the significant dollars spent by the company, are there controls that protect against misuse of the company's assets? Specifically, are there controls over:
21. Cash flows?
22. Accounts receivable collections?
23. Accounts receivable aging?
24. Bad debt write-offs?
25. Inventory levels?
26. Inventory obsolescence?
27. Fixed asset acquisitions?
28. Research and development?
29. Accounts payable aging?
30. Tax payments (timely)?
31. Payroll: new employees hired?
32. Overtime?
33. Percent of billable time?
34. Any other areas? If so, list and append to questionnaire.

ORGANIZATION AND ORGANIZING

1. Has the company a differentiated organization structure; that is, has it been compelled to divide the total work into individualized and distinctive tasks?
2. If no, does it appear the company should move in the direction of greater differentiation?
3. Are there more than two levels in the formal structure? If answers to 1, 2, and 3 are no, go to next section.
4. Does the company know what its activity needs are; that is, has it identified the kinds of work it needs to do to secure and extend its markets?
5. Is there a well-defined philosophy of organization; that is, does the company have the benefit of basic guides for designing its organizational structure?

6. Has activity analysis ever been performed in the company; that is, has systematic study of what is required to "get the product out the door" ever been made and used as the basis of job design?
7. Has the corporate structure been altered from time to time on the basis of what is thought to best meet the changing conditions?
8. Have formal organization charts been drafted and issued?
9. If no, has the lack of charts been justified; that is, have substitutions for the charts been provided in the form of unambiguous statements of management and organization philosophy?
10. Is a definite attempt made to define jobs only in relation to the whole; that is, is the approach to organizational design made on a system basis?
11. Are all executive positions covered by written job descriptions in the hands of each person whose job is described?
12. If yes, are the descriptions generally up to date, that is, less than two years old?
13. Is a program of regular review of job descriptions in effect?
14. If no, is one being developed or contemplated?
15. Are reasons or excuses for nonperformance given or traceable to deficiencies in organization structure?
16. Does every department or section appear essential; that is, does each organizational subunit appear to have significant work to do?
17. Could the work of any department or section be combined with that of another part of the organization; that is, will any benefit, such as foreshortened lines of communication, issue from combining two organizational units?
18. Could certain functions of any department or section be combined advantageously with those of other departments (without eliminating the department or section)?
19. Could any part of any department be eliminated; that is, is any work that is no longer essential being done?
20. Does the formal organization take as much advantage of individual capabilities as it should?
21. Are there any make-work positions; that is, does the company recognize "obsolete" employees and fail to find significant work for them to do?
22. Have responsibilities and authorities been assigned as far down the line as possible?
23. Are authority and the right to communicate confused; that is, are personnel prevented from communicating freely?
24. Does any manager have more than 12 people reporting to him?
25. If yes, does the resultant work of direction and coordination appear excessive? List in notes the positions with a span of control that appears excessive.
26. Do people reporting to a manager with a span of control of 12 or more have generally similar roles?
27. Does any manager have fewer than three people reporting to him?

28. If yes, does he appear to have enough work to do? List in notes persons with span of control of three or fewer who do not appear to have full workloads.
29. Are provisions for staff positions adequate; that is, are there enough people attending to the generic functions of the business such as planning, recruitment, and industrial relations?
30. Are provisions for staff functions excessive; that is, do staff functions overbalance line functions in the sense of there being too many or too highly placed functions?
31. Have all positions filled by persons retiring in two years been identified? If not, list such positions in notes.
32. Is formal organization designed with sufficient awareness of the informal organization; that is, is structure designed in the presence of accurate knowledge of employee powers, capacities, and roles?
33. Is care taken to couple responsibility with sufficient authority?
34. Is the wage and salary program tied in with organization; that is, does parallelism exist between compensation and job responsibilities?
35. Is structure designed to eliminate dead-end positions; that is, is the organization so designed that all positions have clear lines of progression to the top?

INFORMATION AND COMMUNICATION

1. Is the company dependent upon a large flow of information for current decision making; that is, is the business such that it is dependent on a high volume of accurate decisions?
2. If yes, has that fact been recognized in organizational design; that is, have decision responsibilities and authorities been structured into particular jobs and have the jobs been strategically located?
3. Do the managers generally feel they are provided with the information they need to fulfill their responsibilities and exercise their authorities properly?
4. Are communication channels generally free and open; for example, can personnel readily obtain information from the nearest available source without regard to organization or chain-of-command lines?
5. Is the emphasis of information control on economics and not security; that is, does the company control information to achieve low unit information costs rather than to keep it out of people's hands?
6. Has the question of information security been clearly and rationally defined; that is, have practical and reasonable decisions been reached about what constitutes confidential information and how such information is to be treated?
7. Do personnel give evidence of knowing the company's procedures, policies, rules, and regulations?

8. Has the company collected its procedural and policy documents in readily accessible form—in procedure and/or policy manuals, for example?

9. Is the information received by managers in such form and volume that they need not spend more than a small part of each day assimilating it?

10. Have official lines of communications (that is, rights to communicate) been established with the company's vendors, customers, stockholders, and competitors?

11. Is there a formal, standard procedure for the establishment of a new report?

12. Has a review date been assigned to each report?

13. Are the users of each report consulted on a regular basis about the necessity for improvements, additional requirements, and possible eliminations?

14. Has the number of copies of each report been verified in the last two years; that is, have copies been followed to their filing point to insure that the number of copies generated is necessary and/or adequate?

15. Are the most important report items, which should be seen first, prominently placed?

16. Is the purpose of each report clearly indicated by title, column headings, and arrangement?

17. Are preparation, routing, or handling instructions printed on each report and each copy whenever possible?

18. Do operating managers have to further process or analyze reports to obtain needed information?

19. Do recipients find reports to be timely?

20. Do recipients find reports to be accurate?

21. Are all the copies of reports used by the individuals who receive them?

22. Are reports that are voluminous in content avoided?

23. Are voluminous reports reduced to comprehensive summaries?

24. Are exception-highlight principles used in report writing?

25. Do key employees have their own job descriptions and copies of those of their subordinates?

26. Do the job descriptions clearly specify major responsibilities and authorities?

27. Are reviews of position activities made periodically, and are job descriptions updated?

28. If the company has a computer or is using a service bureau, are those needs capable of being served by input-output terminals?

29. If a computer is used, is a video display unit with printout capacity used?

30. Is such a video display unit feasible?

31. Is there a feeling of communication moving down (objectives, policies) and up (feedback)?

32. Are there regularly scheduled meetings at different management levels?

33. If yes, at what intervals are the meetings scheduled? _____
34. Is an agenda of items to be discussed handed out far enough in advance of a meeting to give people a chance to peruse it?
35. Are minutes distributed after a meeting to document assignments and due dates?
36. Do senior executives meet with lower levels on a regular basis, formally or informally (lunchtime and so forth)?
37. Is there a method for periodically reviewing the information system?
38. Is the information system periodically costed out—forms cost or labor cost, for example?
39. Does the company have communication needs that can be served by auxiliary telephone services such as TWIX and Telex?
40. If yes, have such services been provided or are they under consideration?
41. Are manufacturers of office equipment and supplies periodically invited in to survey equipment and systems that generate, convey, receive, process, and store information?
42. Do you know the date of the last review of office machines? If yes, enter here: _____
43. Are meeting rooms available for conferences?
44. Are the people who must work together located close to each other?
45. Are devices like tape recorders available?
46. If not, should they be?
47. Does the general layout of the office lend itself to the normal flow of information? If not, explain in the notes.
48. Does the company have a suggestion box?
49. Are submitted suggestions reviewed?
50. Are submitted suggestions reviewed at a reasonable level of authority?
51. Are the suggestions that pertain to specific and, perhaps, technical areas given proper cognizance before being disposed of?
52. Is the receipt of each suggestion acknowledged?
53. Is the dispostion of each suggestion acknowledged to the author?
54. Are accepted suggestions rewarded?

Forms

55. Is a large number of different forms in use in the company?
56. Are forms under the control of one person?
57. Can recurring information be printed within boxes so that appropriate items can be checked?
58. Are forms sizes generally convenient for filing?
59. Is spacing correct for handwriting or typewriting?
60. Are forms that should be assembled in pads or with carbon paper so arranged?
61. Are blanks aligned vertically in such a way that typewriter tab stops can be used to facilitate completion of the form?

Questionnaires

62. Are forms arranged whenever possible to permit simultaneous preparation of invoices, accounting copies, loading orders, labels, and billings?
63. Have economic order quantities been established for all forms in consideration of rate of use and probability of revision?
64. Have forms that should be consecutively numbered or have a place for inserting a number been so arranged?
65. Are all outside contact forms capable of being mailed in a window envelope so designed?
66. Do forms designed to take information from or pass information on to another form have the same sequence of data?
67. Are continuous forms in use wherever they can be used advantageously?
68. Can any of the blanks on forms be preprinted with fixed data to reduce the number of items to be filled in by the user?
69. Are snap-outs designed to make manipulation and distribution of forms possible with fewest handlings?
70. Are less expensive methods of form production, such as multilithing, used?
71. Have all forms been tested as to their need? That is, what information is being transmitted (type of form); who must receive it (number of copies); when must it be received (time frame); and what is the file destruction schedule?
72. Is the same color ink used in printing all the company's forms?
73. If no, is it necessary to use more than one color? If so, explain in notes.
74. If more than one color of ink is used in printing forms, are individual forms printed in the one color?
75. If no, is it necessary to print those forms in more than one color?
76. Are forms printed on colored paper whenever possible to speed up writing, distribution, sorting, and filing; to designate departments or branch offices; to indicate days, months, or years; to distinguish manifold copies; or to identify rush orders?

RESEARCH AND RENEWAL

1. Are all managers given the opportunity to express their views on matters they think important to the company?
2. If yes, is there a formal method or established procedure in effect to solicit such views or insure that they are heard? If so, describe it in notes.
3. Are all departmental and formally established routines reviewed at planned, regular intervals for necessity and possibility of improvement or elimination?
4. Is EDP service available for research activity?

5. Are decisions based at least in part on calculations?
6. Are calculated risks taken without anyone having made the calculation?
7. Does the company receive research-based economic reports from reputable sources, such as The Conference Board?
8. Does the company have a program for encouraging new ideas from everyone? Describe in notes.
9. Does the company use secrecy agreements or similar inhibiting techniques that might discourage free expression?
10. Does the company protect ideas from piracy by outside influences?
11. Has the company successfully added any new products or services in the last five years?
12. Has the company discontinued any products or services in the last five years?
13. If no, has there been a consistent effort to improve the product line in those years?
14. Does the company have specific, ongoing research programs such as in product, market, acquisition, consumer, and manufacturing areas?
15. Does the company sponsor outside research projects by nonprofit organizations or companies having expertise in specific knowledge areas?
16. If yes, are research funds provided in sufficient quantity to insure effective research activity (a) on a long-term basis and (b) by projects rather than time periods?
17. Do research expenditures compare favorably with those of others in the industry?
18. Are resources (physical and human) inventoried and shifted as new needs arise?
19. Does the company have an incentive program that rewards innovative success?
20. Does the company sponsor skill-improvement programs?
21. Does the company utilize newly acquired skills of its personnel to the satisfaction of those who feel qualified to assume greater responsibilities?
22. Are new personnel with related but broader capabilities sought?
23. Are new approaches sought for company organization, advertising, packaging, outlets, vertical integration, related lines, simplified processes, improved equipment, and financing?
24. Is there a suggestion system?
25. Is it actively in use?
26. Has it produced anything of value? If yes, explain in notes.
27. Does the R&D program tie in with corporate goals?
28. Is there a relation between R&D and market research?
29. Are R&D projects based on subjects or areas related to existing technology, markets, or production skills of the business?
30. Since few companies can afford only research, have R&D projects resulted in products or services that have been commercially developed?

Questionnaires

31. Are projects controlled by budgets?
32. Is the turnover of R&D personnel less than that elsewhere in the industry?

PERSONNEL

General

1. Are human relations considered as important to the firm as production, selling, and other major functions of the business?
2. Has the makeup and organization of the personnel function been arrived at gratuitously or consciously (in accordance with corporate values and industry standards)?
3. Is responsibility for the basic formulation of the personnel program recognized as a corporate management function?
4. If yes, is the responsibility clearly identified and allocated?
5. Have the responsibilities and authorities within the personnel department been clearly delineated and documented?
6. Is the personnel department sufficiently staffed to fulfill its assigned responsibilities?
7. Have the department's relationships to other elements in organizational structure been made clear to all other departments?

Manpower Supply

8. Is there a manpower planning document that identifies manpower replacement and addition needs?
9. Are future manpower needs forecast sufficiently well to minimize emergency recruiting?
10. Are all tenures in positions of ten years and over reviewed annually to detect cases of career arrest?
11. Does there appear to be an adequate reserve of trained talent for key executive replacement?
12. Does the company have any kind of formal performance appraisal program?
13. Is performance measured against preestablished and known standards rather than opinions as to the worth of individual effort?
14. Is some form of appraisal of *executive* performance regularly made?
15. Are performance appraisals oriented to promotion possibilities?
16. If there is a performance appraisal program, are sessions with employees held at least annually for the purpose of reporting the results of appraisals and counseling on how to improve performances?
17. Are supervisors trained to handle the appraisal interview for maximum benefit?

18. Are personnel limited in their career development by the trend of their experience; that is, are employees prevented by long functional or specialization tenure from being considered for promotion to opportunities elsewhere in the organization?

19. Is there a clearly formulated promotion policy and is it circulated among employees?

20. Are personnel promoted according to their contribution, rather than because their performance follows a prescribed, acceptable pattern?

21. Are promotions to supervisory positions made on the basis of the employee's supervisory and leadership potential as well as his technical capacity?

22. Is there a formal training program covering all classes of employees and organizational echelons below the top level?

23. Does the training program have the support, in a concrete way, of top management? (For example, does top management make itself available to participate in training courses?)

24. Are new training techniques actively sought, researched, and tried out when they appear feasible?

25. Are operations people involved (through some kind of formal medium such as a committee) in the determination of training needs and the formulation of training programs and training priorities?

26. Is advantage being taken of the assistance of government agencies to help train employees?

27. Have the firm's suppliers been requested to lend a hand in developing and providing training and training aids?

28. Have line supervisors been given the opportunity, individually or collectively, to acquire knowledge of the management process?

29. Are the results of training checked in a systematic, realistic way, such as testing employees to see what they have been taught, and are the results used to adjust training activities?

30. Are supervisors helped to recognize and are they given assistance in carrying out their responsibility for on-the-job training?

31. Is there an understudy identification and development program?

32. Is there a tuition assistance program?

33. Is the program adequate, and is it promoted internally?

34. Is enough time set aside during the day for holding in-house training meetings?

35. If no, are special arrangements made, such as holding meetings at the end of the workday or in the evening?

36. Are optional training programs available to employees who desire to change their line of work or to progress faster?

37. Are the needs of employees who face skill obsolescence because of technological changes recognized in the training program?

38. Is there need for an apprentice training program?

39. If yes, are the terms (length, stages, and content) of the program realistic?

40. Is care taken to insure that there is an adequate number of apprentices in training at all times?

Questionnaires

41. Do new employees receive formal indoctrination within days after joining the firm?
42. Is a real effort made to fill job openings with qualified employees from within the company before recruiting from the outside?
43. Is there a procedure for approving (certifying as needed) requisitions for new employees?
44. Are all recruitment ads placed by the same person or agency after being checked for content and format?
45. Do employment interviewers generally outline clear and realistic specifications covering the jobs for which they are interviewing?
46. Do application forms comply with government regulations?
47. Do application forms require sufficient information on past work history and related data so that employment qualifications or risks are made readily apparent and screening is facilitated?
48. Are future supervisors of new employees brought into the selection process so they feel a sense of responsibility for success of the newcomer?
49. Does the company use some form of aptitude testing as part of the selection and placement process?
50. If yes, do they serve the function of establishing necessary qualifications (that is, have they been validated)?
51. Does your operation meet all legal requirements for work by women?
52. If minors are considered for hire, is there a procedure for assuring compliance with legal requirements such as relate to working papers, recording of hours, rest periods, approved work, and posting of notices?
53. Has one person, such as the chief personnel officer, the final responsibility to hire and fire, or is the responsibility widely held?
54. Are sufficiently detailed health history statements taken and are adequate physical exams conducted to protect both the health of the employee and the liability of the employer?
55. Do hourly employees enter a probationary period followed by formal evaluation when hired?
56. Has a procedure been established to force effective use of the probationary period?
57. Is there an alert system to remind supervisors of the end of the probationary period?
58. Are applicants being given full courtesy; that is, are they being received well and given adequate information about the company and the job opening and a realistic understanding of their chances of employment?
59. Does the employment office provide the desired impression for applicants?
60. Are reference checks thoroughly made and completed before applicants are hired?
61. Are newly hired employees told what their actual duties and responsibilities will be?

62. Is care taken to make clear their rate potentials, fringe benefits, and working conditions before employment?

Manpower Employment

63. Are checks made to see that employees generally are receiving adequate instruction to enable them to do their jobs satisfactorily?
64. Are employees regularly informed as to the state of the business, company needs and future development?
65. Do supervisors have definite objectives covering their activities and are milestones set for accomplishments?
66. Are these goals offshoots of (integrated with) the larger goals of the business?
67. Do your supervisors genuinely recognize and act in accordance with their responsibility for training and developing their subordinates?
68. Do your supervisors really know what their authorities are and are they trained in using them?
69. Is supervisory advice sought and acted upon before major procedural or organizational changes are promulgated and implemented?
70. Are supervisors trained in the detection and reporting to management of employee dissatisfactions?
71. Do supervisors have the means to readily and conveniently talk with management concerning their own and employee problems?
72. Is there a formal, well-understood procedure that allows employees to air complaints or problems?
73. If no, is there anywhere at least an appellate authority to whom all disputes between supervisors and their subordinates (both hourly and salaried employees) can be brought?
74. If yes, has either party the privilege of appealing?
75. Is there a uniform and consistent policy of discipline for employee misconduct?
76. Are supervisors trained to recognize and deal effectively with disciplinary problems?
77. Are supervisors required to check with the personnel department or personnel function before taking disciplinary action?
78. Are all forms of discipline promptly made a matter of well-documented and comprehensive written records?
79. Do employees know the company policies and plant rules, written or unwritten?
80. Are checks made to see if supervisors are consistently and fairly executing company policies?
81. Is an employee treated as an individual or primarily as a member of a group?
82. Is an effort made to acquaint supervisors with the basic principles of human relations and employee motivation?
83. Is there a person to whom is assigned responsibility for keeping current on legal regulations affecting employee relations?

Questionnaires

84. Has it been made clear to all managers and supervisors that the Wage-Hour, Equal Pay, and Civil Rights laws must be complied with and have they been given training concerning compliance with Wage-Hour, Civil Rights, and other pertinent state and federal labor laws?
85. Is responsibility fully assigned for maintenance of adequate and legal working conditions (especially regarding inspection)?
86. Are rest periods that might become precedent (especially with regard to future union negotiations) informally granted?
87. Is a nondiscrimination policy clearly stated and properly posted?
88. Do the employees have the right to initiate consideration of their transfer when they feel they are not properly placed?
89. Is a qualified and experienced person assigned to the development, maintenance, and application of wage and salary policies?
90. Does management show willingness to share in any fashion the contributions to profit made by employees? If yes, list in notes the forms the sharing takes.
91. Are efforts made to stabilize work schedules in order to prevent layoffs and thus effect savings through lower unemployment compensation tax rates and earn a reputation as a good, steady employer?
92. Is there a standby plan that becomes operative in the event of layoffs?
93. If yes, does this plan recognize seniority, etc.?

Administration

94. Does the company maintain adequate personnel files; that is, is a record kept for each employee on an up-to-date and comprehensive basis (including all vital data and appraisal results)?
95. Is there a policy regarding retention of personnel records to fulfill practical and legal requirements?
96. Does the company maintain a head count of employees?
97. Is there a breakdown by category?
98. Is there a means by which education and skills of personnel can be related for purposes of comparison?
99. Are measures (opinion and attitude surveys, exit interviews, evaluation sessions) of employee feelings taken?
100. Are turnover and absentee rates by class of employees known?
101. Do you know how the turnover and absentee rates compare with those of other employers?
102. Do you know your costs for turnover and absenteeism?
103. Do you have a program for coping with absenteeism and turnover?
104. Do you have a method of evaluating your employee communications?
105. Is there a current calculation of the overhead factor per employee?

106. Are jobs defined to make the fullest use of each employee's abilities consistent with needs of the business?
107. Is there a clear definition of exempt and nonexempt classifications (to avoid legal and morale problems relating to payment for hours worked)?
108. Has objective knowledge of what each supervisory-managerial job requires been acquired; that is, have job specifications (educational requirements, experience, skills, and so forth) been established for most supervisory and managerial jobs?
109. Is the material well written, organized, and distributed?
110. Is it kept up to date?
111. Is a personnel policy manual kept on a current basis, adequately distributed, and properly used?
112. Does the company seek to "know" its people through the use of tests, interviews, or similar means?
113. Does the company make a serious effort to become aware of its employees' capabilities, inclinations, and job goals?
114. Are all rank-and-file jobs classified into grades according to the skills and experience required, and are the wage rates appropriate to the grades?
115. Are present forms of communication, that is, upward as well as downward, effective?
116. Are the company's goals and objectives spelled out and communicated in some meaningful fashion to all employees?
117. Is there an up-to-date employee handbook that explains policies, practices, rules, and benefits so they will be understood by all the employees?
118. Are there formal staff meetings to insure effective communication of relevant information to supervisors?
119. Is there meaningful contact between management personnel and workers outside the minimum requirements; for example, do top and staff managers occasionally walk through all areas of the operation and talk with employees?
120. Are personnel policies as set forth in the employee handbook honestly and uniformly applied?
121. Is needed information collected to realistically and effectively present personnel policy and formulate additional policies?
122. Are personnel policies periodically reviewed and evaluated with supervisors and management?
123. Are your supervisors advised of and given an explanation of general policy changes before a general announcement is made?
124. Do personnel policies emphasize the mutuality of interests of customers, employees, community, and business owners?
125. Is there a company publication that is more than a gossip sheet and that informs employees of your company and its benefits and does not overemphasize executive activities?
126. Are employees actively encouraged to make suggestions, however large or small, for improvement of the business?

127. If yes, do all suggestions for improvement receive full consideration and are the decisions made in respect to them reported back to the originator, as opposed to an anonymous suggestion box?

128. Are efforts made to inform employees before organizational and procedural changes are made in operations affecting them?

129. Are hiring rates sufficiently competitive within the community and industry that good people can be attracted?

130. Are fringe benefits explained to new employees upon hiring, and are changes carefully explained to all employees?

131. Are employees helped to realize the value of the company's fringe benefits in meaningful terms, such as what it would cost them to secure the benefits themselves?

132. Are fringe benefits chosen on some objective basis such as knowledge of which benefits are most important to employees?

133. Is it known what percent of payroll dollars is being spent currently on fringe benefits?

134. Are administrative procedures periodically reviewed to detect delays in processing employee claims and abuse of benefits by employees?

135. Are steps taken to spell out eligibilities for benefits?

136. Are costs of premiums for life, health, hospitalization, and accidental death insurance shared on a basis that tends to hold good employees?

137. Do you have a procedure for monitoring unemployment insurance premium rates to assure that you are not overcharged in error?

138. Are your fringe benefit programs competitive locally?

139. Are your employees aware of the extent to which the company pays for fringe benefits?

140. Are the content and costs of the benefit program periodically reviewed to see that they are in line?

141. Are your wages periodically reviewed to determine intraoperation wage equity competitiveness?

142. If you have wage incentives, do they really serve as incentives to greater productivity or are they just built-in payroll costs?

143. Are your employees' work hours and overtime pay practices in line with your competition?

144. Is there a pay scale for grades of work?

145. If yes, do you know to what extent it is in line with the going rate?

146. Are wage rates periodically compared with competing community rates?

147. Is a review of exempt salaries formally and periodically made?

148. If yes, do its provisions appear adequate and reasonable; that is, are review periods about the right length, are salary ranges realistic, and are compensation factors reasonable?

149. Are outstanding employee performances, employee anniversary dates, and long years of service recognized in ways meaningful to employees?

CLERICAL OPERATIONS

Personnel and Organization

1. Does staffing appear to be tailored to the clerical workload; that is, are there sufficient numbers of personnel and is there a sufficient variety of talents?
2. If no, have steps been taken or are they being taken to correct the shortages?
3. Are overqualified personnel hired for routine jobs?
4. Is clerical-employee recruitment, screening, and hiring under one person's control?
5. Is there any measure of turnover rate?
6. Are rate ranges established for jobs and maintained by periodic survey?
7. Are the employees who carry out procedures consulted for their views before changes are made in procedures?
8. Are employees in view of or readily available to their supervisors, and vice versa?
9. Is there a chain of supervision (and promotion) that goes into effect when absence or termination occurs?
10. Are employees grouped together on the basis of a common factor, such as common supervision, utilization of common machines, or participation in the same work flow?
11. Are working units, groups, or subgroups located as much as possible according to how they fit into given work flows (Note: Preparatory work relating to this question would be an office plan showing work stations as they relate to function performed.)
12. Are there any formal training programs?
13. If yes, are they geared to employee as well as management needs?
14. Are performance reviews made periodically and objectively?

Procedures and Work Flow

15. Is each job documented so a new employee has written instructions of some kind to follow?
16. When manual procedures are employed, have one-write systems been explored or exploited to the full to eliminate repetitive entry of the same data?
17. Are reports designed to produce answers rather than detail?
18. Do employees work on many different jobs during the day?
19. Have clerical personnel been instructed in the use of the equipment they are likely to operate?
20. Has responsibility for work flow analysis and design been specifically assigned to an individual or group?
21. Are valuable business records adequately protected from fire and theft?
22. Have steps been taken to reduce the transportation of documents to the shortest amount of travel distance and time?

23. Has work been designed to reduce detail to the necessary economic minimum?
24. Is there a standard of production for the measurable tasks?
25. Do information, facts, and data supplied to clerical employees arrive in condition suitable for use? (See questions about forms and reports under Information and Communication.)
26. Can the originator supply more or better information that would make subsequent operations easier?
27. Do clerical operations appear to be free of duplication in any one procedure?
28. Is the information leaving clerical operations in as good a form or as complete as necessary?
29. To the greatest degree possible, is work brought to the worker rather than have the worker go to the work?
30. Is there a regular review of the need for or modification of reports being produced?
31. Have departmental objectives been established?
32. Are they in writing?
33. Is accomplishment or nonaccomplishment of objectives reported to management regularly?

Space and Facilities

34. Is the office clean and free of distracting noise?
35. Is the office air-conditioned for proper temperature, humidity, and circulation?
36. Is space allocated for peak loads rather than normal or minimum requirements?
37. Is space larger than required for efficient production and appearance; that is, can it be reduced without sacrificing those elements?
38. Has space been left for later expansion or adjustment?
39. Are aisles wide enough for the traffic?
40. Are aisles wide enough for vault trucks and other carriers?
41. Are there at least two exits from rooms housing a group of employees?
42. Are coat lockers near the exit for least disturbance?
43. Are restroom facilities adequate and convenient?
44. Does every employee have direct access to an aisle wherever possible?
45. Are lighting standards adequate, particularly for employees doing figure work, or are special provisions made for such workers?
46. Are adequate facilities provided for visitors and others who must wait to be seen?
47. Do employees who do a lot of interviewing have sufficient space and privacy for visitors?
48. Are individuals who receive frequent visitors located as close as possible to the main entrance?
49. Are services or service units nearest to the departments that use them most?

50. Is there a need for conference facilities? If yes, have they been provided?
51. Have clear openings been substituted for doors wherever practical?
52. Are doors so placed as to preserve wall lengths?
53. Have file cabinets been used to separate work units where practical?
54. Could modular or unitized furniture be used to substitute for partitioned offices to save space?
55. Are private offices so placed that they allow maximum light and ventilation for adjoining outer offices?
56. Have confidential areas been sufficiently isolated from the public?
57. Are security procedures adequate?
58. Are there enough drinking fountains and sanitary facilities to minimize unnecessary walking?
59. Are there enough private offices, but not more than necessary?
60. Does the space have a minimum of offsets and angles?
61. Are the facilities that serve the entire office easily accessible to all?
62. Are the units that use noisy equipment adequately sound-treated and sufficiently segregated to avoid disturbing others?
63. Are work stations kept in an orderly condition to improve office appearance and reduce the time spent in seeking papers?
64. Are electrical outlets adequate for serving the mechanized equipment?
65. Is office equipment appropriate to the clerical workload? (For example, would the addition of special devices, such as ten-key decimal tabulators for statistical typing, help? Would electrically driven equipment prove more economical than manually operated equipment?)
66. Does electrically driven equipment (such as posting machines) disturb the office?
67. Are there enough telephones for those who use them frequently?
68. Is there a procedure for answering the phone when the person called is absent?
69. Is desk top equipment adequate to the needs of each worker?
70. Is heavy equipment against walls or columns?
71. Are partitions movable whenever possible?
72. Have supply and storage cabinets in sufficient numbers been conveniently located?
73. Have work stations been designed for efficiency? For example, have modular or L- or U-shaped stations been studied?
74. Do typists have left pedestal typing platforms wherever possible?
75. Do all workers have chairs that are fully adjustable for correct posture?
76. If many files are involved, have five-drawer cabinets or open shelves been considered to conserve floor space?
77. Can gathering and sorting aids be used for paper assembly tasks?
78. Are machines being operated at maximum capacity?
79. If no, can machines be used jointly by two or more departments?

Questionnaires

80. Are numeric and terminal digit filing methods employed when they are appropriate?
81. Are photocopies generated prolifically?
82. Does anyone review new equipment releases for applicability to existing operations?
83. Are machines being regularly maintained by qualified maintenance men?
84. Is there a machine review in effect to insure the replacement of machines when they reach a certain age or condition?
85. Does equipment appear to be placed in the right location and at the proper height for efficient operation? Specify exceptions in notes.
86. Is proper use being made of dictating machines as a means of saving clerical time?
87. Is the most efficient duplicating system being used? (For example, the spirit process is less expensive for short-run requirements than the stencil process.)
88. Are two-drawer file cabinets in or by desks necessary; that is, can centralized, readily accessible files be substituted?
89. Have sorting trays and fixtures been acquired under a plan for speeding the transfer of working papers between operations?
90. Are counters equipped with file drawers, cabinets, and shelves?
91. Are all personnel who do the same job provided with comparable equipment?
92. Is a formal record retention and destruction policy in effect?
93. Have steps been taken to eliminate or reduce duplicate filing to a minimum?
94. Are users charged for efforts of service departments?
95. Is forms control a centralized responsibility?

MANUFACTURING

General

1. Does the company have a manufacturing operation?
2. If no, does it assemble and package? If answer to both this and question 1 is no, leave this section.
3. Is plant production per employee, per dollar of wages, and per dollar of plant investment known?
4. If yes, do the figures show that plant efficiency has kept pace with or risen faster than that of others in the industry?
5. If no, are steps being taken to improve efficiency?
6. Can vendors or customers be helpful in making operations easier and more economical?
7. If yes, are they being consulted?

8. Does production complain about inadequate designs, designs that cannot easily be fabricated, or too frequent design changes?
9. Does production complain about late deliveries of new designs and design changes that alter production schedules or delay production?
10. Are there long-standing, high-cost production situations in the plant that indicate unsolved engineering problems?
11. Does accounting give manufacturing the costs by product on a monthly basis?
12. Is reporting adequate; that is, are reports accurate and prepared early enough for corrective action by the right people?
13. Are manufacturing reports actually used by management?
14. Is the material cost (percent of production cost) known?

Production Control

15. Are sales forecasts communicated to production so that schedules can be developed to authorize production to best meet customer requirements, order patterns, and inventory requirements?
16. Are sales forecasts prepared in the detail needed for ready translation into a specific production plan? If yes, secure a copy of such a forecast and append to this page.
17. Are production schedules maintained in the degree of detail and accuracy needed?
18. If yes, are the schedules permanently displayed or effectively communicated so that their content is widely comprehended?
19. If effective schedules are produced, are they followed and acted upon?
20. Are changes likely to significantly affect the sales of products communicated quickly to production in writing?
21. Is up-to-date and accurate vendor or procurement lead time available to production schedulers so that needed parts are on hand and do not cause delay in production?
22. Is delivery given appropriate importance in vendor selection?
23. Under certain conditions, can delivery supersede quality and price?
24. Are the lead times used for scheduling reasonable and in accordance with management policy?
25. Does planning predict the workload for each machine in sufficient detail to permit early forecasting of manpower and/or machine priority needs?
26. Have production standards been established to facilitate correct machine loading and the minimizing of bottlenecks?
27. May machines be selected for use regardless of manufacturing cost per unit?
28. Are machine speeds prescribed to prevent workers from setting their own speeds?
29. Is there a means by which the current status of each job can be readily determined; that is, can the progress of any job be checked readily?
30. Does production control check the accuracy of its records?

31. If component parts and subassemblies are produced, do their production schedules tie in with end-product schedules?

32. Are schedules checked for materials availability before release to production?

33. Is there in effect a work order or similar system that requires written orders for all major production jobs?

34. If yes, and if shop work order numbers are used, can they be eliminated by identifying parts by number on the schedule?

35. Are work orders ever started through manufacturing with parts missing?

36. If yes, is production control reasonably sure that the missing parts will be received and processed when the rest of the order reaches assembly?

37. Is there a need for quality control in the company?

38. If yes, is there such a program?

39. Are reports that permit the prompt identification of quality problems and the taking of timely corrective action prepared?

40. Is there a measurement of the cost of the quality control department?

41. Is information available to management on the utilization and efficiency of machines and manpower by department?

42. Does management take action to raise efficiency when the figures show deficient utilization (total potential hours versus actual hours used)?

43. Do all major jobs and operations have time standards established by industrial engineering methods?

44. Does the industrial engineering department establish standard time data to minimize the amount of time studies that must be made?

45. Are manufacturing department people in agreement with the time standards used?

46. Is there a continuous program to review and revise methods and standards?

47. Was there economic justification for original purchase of machines? Has it since been tested?

48. Are there enough direct labor time codes to cover all machine situations?

49. Is there a need for management to improve time recording accuracy and responsibility? If so, prepare a separate schedule.

50. Does the work order system provide documents for cost control of job progress, machine repair records, and closeout control upon completion?

51. Is the actual production compared with the planned production and are deviations noted?

52. If a delay is encountered, is it communicated to the departments affected?

53. Are make-or-buy decisions reviewed so that proper consideration is given to purchasing, production, and engineering viewpoints?

54. If yes, is the review process structured so that make-or-buy decisions are quickly made?

55. Are requirements for common parts consolidated into schedules so that there is no undue repetition of setups for production of the same items?
56. Are bills of materials or usage formulas that are up to date (reflecting the latest engineering changes) the basis for determining parts requirements?
57. Is someone responsible for keeping drawings and bills of materials up to date?
58. Is a record of scrapped items maintained?
59. If yes, is it used to measure the effectiveness of the supervisor, to measure the effectiveness of employees, to determine cost to the company, and as a guide in reducing its cost?
60. Are scrapped parts replaced by a requisition that is approved by the department foreman and reviewed later by the manufacturing manager?
61. Does the company have a formal value analysis program seeking substitution of less costly materials, ways of using the same part and insuring that qualities of parts do not exceed usage requirements of end products?
62. Are idle-time reports prepared for machines and men? Do they contain the reasons for idleness?
63. Have make-or-buy decisions been reviewed within the last year?
64. Is there a method of following a product through the factory?
65. Once a machine has been installed, is there follow-up to see if it performs according to specification?

Operations

66. Does each production step or manufacturing operation appear to be essential?
67. Does there seem to be a possibility of combining certain steps to form a single step?
68. Can any operation be subdivided, and can the various parts be added to other operations?
69. Does the sequence of steps appear to be the best possible?
70. Do there appear to be delays that can be reduced or idle time that can be eliminated?
71. When materials can be checked for accuracy, can a sampling method be used?
72. Are economic lot sizes known?
73. If yes, is that knowledge used; for example, is the knowledge used to reduce fixed costs (set-up time, and so on) to acceptable levels?
74. Is value of past usage considered so that neither excessive inventories nor stock-outs occur?
75. Are those responsible for setting up schedules aware of plant capacity in terms of product categories, so that unrealistic production schedules, frequently recurring "emergencies," uneconomical production due to machine set-up breaks, missed delivery dates, and loss of customer goodwill do not result?

76. Is there a formal procedure for inspecting returned products?
77. Are there formal procedures for recording excess labor, computing its cost, and minimizing it?
78. Is materials handling examined to reduce its cost by use of floor trucks, skids, pallets, hydraulic lift trucks, hoists and forklift trucks? Also by conveyors: belt, roller, skate-wheel, overhead chain, and floor-to-floor?
79. Are parts received in unitized loads as specified?
80. Are they put in stock as a load and issued later in the same way? (The purpose is to eliminate counting.)
81. Are small parts counted on a scale?

Facilities and Equipment

82. Is the manufacturing area kept in an orderly fashion; that is, are wastepaper and other debris constantly cleared and stored?
83. Is warehouse space availability known so that blockage of warehouse aisles, which invites excessive handling and warehouse overflow that forces production shutdowns, can be avoided?
84. Do proper safety precautions appear to be exercised in the manufacturing area; for example, are aisles clear and are machines always operated according to safety standards?
85. Are cranes, scales, benches, and machines effectively used?
86. Are spare parts stored conveniently and properly?
87. Is everything that is needed to perform a particular operation where it should be when it should be?
88. Are tests on the efficiency of the machines, standard to manufacturer's specifications, periodically conducted?
89. Are scales checked periodically for accuracy?
90. Is height of the building used effectively for storage with the aid of racks and forklift trucks?
91. Is the warehouse divided into two areas, active and reserve stocks, for the purpose of reducing time to pick customers' orders?
92. Are washrooms and lavoratories clean and adequate for the size of the workforce?
93. Are the dressing rooms equipped with lockers; are they clean and adequate for the size of the workforce?
94. Are lighting conditions throughout matched to the work performed or functions involved?
95. Is machinery as technologically modern as is economically feasible?
96. Are repetitive actions reviewed from the standpoint of automating the function?

Personnel and Organization

97. Is the production manager included in the planning group?
98. Does the production manager keep in contact with the sales effort?
99. Does management have the right to transfer operators to various jobs and machines so that operations can be performed by individuals with the best labor rates?

100. Must foremen have the authority of the manufacturing manager for overtime work?
101. If yes, do policies exist so that overtime does not become excessive?
102. Is the ratio of supervisors to hourly workers such that productivity is high and supervisors are in a position to take care of their non-supervisory duties?
103. Does each machine critical to sustained output have a backup operator?
104. Are supervisors providing enough job direction; that is, are they sufficiently free of other obligations to provide the amount and quality of supervision needed?
105. Are there backup people for the manufacturing manager, supervisors, and foremen?
106. Are hourly workers adequately supervised on evening shifts?
107. Is the ratio of apprentices or helpers to journeymen determined by work requirements?
108. Are clerical positions in the manufacturing branch created when justified by clerical workload?
109. Is there a systematic program in effect to create supervisory attitudes favorable to cost control and problem solving?
110. Have qualified hourly workers real opportunity to move into the supervisory ranks?
111. Are lines and qualifications for progression within supervisory ranks realistically defined and communicated?
112. Are the methods used in selecting supervisors objective, reasonable, and fair to all?
113. Have positions occupied by foremen who will be retired within two years been identified, and are potential replacements undergoing training for the posts?
114. Are positive steps being taken to raise hourly workers' morale and work interest to high or higher levels?
115. Does turnover of hourly workers appear under control; that is, does it appear normal for the industry or better?
116. Is there a well-administered hourly worker qualification training and test program in effect?
117. Is there a set procedure for training new employees?
118. Are employees' capabilities matched to the task when necessary?
119. Is there a set procedure for obtaining tools and materials to discourage pilferage?
120. Is all garbage or other disposable material checked to see that it is to be thrown away?
121. Are production records checked against issued materials to see that the materials were used, returned to stock, or scrapped?
122. Are shipping and receiving docks under constant surveillance?
123. Do employees have access to their cars in unsupervised areas?
124. Are visitors and truckers allowed to wander around company property?
125. Are inventoried items fenced off?

Questionnaires

126. Are loadings and unloadings checked?
127. If a weightmaster is employed, what controls are exercised over him; that is, does he weigh the material himself?
128. Is someone responsible for keeping abreast of new production methods?

MARKETING AND SALES

Sales Information

1. Are sales volumes for each of the preceding ten years known and readily available? Obtain the figures and put them in notes.
2. Has sales volume in the last ten years risen 50 percent or more?
3. In the last five years at least 25 percent?
4. Are sales figures for the industry known?
5. If yes, has the company's share of the market been measured and correlated with the industry trend?
6. If no, is a plausible reason given?
7. Is sales analysis in any form performed?
8. If yes, does it appear to fully exploit the advantages offered by the information available?
9. If no, is a sound reason given?
10. If there is no sales analysis activity, are there plans afoot for starting it?
11. Are sales forecasts made each year for each product class?
12. If yes, are they made for at least two years ahead by both dollars and units of sale?
13. Do the sales projections appear soundly based and realistic; for example, are they developed only after adequate market and economic research?
14. Are the projections prepared in sufficient detail to allow performance to be measured against them?
15. Is average dollar sales volume by salesmen known? If yes, what is it?
16. If the company owns or has access to one, is the computer programmed to take advantage of mathematical forecasting and modeling methods?
17. Is the range of salesman dollar volume known; that is, is the percentage difference between highest and lowest ranking volume known?
18. Are the average earnings of salesmen known?
19. Is the dollar range of salesman income known? If yes, what is it?
20. Is the average salesman tenure known? If yes, what is it?
21. Does tenure seem balanced; that is, does it seem well distributed so that the company, for example, will not be hit with a high percentage of retirements in one period?

22. Are call reports prepared by salesmen?
23. If yes, is the information they contain productively used?
24. If no, is there a good reason why not?
25. Is there a means of measuring profitability by salesman or sales territory?
26. Is profitability by customer calculated?
27. Are freight allowances regularly checked?
28. Has the percentage of sales returns and allowances taken as a percent of total sales changed in the last two years? (If yes, describe changes in notes.)
29. Were the company's own manufacturing defects a major reason for allowances of sales returns?
30. If yes, has corrective action been taken or is it being taken?
31. When defects are due to vendor-supplied parts or materials, do vendors reimburse the company for defective products returned? If yes, list the percent of value of products returned.
32. Can sales be correlated with purchases (or production) and inventories?
33. If yes, are such correlations performed?
34. Is the marginal income (net sales less all direct costs) for each salesman, customer, territory, or market known?
35. Is market research done at all?
36. If yes, is it a continuing function as opposed to a one-shot operation?
37. Does the company make a profit on spares, parts, and so forth? (If yes, give percent of gross profit due to that source. _____)
38. Do salesmen know which department to call on at a customer's office: purchasing, management, R&D, production, maintenance?
39. Do salesmen feed back to marketing management, engineering, and production knowledge of what customers think they need in the way of product design?
40. Is management regularly informed about the status of current orders so they can see the effects on the sales forecast and take such action as is needed to protect profitability?
41. Does the company have a means of quickly learning about fast- or slow-moving items from their customers?

Sales Promotion

42. Is an advertising-sales promotion budget regularly provided?
43. If yes, is it soundly constructed and usable as a performance tool?
44. Has the sales department adhered to the budget within 5 percent in the last five years? If not, list the variances in notes.
45. Is there in effect a procedure that insures that amounts budgeted for programs abandoned, deferred, or curtailed are used to reduce the budget and not allowed to be used for unauthorized projects?
46. Are advertising expenditures made by the company's agency reviewed to be sure that advertising billed has actually been run, that the proper rate applications have been made, and so forth?

Questionnaires

47. Is any form of value analysis employed to measure program effectiveness?
48. Are invoices for space, time, and printing checked for accuracy?
49. Does the sales department get innvolved in handling customer problems, such as inquiries about delivery dates?
50. Is the pricing structure comparable with that of the industry in respect to discounts, rebates, and so forth?
51. Do warranties and guarantees exist? If yes, describe in notes.
52. Are warranties and guarantees in line with those in the industry? Give exceptions in notes.
53. Does the company provide product service?
54. Does engineering provide product technical support?
55. Is sales (technical) literature adequate?
56. If no, are plans for improving the literature in existence or are they being formed?
57. Is the determination of where to advertise or exhibit made on a factual, planned basis?
58. Are any payments received from other manufacturers in the form of reimbursement for cooperative advertising allowances to the company's customers?
59. If yes, do controls exist to insure that the advertising is placed as claimed by customers and that reimbursement equals payment?

Sales Management

60. Are accounts receivable with zero balance sent to the sales department?
61. Has corrective action been taken on delinquent accounts?
62. Does the company know why growth accounts are improving?
63. If yes, has the knowledge been applied to nongrowth accounts?
64. Are there direct salesmen? If yes, how many? _____
65. Is there a sales manager?
66. If no, should there be one?
67. Is a sales quota set for each salesman?
68. If yes, is the quota meaningfully used?
69. Do the salesmen participate in planning quotas?
70. Do salesmen work on an incentive basis that is realistic in terms of what the company can offer?
71. Does the compensation plan take into account the potential market versus market share? The profitability of items rather than volume alone?
72. Are salesmen encouraged to call in the sales manager or other salesmen to handle an account or help close a sale in their territories?
73. Does the sales manager manage the sales force rather than "sell"?
74. Is there a set pattern for customer follow-ups?
75. How are new markets explored? Describe in notes.
76. How old does a product have to be before no more spares are inventoried? State age in notes.
77. How often are sales territories evaluated? _____
78. Is the back order information system adequate?

79. Are salesmen asked to pursue delinquent creditors, resolve disputes on specifications and deliveries, and control inventories consigned to customers? Follow up performance of major deliveries? Be alert for novel applications of company product?
80. Are the company's sales efforts devoted to the products or services of the future (as opposed to the past)?
81. If yes, does the company know how to differentiate between those two types of products?
82. Are sales agents used at all? If yes, indicate percent of sales going through agents. _____
83. Does the company sell through distributors?
84. If yes, are relationships with distributors productive? Does the company have a formal program of distribution contact and support?
85. Do distributors who have part of company product line find themselves competing against other distributors with other parts of company line?
86. Does the company export?
87. If yes, how are exports handled? List in notes international sales, franchises, agents, tax advantages used.
88. Are salesmen completely familiar with entire product line?
89. Do salesmen make calls on customers in relation to profit potential rather than just volume?
90. Are quotas set and compared with actual periodic results?
91. Do comparisons result in corrective actions?
92. Do salesmen participate in planning expense allowances and number of calls?
93. Is tight control exercised over variances from established prices?
94. Are customers' orders subject to review and approval before acceptance by sales or order department or by credit department?
95. Does the company have an initial training program for its salesmen?
96. Does it have a continuing program?
97. Has a customer profile been developed?
98. Are there regular sales meetings wherein the salesmen are encouraged to discuss their problems?
99. Is sales service part of the sales department?
100. If no, is it part of the engineering or another department?
101. Is warehouse location a matter for periodic, formal review?
102. Is a senior officer responsible for review and correction of weaknesses revealed by analysis of complaints and returns?

ENGINEERING

General

1. Does the engineering department develop and maintain long-range plans covering investment, overhead, recruitment, personnel development, and facilities?

2. If yes, are the plans developed on an integrated basis with corporate plans?
3. Does the engineering department operate under a budget system tied in with a projection of workload?
4. If yes, is the projection dependable; that is, does it result from careful consideration of all the factors involved?
5. Are supervisors involved in developing their own annual operating budgets?
6. Is the department's annual budget broken down in sufficient detail that control is possible?
7. Is the engineering department's annual budget formally reviewed by a qualified group before it is approved?
8. Are periodic checks made, for example, quarterly, by the department management of operating cost trends versus budget forecasts?
9. Are supervisors given regular feedback of operating costs versus budget to date with variances shown of items for which they have responsibility?
10. Is it possible and is there a tendency to switch funds from one budget item to another as long as the total budget is not exceeded?
11. Do fixed costs in the engineering budget (rent, corporate management, insurance) appear reasonable both in themselves and in comparison with those of other departments?
12. Is the engineering department operated on a cost center basis?
13. Are engineering cost centers usefully determined (neither too small nor too large) so that costs by center can be conveniently determined and controlled?
14. May overtime be authorized anytime by a supervisor?
15. If there are projects with long lead times, are there any controls on commitments in addition to expenditures?
16. Does accounting provide engineering with the data necessary for the development of cost and project progress reports in time for the reports to be of use?
17. Upon project completion, does accounting provide a full cost report with complete project costs?
18. When requested, will accounting provide costs to date on projects, contracts, and special activities?
19. Are project estimates revised as the project progresses?
20. When on-going project costs substantially exceed approved estimates, is there a formal procedure and investigation before additional funds are assigned?
21. Are all engineering charges expensed rather than capitalized?
22. Are there some engineering charges that should be capitalized?
23. Does purchasing make material or equipment substitutions without consulting engineering?
24. Is engineering allowed to specify manufacturers or suppliers when it deems necessary if it can support its decision?
25. Is there a body of well-considered and communicated policies within which engineering decision authorities are spelled out?

26. Are potential replacements for men who hold key professional, technical, and managerial positions and will retire in the next two years now undergoing training?
27. Can engineering and drafting supervisors handle their paperwork, returns, nontechnical reports, and so forth, in one hour or less a day on the average?

Controls

28. Are project estimates, covering cost, time, and finishing dates provided for all identifiable projects over a certain size?
29. Are project estimates made up by persons other than those who will work on the project?
30. Is there enough estimating work to keep at least one person busy full time?
31. If yes, is there an estimator specialist or a group of project estimators within engineering?
32. If no, should there be one?
33. Does the department maintain updated and well-organized files of standard costs, past project costs, materials and equipment cost data, and similar information useful in estimating?
34. Are records kept of current labor costs (in-house, field, and so forth) and standard overhead rates for use in project estimates?
35. Is a computer (in-house or service bureau) used to receive and make use of estimating data?
36. If no, does it appear that a computer can be used with benefit? If yes, indicate in notes.
37. Are estimates developed in sufficient detail for planning and control purposes?
38. Has the accuracy of recent estimates been satisfactory to department management?
39. Have complaints about estimate quality been heard outside the department?
40. If estimates vary erratically, have steps been taken or are they being taken to correct the conditions producing them?
41. Once approved, are plans for major projects prepared in sufficient detail to facilitate the establishment of effective controls?
42. Are there procedures for revising approved plans for major projects?
43. Are schedules and other controls changed when plans are revised?
44. Are authorities spelled out for approving work in various cost categories; for example, are maximum cost approval levels set and are approval authorities granted?
45. Are in-house and out-of-house labor and material charges accumulated by individual projects by accounting?
46. Is nonproject work covered by open work order numbers?
47. Are status reports regularly prepared for major projects to foster comparison against target, schedules, and budgets?

48. Is there a standards group, committee, or assigned responsibility in the department concerned with design, component, construction, drafting, and other forms of standardization?
49. Does the standards work have specific and known objectives such as component cost reduction, work simplification, and inventory control?
50. Is the standards group or activity also concerned with methods such as drafting simplification, drafting symbols, use of photography, elimination of unnecessary detail, and perspectives?
51. Are records maintained to facilitate modification of work standards as needed?
52. Is the standards activity concerned with materials testing and product evaluation?
53. Is scheduling performed by someone other than the persons responsible for project execution?
54. Are engineering projects assigned priorities and regularly reviewed against due dates?
55. Is there a realistic priority system in effect as an aid to work scheduling?
56. Does planning predict the department's workload to permit early forecasting of manpower or craft bottlenecks and the need to adjust priorities?
57. Are engineering schedules coordinated with construction or production schedules? If no, should they be?
58. Are CPM, PERT, and similar scheduling techniques applicable to projects for control purposes employed?
59. If no, is use of such techniques being planned?
60. Are determinations routinely made of the total man-hours of work in process, man-hours available for scheduling, and man-hours ahead or backlogged by discipline or specialty?
61. Is the number of men available for scheduling purposes known each week?
62. Is the percent of actual hours worked on scheduled assignments 90 percent or better?
63. Are comparisons of actual labor hours with estimated hours regularly made and analyzed?
64. Can work imbalances be forecast in time to adjust them?
65. Are work authorization procedures in effect screening out redundant or unnecessary work?
66. Is the percent of total engineering man-hours for overtime more than 5 percent? If yes, put actual figures in notes.
67. Is there a routine, thoroughly understood procedure for change orders?
68. Is the parts-numbering system understood and commonly used by engineering and production?
69. Are adequate procedures that control the design and issue of forms and numbers of copies of documents reproduced, distributed, and filed in effect?

70. Are time expenditures by engineers, technicians, and draftsmen routinely charged, as applicable, to projects?
71. Does engineering have adequate safeguards for confidential materials, drawings, process data, and so forth?
72. Are cost records maintained so that management can determine make-or-buy decisions, that is, in-house versus contract for design engineering work?
73. Does engineering participate directly in the preparation of plant capital expenditure estimates?
74. Is it clearly understood what engineering charges may be capitalized versus expensed?
75. Is there a staff group or other specific assignment of responsibility for cost-reduction and methods-improvement studies?
76. Is any form of value analysis used to arrive at the best product cost?
77. Is value analysis applied to major manufacturing processes equipment groups or units for the purpose of lowering production costs or achieving improved quality relationships?
78. Are engineering costs charged to the departments or cost centers benefiting directly from the incurred expense?
79. Does accounting use an average rate to distribute engineering labor?
80. Is the engineering staff generally free to accept change in assignment? State in notes the percent of man-hours not available for regular scheduling owing to fixed assignments.
81. Do adequate field data such as costs and work progress come in so that an accurate assessment of materials, deliveries, and construction progress is possible?
82. Do estimators occasionally visit construction sites to verify, firsthand, that conditions are as reported?
83. If projects are not on time and cost schedule and the project manager refuses to take remedial action, may estimating go direct to engineering management?
84. Is a summarized monthly project status report prepared for engineering management to highlight deviations from estimates on an exception basis?
85. Are closed-out-project cost reports analyzed to spot recurring high-cost problems?
86. Once recurring problems are identified, are they turned over to specialists for investigation?
87. Are causes for deviation from schedules and deviation from estimates determined and followed·up?
88. Do project managers adequately recognize their "business" responsibilities and not get too deeply involved in design detail?
89. Is there a review of proposed projects prior to authorization by a qualified group to determine cash needs, profitability, product life, and similar criteria sufficient for assessment of the priority and value of the project to the company?

90. Is a satisfactory project cost code adequate to break down and assign project costs for purposes of amortization, depreciation, maintenance controls, and other criteria in effect?

Product Engineering

91. Is there regular feedback from marketing about product performance, client complaints, competitive designs, and suggested improvements?
92. Are the results of quality control, product testing, and evaluation passed on to engineering?
93. Are concepts of configuration management employed?
94. Is there a review procedure for determining manufacturing parts obsolescence?
95. Is it clearly understood who may contact customers and under what circumstances?
96. Is it clearly understood who may contact subcontractors and for what purposes?
97. Is subcontract work inspected and checked against drawings?
98. Is engineering regularly represented at product planning meetings?

Plant Engineering

99. Is the engineering department serving the company's plant engineering needs?
100. If no, are plant engineering needs being thwarted from within the company or by outside sources? If yes, stipulate source in notes; if no, go to next section.
101. Are equipment purchases, material selections, and project design decisions influenced primarily by first-cost considerations?
102. If no, do the decision models appear adequate in the sense of including all the relevant variables?
103. Is there an understanding between plant engineering and engineering department as to responsibilities, authorities, and so forth?
104. Are functional responsibilities between plant engineering, quality control, pilot plant engineering, R&D, and other adjacent activities clearly delineated and understood?
105. Can plant engineering be further incorporated into the central engineering department?
106. Do plant engineers get transferred into and from the engineering department sufficiently to establish mutual rapport and understanding of each other's problems?
107. Are capital additions and major changes in plant layout and design over a certain cost subject to engineering review prior to final approval?
108. Are machines and process equipment design modifications over a certain value subject to engineering review prior to final approval?

109. Is a machine and equipment standardization program in ef under engineering department control?
110. Do the spare parts interchangeability program and the i... and equipment standardization program have influence on the design of all new construction and purchases of equipment?
111. Is the parts interchangeability and equipment standardization program taken into full account when plant or machine modifications are made?
112. Can production requisition and receive engineering assistance on problems that cannot be solved by the production department?

Drafting

113. Is drafting centralized in a group or groups to permit its optimum employment?
114. Is there a satisfactory drawing numbering system that permits easy reference, storage, and retrieval?
115. Is the drawings storage area (vault) adequate for current and near-term future use?
116. Are vault controls in force to limit access to and the removal of drawings?
117. Is protection over original drawings in force, and is their safe custody assured?
118. Is the vault periodically purged of dead drawings, and is there a system in force for permanent storage of drawings that should be microfilmed?
119. If yes, is purging done at least annually?
120. Are drafting productivity studies ever made?
121. If yes, are the results used?
122. Are all drawings checked for accuracy, compliance with standards, and customer requirements?
123. Are drawings systematically checked by a responsible person prior to release?
124. Is drafting conveniently located for engineers who rely on it heavily?
125. Are lighting, boards, furniture, and elbow room adequate in drafting?
126. Are drawings released to contractors, plants, and vendors in packaged form in proper sequence?
127. Are drawings accompanied by materials bills per individual drawing or adequately cross-referenced?
128. Are drawings released to production in accordance with schedule and to tie in with production schedules and project priority?
129. Are plant drawing files complete and in good order?

Services and Facilities

130. Is there a technical library of any kind?
131. If yes, is it kept current and under reasonable supervision?

132. If no, is a library justified by the volume of information kept on hand or needed for reference?
133. Do engineers have access to on- or off-line computers?
134. Are aperture card devices used?
135. Is microfiche used?
136. Are vendor catalogs and research material on microfilm?
137. Are files for engineering data and correspondence adequate?
138. If yes, are the files within reach of those who use them?
139. Are reproduction facilities adequate and conveniently located?
140. Is there enough suitable reproduction equipment?
141. If yes, is the equipment under proper control?
142. Are the administrative functions in engineering under one supervisor (clerical, mail, filing, vacation schedules, telephone extensions, and so forth)?
143. Do other departments make extensive use of engineering department's graphics, model shop, and other facilities?
144. Is all engineering under one roof?
145. If no, is it unnecessarily dispersed?
146. Are models used as extensively as is practical (for piping, for example)?
147. Are model facilities adequate?
148. Are departments that use engineering facilities charged for the use of those facilities?
149. Is the technical library within reasonable proximity of those who need it?
150. Are cameras and dictating machines used to aid better and faster communication?
151. Is engineering adequately equipped with dictating machines and other necessary office equipment?
152. Are public rooms (conference, training, waiting) adequate for the engineering department needs?
153. Are engineers given privacy for their work that requires freedom from distracting noise and movement?
154. Are adequate security systems and procedures in force?

Organization

155. Is the department formally structured; that is, does it have segregation of work?
156. If yes, are personnel so grouped that related functions come under a single supervisor as far as possible?
157. Is the division of responsibility between production control and engineering clearly spelled out?
158. Is the division of responsibility between quality control and engineering clearly spelled out?
159. Are relations between engineering and customer service harmonious and are responsibilities clearly defined?
160. If the department has organization charts, are they accurate and distributed to those concerned?

161. Have studies been made to discover ways to organize engineering work more effectively?
162. Is periodic review made of the distribution of work and authority relationships for the purpose of finding organizational impediments?
163. Have steps been taken to improve the utilization of engineers by providing more technical support help?
164. Can work be organized along project lines?
165. If yes, is it?
166. Are responsibilities and authorities the result of analysis?
167. If no, is that the result of following traditional organizational patterns?
168. Are current job descriptions covering his own, his supervisor's, and his subordinates' positions in the hands of each person with supervisory responsibilities?
169. If no, does each man assigned to a project have clearly stated descriptions of project objectives and his responsibilities as a project member?
170. Do provisions for staff jobs such as planners, schedulers, and office manager appear adequate, as attested by engineers being free of clerical and auxiliary duties?
171. Is management direction diluted by the presence of union leadmen or similar classification that prevents direct instruction from manager to draftsmen and engineers?
172. Does the ratio of supervisors to workers—including engineers, designers, draftsmen, and administrative personnel—appear to be in balance? List ratio in notes.
173. Does the ratio of graduate engineers to nongraduate technical personnel (designers, tech aides, and so on) and draftsmen appear reasonable? List ratios in notes.
174. Has an effort been made to assign technical work to draftsmen, tech aides, designers, and similar nongraduates to permit graduates to concentrate entirely on design engineering?
175. Are there specialized groups (HVAC, mechanical, electrical, instruments, corrosion, soils, structural, communications, and so forth) within the engineering department?
176. If yes, do they appear justified?
177. If engineering is concerned with field work—construction, for example—is there adequate engineering representation in the field?
178. Do project managers appear to have the authority necessary to manage their projects?

Personnel

179. Are technical and professional staffs generally employed in work that matches their pay grade and skill classification?
180. Have supervisors been given training in cost control and problem solving?
181. Can employees without engineering degrees move into engineering positions?

182. If yes, is there a procedure for identifying the technical abilities or potentials of these employees?

183. Have specifications for supervisory positions been defined and made public?

184. If yes, are the specifications followed in selecting supervisors?

185. Does engineering have a procedure for receiving and testing suggestions for solving work and technical problems from other departments in the organization?

186. If yes, are the suggestions received acted upon or are reasons for not acting upon them quickly given to the originators?

187. Has the supervisory group been given adequate training in management principles and fundamentals?

188. Is there a formal program for the indoctrination and training of new employees?

189. Is turnover of department employees equal to or better than industry average? State turnover rate in notes.

190. If turnover is in excess of industry average, does it appear that salaries and other rewards are insufficient to retain and motivate competent engineers, technicians, and draftsmen?

191. Is the company seeking to reduce the problem of the obsolescence of engineers by updating the education of engineers with 10, 15, or 20 years of experience?

192. Must engineers become managers to obtain recognition beyond middle-management levels?

193. If yes and if compensation is equal to or better than the going rates, is the quality of department administration at fault?

194. Are annual appraisals made of supervisory performance?

195. Are project results appraised by a group?

196. Is there a well-defined plan to upgrade professional skills through company-supported plans and courses, especially those of young engineers?

197. Are nongraduates, technicians, and draftsmen encouraged and given assistance to improve their skills and qualifications?

198. Are competent professionals who lack skill or interest in supervision given work that entitles them to equal pay for equivalent contribution?

199. Is the assignment of secretaries and clerical personnel consistent with best employment of those personnel?

200. Are professionals encouraged to publish, seek patents, lecture, and in other ways promote their professional status?

201. Are professionals encouraged to join professional societies?

202. Are vacation schedules in keeping with engineering planning and known peak loads?

203. Are engineers given the opportunity to transfer to other departments to broaden their experience?

204. Can professional managers who lack engineering degrees become managers of the engineering department?

205. Are engineering department personnel, occasionally including non-engineers, given tours of production facilities, newly constructed

sites, and so forth to broaden their understanding of what design engineering is really about?

ELECTRONIC DATA PROCESSING

1. Is data processing automated in the company? If yes, describe the installation, including its equipment configuration, in notes.
2. If no, does it appear that automated data processing is becoming economically feasible? If answers to questions 1 and 2 are no, go to another section.
3. If there is an internal audit department or other agency that evaluates the company's data processing function, have you obtained its most recent study of data processing?
4. Was the question of lease, lease-buy, or buy studied before the present installation was acquired?
5. Have any major changes in the data processing system been made in the last two years?
6. If no, has the system been reviewed in the last two years?

Organization and Staffing

7. Is there a table of organization? If yes, attach a copy. If no, rough out a copy and attach to this questionnaire.
8. Is the department staffed in accordance with the table of organization?
9. Is there appropriate separation of duties between operating, programming, control, and system personnel?
10. Is there a program for the systematic rotation of operating personnel from job to job to provide operator backup. If yes, is it being carried out effectively?
11. Is there a program to train computer operators as programmers?
12. Have formal job descriptions for all positions been written?
13. Is a control or dispatch group responsible for controlling the flow of data to and from the data processing department?
14. If yes, does the control group have either the direct authority or the management backing necessary to enforce adherence to controls both within the data processing area and outside it?
15. Are programmers on call to cover emergencies in computer operations?
16. If yes, is there a procedure for determining on whom to call?
17. Is the operator restricted from assuming the responsibility for deciding whether or not processing should be continued when program or machine errors have interrupted the normal flow?
18. Does the procedure include estimated and actual cost for system design and operation?

Questionnaires

19. Is membership in professional organizations encouraged?
20. Is a job request procedure utilized?
21. Does the procedure include estimated and actual cost for system design and operation?
22. Is a complete log of job requests maintained?
23. Is there an adequate method for reporting actual development time for a particular job?
24. Is a program maintenance group assigned to computer operations?
25. If no, how are modifications and one-time programming needs that require less than one month to implement handled?

Documentation

26. Is there a requirement that each program be documented?
27. Does a thorough check show documentation for each program?
28. If no, is the lack of program documentation recognized by EDP management?
29. If there is program documentation, does it include all of the following: logic flow chart, coding sheets, controls, compiler printout, form and record layouts, and a signoff sheet for program changes? If no, record what is missing in notes.
30. If there is documentation, is it in a form understandable to an outsider? Is it required to be in standard form?
31. Are run books containing a complete listing of instructions for each run, the flow charts, and so forth maintained?
32. Does the computer operations manager have the authority to sign off on new run book manuals?
33. Are run books used when the runs are being made?
34. Have provisions been established to insure that all documents are kept up to date?
35. Is there an operations schedule?
36. Are copies of all reports that have been issued maintained in a reports manual?
37. Is a complete machine log maintained?
38. If yes, does it identify rerun time, down time, and production time?
39. Are report distribution and binding instructions in writing?
40. If yes, do they refer to recipients by title?
41. Is a shift-turnover log maintained?
42. If yes, is it used to fix responsibility in the case of reruns or errors?
43. Is a complete log of job requests maintained?
44. Is there a standard method for reporting actual development time for a particular job?
45. Are control points documented? Does the documentation explain where and what the controls are?
46. Is a standard for control spelled out in a comprehensive format?
47. Are all requests for special processing received from the originating department in writing?
48. If yes, is processing performed only on the basis of a signed written request?

Utilization and Output Quality

49. Is the computer equipped with a main frame clock that prints time in, out, and elapsed on the console typewriter?
50. If yes, is the clock used? If yes, explain in notes what is done with the printout.
51. If there is no clock, does management have any idea of the number of hours the computer is used each month?
52. If the equipment is rented, is usage greater than the base rental hours per month?
53. If the equipment is rented, is usage less than the base rental hours per month? If yes, state in notes the number of hours less than the base rental hours.
54. Is a record kept of reasons for reruns and equipment failures, and are the failures followed up by preventive actions?
55. Is traffic through the data processing area controlled, or are people allowed to wander about?
56. Are all security forms such as payroll checks serially numbered?
57. Are adequate controls exercised over security forms?
58. Are all security forms accounted for after processing?
59. Are all source documents initially created by departments other than the data processing department?
60. Are batch listings prepared for all input data? Explain in notes.
61. If no, is there a valid reason why not?
62. If yes, does the data processing control group review and balance batch listings?
63. Are manual controls, such as batch header cards, over dollar amounts of item counts established for all input data before the data are forwarded to the data processing department?
64. Are all processings performed on the computer and all decisions made by the console operator recorded on the daily log or console typewriter?
65. Is a checkpoint restart ability built into long runs, such as master file updates?
66. Are all log sheets serially numbered?
67. If yes, are all serial numbers accounted for daily?
68. Is the log reviewed and signed at the end of each shift by the supervisor?
69. Are the logs filed as a permanent record?
70. Does the program check the header label to make sure that the proper tape-disk pack is mounted?
71. Does the console typewriter notify the operator when an incorrect tape-disk pack has been mounted?
72. Is there a standard procedure to be followed when the tape-disk pack is unreadable?
73. Is there an audit trail with complete controls over the computer as well as the people and data?

Questionnaires

74. Do any of the personnel responsible for establishing input controls have ready access to the computer?
75. Are record counts for sorts printed and checked?
76. Do the run logs identify the operator who runs each job?
77. Are control points from run to run printed and balanced?
78. Is the processing area provided with independent temperature and humidity controls maintained by a separate circulating system?
79. Does the equipment meet or exceed the computer manufacturer requirements? (Usually explained in a manual.)
80. Is the library of tape-disks or cards under environmental control, that is, air conditioners and humidifiers?
81. Are supplies, such as cards, forms, stock paper, and ribbons, maintained under environmental control?
82. Are the supplies at a location convenient to the processing area?
83. Have policies controlling housekeeping, smoking, and the availability of the computer room to visitors been established?
84. If yes, are the policies adhered to?
85. Are optical and other special input–output devices employed?
86. If yes, is the utilization rate of the special devices known?
87. If yes, does the rate or other special circumstance justify the presence of the device?
88. Is the EDP department installation run on an economic basis, that is, as an investment or cost center?
89. Is there an operating budget?
90. If yes, is it adhered to as attested to by the fact that variances have not exceeded 10 percent?
91. Are any of the major programs run in compatibility mode?
92. Are data processing services charged back to the different departments?
93. If yes, show in notes what percent of data processing is charged to each department.
94. If no, list in notes the departments for which data processing is performing a service and to the best knowledge of management what percent each department represents.
95. Are the user departments aware of their responsibility for data generation?
96. Are the user departments satisfied with the way in which their specific needs are handled by data processing? Explain in notes.
97. Do top-level executives in all areas of the business play an active role in deciding how data processing will be used?
98. Is there a definite degree of management involvement in data processing?

System Security

99. Are input tapes processed to the main files only after all batches have been reviewed and balanced?
100. Are controls on rejects maintained outside the data processing department until they are ultimately cleared?

101. Is input keyed from original source documents or clerical transcriptions? Explain in notes.
102. Is keypunching direct to tape (keytape) used?
103. Is verification of keypunch sufficient, but not excessive?
104. Is statistical sampling used in verification when possible?
105. Are all plastic rings (inserted on the tape for writing) removed from the tapes when the tapes are placed in the storage to guard against accidental misuse of the tapes?
106. Is more than one generation of tape-disk packs stored in an area geographically separated from the processing center? If yes, how many?
107. Is a duplicate set of important tape-disk packs stored in an area geographically separated from the processing center?
108. If yes, have provisions been made to keep it up to date?
109. Are all computer programs maintained in an instruction tape-disk?
110. Is there a special corrector routine established for changing the instruction tape-disk pack to prevent any invalid or unauthorized changes?
111. Are all changes to the instruction tape-disk packs made by persons outside the data processing operations group?
112. Are duplicate instruction tape-disk packs maintained to insure that the programs would not be lost if a tape-disk were lost or destroyed?
113. If yes, is the location outside the computer area?
114. If yes, are the instruction tape-disk packs updated periodically?
115. Are gummed labels attached to the outside of each reel of tape or disk pack for distinct and clear understanding?
116. Are magnetic labels recorded on the tape-disk for identification of the label if the gummed label falls off and for program verification?
117. Is control maintained over access to the tape-disk pack library?
118. Is there a tape-disk retention schedule so that it is always possible to recreate a tape-disk still needed for future processing in the event of loss or accidental destruction?
119. Are all corrections of rejected input made by personnel other than those of the data processing department?
120. Are all corrections of input data batched separately?
121. Are batch numbers assigned to correction batches to facilitate better control?
122. Is there an adequate operations schedule, and is it adhered to?
123. If changes in schedule are made, are they made only after the manager of the department has approved them?
124. Is an adequate inventory of supplies, such as cards, ribbons, and forms, maintained on a regular basis?
125. If yes, who is responsible for the inventory?
126. Is insurance coverage adequate in the sense that not only is physical equipment covered but the value of all records and programs and the cost of using backup equipment until the equipment is replaced are covered as well?

Questionnaires

127. Is there a formal backup arrangement for an alternate computer in the event of a prolonged breakdown of equipment?
128. Does the company buy additional computer time at other locations to meet peak loads or for special one-time long-run jobs?
129. Does housekeeping in the data processing area appear to be satisfactory; that is, is there a place for everything and is everything in its place when it is not actively in use?
130. Are program source decks and tapes maintained in secure file cabinets?
131. Are source decks or tapes properly numbered or labeled?
132. Are the file cabinets clearly identified?
133. If the life of the company, for example, airline reservations service, depends on EDP, is there an auxiliary power supply?
134. Is the sale of cards and other salvage material handled outside the data processing function?
135. If computer time is sold, is it so controlled as to insure accountability?
136. Does the librarian have up-to-date lists of all tape-disks and their current status?
137. Are confidential tape-disks stored in locked cabinets?
138. Are all shifts covered for library access?
139. Are programmers required to obtain written authorization for hands-on time?
140. Is there a rigid set of edit rules for data entry?
141. If yes, is it understood by all concerned—programming, systems operations, control, and outside departments? Explain in notes.
142. Are records of the number and frequency of input errors maintained?
143. If yes, is proper corrective action taken to prevent the recurrence of errors?
144. Is the control to assure correction and reentry of invalid data adequate?
145. If yes, is the procedure followed?
146. Are government requirements known? If yes, are they adhered to?
147. Is access to the computer room and tape-disk storage controlled by mechanical means, such as locked doors or electronic badge readers?
148. Are magnet-detecting sensors used to prevent accidental or deliberate attempts to destroy tape-disks?
149. Are all data processing personnel screened to prevent a disgruntled employee from causing damage?
150. Is the computer site off limits to casual or nonscheduled visitors?
151. Is access to the backup tape-disks in another geographical site controlled?
152. Are maintenance personnel who are required to work in the computer site screened?
153. Is security good enough to prevent *anyone* from removing a reel of tape or a disk pack?

154. Are *some* of the custom forms (such as invoices, statements, checks) kept at a site safe from fire or accidental sprinkler damage?
155. Are any programs audited by writing a program of errors and running it?

COSTING AND PRICING

Costing

1. Does the company have a cost accounting system now? If yes, describe (a) how it is developed, (b) the supporting documentation, and (c) the methods of cost accumulation and reporting. Prepare a detailed flow chart.
2. If no, would a cost system be of value? Explain in notes.
3. Describe, in the space provided for notes, the type of cost system used: (a) job cost, (b) process cost, (c) standard absorption cost, (d) standard direct cost, or (e) a combination of types based on product or services mix?
4. Is the type of cost system used justified by the nature of the business?
5. Does the company rely on historical data only?
6. Are cost standards based on time studies or other engineering methods?
7. Can the company reasonably estimate the cost of a job or process before it is begun?
8. If yes, do cost estimates show both hours and dollars?
9. Are actual costs reported? If yes, are they compared with estimates or standards?
10. Does the cost system pinpoint variances by employee, process, or department?
11. Do comparisons generate any action? Explain.
12. Are reports prepared in responsibility-accounting format?
13. Are cost standards reviewed and revised periodically? If yes, describe frequency and basis for revision.
14. Are cost standards used in administrative and clerical areas as well as production?
15. Is the cost system used in budget preparation or other forecasting areas?
16. Is the cost system used to record profitability on the general books of account?
17. Are variable and fixed costs separately identified?
18. Can the direct-costing method be profitably employed?
19. Does the company know and regularly review its breakeven point? If yes, by product line?
20. Is return on investment measured regularly? If yes, by product? By project?

21. Are distributions and allocations of costs based on causal relationships?
22. If expenses are allocated, are they grouped into a few significant categories for distribution on some uniform basis? Is the allocation basis realistic?
23. Is the profitability of product lines disguised by use of allocations?
24. Is there a management-administered cost control program?
25. If yes, is the cost control program related to budget plans?
26. Is it production-oriented?
27. Is it applied to administrative and clerical areas?
28. If a standard cost system is used, is a complete variance analysis provided each month?
29. Are standard costs revised each month?
30. Is there a cost-reduction suggestion box?
31. Are cost savings that result from suggestions shared with employees?
32. Are there media (house organs, periodic memoranda) for periodically communicating past, current, and future cost reduction efforts as well as employee awards?

Pricing Policies

33. Are pricing policies integrated into long-range planning?
34. If yes, are policies reviewed in order to avoid legal difficulties?
35. Is consideration given to overall benefits to the company as opposed to parochial interests of particular units of the company?
36. Are the company's prices less than the prices of its competitors?
37. If no, are they equal to or higher than competitors' prices?
38. Does the company have a pricing policy covering its general level of prices, such as premium and bargain prices, in relation to competitors?
39. Does the company meet competition as closely as possible?
40. Does the company monitor competitive prices on a frequent basis?
41. Is customer order volume a factor in pricing policy?
42. Are costs of special tooling factored into the selling price, priced as a separate item, or absorbed? Specify in notes.
43. Does the company monitor its comparative share of the market and the effects thereon of price changes?
44. Are a variety of markets such as brand name versus private label production or sales to discounters considered to permit better pricing on basic or branded lines or to generate higher overall return?
45. Are geographic differentials employed to advantage?
46. Is cost-plus used to set prices?
47. Is cost-plus the only criterion used to set prices?
48. Are product line price relationships based on varying demand rather than fixed cost plus?
49. Is pricing flexible enough to create volume during slack periods and to benefit from heavy demand during others?
50. Are discounts or other price concessions employed in an attempt to gain volume and maximize overall return?

51. Are meaningful, timely sales analysis reports prepared for management review and action?
52. Does the company know the historical results on profits from increases and decreases in individual item prices and product line prices?
53. Is a computer used to predict effects of changes, to measure risks, and to assist in decisions?

PURCHASING

1. Is a department or a single organizational unit engaged in purchasing? If yes, prepare a departmental organization chart identifying positions and reporting relationships.
2. If no, is the purchasing function completely decentralized? If yes, identify responsibilities and describe the purchasing system used.
3. Does the present degree of centralization or decentralization of purchasing appear justified? If no, list reasons why in notes.
4. Are there written purchasing policies?
5. If yes, have purchasing policies been established at (a) corporate level, (b) divisional level, (c) local plant management level, and (d) departmental level? Describe exceptions in notes.
6. Have purchasing procedures been documented?
7. Is the documentation up to date and in the hands of users?
8. If yes, do the procedures cover all of the following?
    (a) Requisitioning.
    (b) Bid requirements and method of vendor selection.
    (c) Authorizations and signatures required.
    (d) Necessary forms, reports, and files.
    (e) Organizational and operational relationships with (1) accounting department, (2) receiving department, and (3) inventory planning and control departments.
    (f) Vendor evaluation.
    (g) Buyer evaluation.
    (h) Purchase of capital goods or equipment.
    (i) Legal considerations, including trade regulation laws, use of uniform commercial code, warranties, product liability considerations, nonperformance.
    (j) Interdivisional and interlocational purchases.
    (k) Purchases from local suppliers.
    (l) Use of blanket orders or long-term purchase contracts.
    (m) Reciprocal purchase arrangements with vendors. Describe exceptions in notes.
9. Have any major purchases recently been made outside the prescribed purchasing routine?

10. If yes, does the circumvention appear justified?
11. In the event of vendors back-ordering materials or supplies, are the purchase orders for undelivered quantities canceled and replaced with new purchase orders? Comment fully on treatment of back orders.
12. Are any accounting functions performed by the purchasing department or by purchasing personnel?
13. Does the purchasing department handle such functional responsibilities as vending machine service or sale of scrap? If yes, describe in notes.
14. Does the purchasing department actively pursue cash discounts?
15. If yes, is there a follow-up procedure to measure or determine the discounts lost?
16. Does purchasing coordinate with inventory control and production planning in establishing systematic reorder points, necessary lead time, inventory markers, and so forth?
17. Have purchase quantity levels been established in connection with inventory control to assure economic ordering?
18. Does purchasing work with the storage and warehousing personnel to establish the most effective inventory controls?
19. Does purchasing coordinate and work with production, engineering, and finance (accounting) to conduct studies in the following areas: (a) product substitutions or value analysis, (b) off-grade or reprocessed materials, (c) make-or-buy studies? Describe exceptions in notes.
20. Does the purchasing department utilize "objective setting" or "plan of purchase"?
21. Is the purchasing department advised of engineering or material changes to prevent overbuying or to minimize obsolescence of inventory?
22. Are there purchasing functions that have been adapted to EDP?
23. If yes, have specific programs (subsystems) been written and made operational?
24. If no, are there areas that should be computerized?
25. Has a purchasing department comparative operations analysis (refer to addendum 1) been performed? When? By whom?
26. Does the purchasing department serve as a source of information from vendors, competitors, and so on?
27. Is the gross dollar value of all purchases made this year known? Put the percent of sales income it represents in notes.
28. Is the dollar value broken down into its principal components, such as raw materials, components, services?
29. Is percent of total purchases (in terms both of purchase orders and dollar value) handled by the purchasing department known? If yes, put in notes.
30. Have you made a distribution of purchase order value, that is, distributed by number and dollar value? If yes, put it in notes.
31. Does the company have guidelines as to ratio of cost to purchased or special skills needed?

32. Does the purchasing department have any voice in the selection of materials, supplies, specifications, and so forth?
33. If yes, has it too much voice?
34. If no, has it too little voice?
35. Is expediting deliveries a major problem?
36. Are overdue deliveries regularly expedited or taken note of in the receiving process and acted upon?
37. Are all purchases delivered to a central receiving location, as opposed to direct delivery to production areas?
38. If yes, are separate records maintained by employees who are functionally independent of the manager?
39. If economic lot adjustments are made, are the excess quantities controlled and applied in order to reduce subsequent requirements?
40. Is batching of small orders routinely done; that is, are blanket purchase orders of commonly used, low-unit-cost items provided?
41. Are purchasing activities so subdivided that no individual has the responsibility for an entire purchasing transaction from beginning to end?
42. Are orders ever divided among a number of vendors?
43. If yes, is any advantage offered by the division?
44. Is each purchase transaction based on the provision of a purchase requisition, and is approval of the requisition required by a duly authorized person before a purchase order is made up?
45. Are purchase order drafts used; that is, are combination orders and order payment forms employed?
46. Is there an approved vendor list for major items?
47. Are there policies that outline the conditions under which vendor selection can take place outside the purchasing department?
48. Are purchase requisitions ever marked rush, emergency, or as soon as possible?
49. If yes, is it known what percent of purchase orders are so marked?
50. Are bids received from the same vendors each time?
51. Are exceptions to lowest bid allowed?
52. If yes, how are such exceptions controlled?
53. Are purchase order blanks prenumbered and properly controlled?
54. Do employees who approve requisitions appear to have enough information to make intelligent approval?
55. Are routing considerations (delivery costs, freight allowances, premium rates) given adequate attention in the evaluation of competitive bids?
56. Are transportation allowances verified?
57. Are efforts made to ship by the most economical methods?
58. Is price included whenever possible in the purchase order?
59. Are prices of items not prepriced verified after receipt of purchase confirmation?
60. Are purchase orders so written that materials received can be easily identified and checked?
61. Is policy with respect to acceptance of gifts from vendors explicit?

62. Does the company investigate for conflict of interest such as ownership by purchasing agent of stock in suppliers?
63. Are materials price variances used as a measure of purchasing agent performance?
64. Are quality control analysis reports used as a measure of purchasing agent performance?
65. Are all purchases made on purchase orders and channeled through the purchasing department?
66. If yes, should they be, for example, on-site, small inventory levels (rack jobbers)?
67. Does a copy of the receiving report go directly to the accounting department?
68. Are receiving tickets prenumbered and is a permanent record kept in the receiving department or is a copy of the purchase order sent to receiving as authorization to accept goods to speed processing?
69. Are returned purchases cleared through the shipping department?
70. Are invoices checked in the accounting department against purchase orders, receiving reports, and inspection reports?
71. Is there a definite responsibility, as supported by evidence, for checking invoices as to prices, extensions, and freight charges? If no, list exceptions in notes.
72. Are purchases made for employees cleared through the purchasing department in a routine manner?
73. Are vouchers prepared for all purchase and expense items?
74. Are vouchers for purchases and expenses examined by a responsible officer or employee to ascertain completeness of attachments and various required approvals?
75. Is postage metered?
76. Is scrap segregated from the rest of the inventory?
77. Is there a clear distinction as to what is scrap?
78. Does someone, other than those who accumulate it, inspect the scrap before it is shipped?
79. Is the scrap weighed or its quantity known in some other fashion before shipment?
80. Is a scrap inventory record maintained?
81. Are competitive bids for scrap received?
82. If yes, are the bids from the same people?
83. Are vendor charge-backs promptly handled?
84. Are vendor charge-backs promptly aged?
85. Are major vendors reviewed from the viewpoint of their potential as customers?
86. Are cumulative statistics of amounts purchased from vendors developed?
87. Are vendors adequately diversified so that the company would not be helpless in the event of a strike or major disaster to the vendor?
88. Does the purchasing officer have awareness of operations research methods that might help improve his performance, such as linear programming and statistical decision-making tools?

89. Does the purchasing agent attend AMA and similar seminars?
90. Does the purchasing agent belong to pertinent professional organizations?

MATERIALS HANDLING

1. Is materials handling a major activity in the company? If no, go to next section.
2. Is materials handling a specialized activity in the company or unit; that is, is at least one person engaged full time in the activity?
3. If yes, are direction and quality of materials handling services the responsibility of one person?
4. Does production planning give warehouse personnel sufficient advance notice of items and stock activity to be expected?
5. Are warehouse personnel notified in advance of planned inventory changes?
6. Is there any indication that the company carries varieties of stocks that lend themselves to standardization?
7. If yes, is any kind of value engineering being practiced or planned?
8. Is there any evidence of an excessive accumulation of materials awaiting repair, rework, or return to vendors?
9. Do inventory records appear to serve a useful purpose beyond accounting; for example, are they used for purchasing materials or for scheduling production?
10. Does someone have the obligation to keep current on new methods of materials handling?
11. If yes, is he encouraged to look in other industries for equipment that could be slightly altered to meet the company's needs?
12. Do materials appear to be standing around piled up unnecessarily on the receiving platform?
13. Do production workers stand around waiting for materials to arrive?
14. Are materials moved more often than necessary?
15. Do skilled workers handle materials; that is, is expensive labor used for unskilled—and often unnecessary—manual jobs?
16. Are delicate parts frequently damaged in transit?
17. Are production areas cluttered with parts and material to be used— or moved to the next operations?
18. Are all materials unloaded mechanically or with machine assistance?
19. If no, do materials that are unloaded manually have to be so handled?
20. Are prepackaged cartons for simplifying counts and materials handling being used?

Questionnaires

21. Are identical items stored in one location to minimize time-consuming searches by stock handlers?

Methods

22. If the warehouse is on more than one floor, are fast-moving stock items concentrated on one floor near the shipping area to minimize travel, retrieval time, and elevator usage?
23. Are storage areas and shipping areas close together so that the storage area can act as an effective feeder to the shipping docks without costly backhauling between storage areas and resultant double handling?
24. If no, can the storage and shipping areas be brought closer together?
25. If yes, does the change appear to be economically justified?
26. Are lifting areas well illuminated?
27. Are all bins clearly labeled to facilitate order picking?
28. Are materials so placed as not to overflow from one location into adjoining aisles, which would require rehandling to free blocked items and show that space utilization preplanning by warehouse personnel may be inadequate?
29. Is merchandise that can be stored uncartoned, rather than cartoned, so stored? (If no, materials handling and production costs may be much higher than necessary.)
30. Are materials available to workers without waste motion? For instance, when large metal castings are to be ground, the pieces should be brought to the operator on a waist-high conveyor to avoid his stooping over. If the bottom of the casting is to be ground, the piece should be turned by means of a special holding fixture.
31. If small pieces are arranged on hangers preliminary to a plating or painting operation, can workers use both hands in placing units? Are pieces fed to the hanger crew by materials handlers, and are hangers fully loaded to avert plating or painting empty hangers?
32. Are bags of incoming materials palletized to avoid handling individual bags?
33. Is there a central locator file?
34. Are large portable bins available to avoid repeated handling of small containers?
35. Are dump trucks in lieu of standard trucks used in unloading bulk commodities?
36. Is crane capacity adequate to lift the heaviest jobs?
37. Are all the main lifting areas covered by craneways?
38. Can forklift trucks be used with benefit in the warehouse and plant? If yes, are forklifts used? If no, have steps to obtain forklifts been taken or are they being taken?
39. If forklift trucks are used, are a sufficient number and variety on hand?

40. Are stacks set up to avoid bottom pieces being crushed by the piling of excessive weight, by leaning towers of materials, or by forklift truck chewmarks?
41. Are traffic personnel aware of the advantages of specialized freight cars introduced in recent years? (For example, one type has "garage door" roll sides that make the interior of the car fully accessible to materials handling equipment.)
42. When material is received, is it properly typed and routed?
43. Is material examined for conformance to specifications when received?

Facilities and Equipment

44. Does storage space (throughout) appear adequate?
45. In multistory plants, are elevators used to move materials between floors? If yes, how long and how often must one wait for an elevator?
46. If materials must be moved from one machine to another, are they moved mechanically? If not, are they best moved manually?
47. Is scrap disposed of mechanically?
48. Are aisles clear, smoothly paved, and well lighted so that traffic can flow smoothly?
49. Do tote boxes, bar stock, or parts of machines project out into aisles?
50. Are storage areas well lighted?
51. Are storage areas marked off into sections?
52. If yes, are sections numbered or lettered for identification?
53. If yes, are records kept of what is stored in each area so that parts and products can be located rapidly?
54. Are products stored in the most easily handled forms and in units in which they will be shipped?
55. Are aisles wide enough to permit free movement of handling equipment?
56. Are storage areas located as close as possible to the production areas they serve?
57. Is there an adequate supply of fire extinguishers?
58. Is warehouse space being utilized for storing materials that are outside the intended scope of storage? For example, is scrap being stored at substantial costs?
59. Are shipments ready for the truckers when they arrive? (If no, a great deal of time is wasted by truckmen.)
60. Are costly, long-carried items stored far from exits?
61. Is a burglary alarm system used for protection through all doors and through all windows?
62. Is there a regular schedule for cleaning the plant?
63. Does the person approving rates have a rate and routing guide covering incoming and outgoing items?
64. If yes, is the guide kept up to date?
65. If yes, is it adequate; that is, does it cover the usual raw material purchases and shipments of finished goods?

Questionnaires

66. Is the company's liability established by reference to purchase order and shipping order?

Freight

67. Are quantities checked to the proper receiving or shipping document?
68. Are rates checked to the guide and shipping order?
69. Are extensions checked?
70. Are bills paid within the specified time limit?
71. Are the controls such as to prevent duplicate payment of freight bills? Describe the essential control features briefly in notes.
72. Are controls over payment of freight charges adequate but not excessive? If no, what corrective measures are necessary?
73. Is a report of premium shipments prepared regularly?
74. Determine amount of demurrage paid by plant for period under examination.
75. What is cause of demurrage?
76. Have arrangements been made to utilize average demurrage agreement credits?
77. What corrective action has been taken to reduce demurrage expense?
78. When minimum carload weights are paid for, for example, 21,000 pounds as 24,000 pounds, could the additional weight of 3,000 pounds have been shipped, in effect, at no cost?
79. Examine loss and damage claims and try to ascertain if there is a pattern for such claims. Can they be eliminated?
80. Are claims settled promptly?
81. If there are differences between carrier's freight and the freight on the sales invoice, is rate and routing guide incorrect? Is it the result of application of incorrect rates or computation? Was customer charged the proper amount for freight?
82. Has the company used the services of an independent freight audit agency as a supplement to or instead of its own freight department?

Inventory

83. Is inventory a significant company investment?
84. Can the quality of inventory management significantly affect the firm's earnings? If answer to both questions is no, go to the next section.
85. Are all material purchases delivered to central stores as opposed to direct delivery to production units?
86. If yes, are the stores records maintained by employees functionally independent of the storekeepers?
87. Is one person responsible for inventory management?
88. If yes, is a different person responsible for inventory verification?
89. Is the gross inventory turnover known?

90. Are the turnover rates for the various inventory classes known?
91. If yes, does it appear reasonable as measured against industry standards, previous levels, and so forth in each case?
92. Are perpetual inventory records maintained with respect to raw materials and supplies, work in process, and finished stock?
93. If no, should they be?
94. Are inventory records maintained on bins or in stock areas?
95. If no, should they be?
96. If yes, is it necessary that they be?
97. Are all inventory items ordered, stored, issued, and controlled on the same basis?
98. If yes, does it appear that the inexpensive items are incurring excessive clerical and handling costs?
99. Are security measures that effectively control pilferage of expensive items in force?
100. Are material items properly identified by part number?
101. Are vendors' counts double-checked by the receiving department?
102. Are prepackaged cartons for simplifying counts and materials handling being used?
103. Does the company have adequate storage facilities?
104. Does the company carry varieties of stocks that lend themselves to standardization?
105. Is any kind of value engineering being practiced or being planned?
106. Is there any evidence of an excessive accumulation of material, that is, material awaiting repair, rework, or return to vendors?
107. Do inventory records appear to serve a useful purpose beyond accounting; for example, are they used for purchasing materials or for scheduling production?
108. Are perpetual inventory records checked by physical inventories at least once each year?
109. If yes, does the system lend itself to cycle counts?
110. If yes, are adjustments to the records made immediately?
111. If yes to Question 110, are such physical counts taken by employees independently of managers and those responsible for maintaining perpetual records?
112. Is there written approval by a responsible employee of adjustments made to perpetual records based upon physical inventories? How much was the last adjustment? What was done about it? Indicate in notes.
113. Does the system include provision for periodical reporting to a responsible employee of slow-moving items, obsolete items, and overstocks? List in notes the action taken in last six months.
114. Are the following classes of inventories under accounting control: (a) consignments out, (b) materials in hands of suppliers, processors, and so forth, (c) merchandise shipped on memorandum, (d) consignments in?
115. Is merchandise on hand that is not the property of the company (customers' merchandise, consignments in, and so forth) physically segregated, clearly marked, and under accounting control?

116. At year-end inventories, are adequate written instructions prepared for guidance of participating employees?
117. At year-end inventories, are the following steps checked on a sample basis: quantity determinations, summarization of quantities, unit conversions, prices used, extensions, additions, and summarizations of detailed sheets?
118. Are records kept for manufactured parts in subassemblies? Do the records appear justified?
119. Is there a cycle-counting program in effect? Describe in notes.
120. Are nonproductive issues to cover scrap, shrinkage, replacement, service, engineering, maintenance, and the like properly reported and classified for accounting purposes?
121. Are selective controls that distinguish the relative values of the items, according to the usage value of the material, in use?
122. Are there any duplications of perpetual inventory records in the company organization? Has their value to the company been reviewed?
123. Are unnecessary entries, such as purchase order date, included with perpetual inventories?
124. Is there effective control over the accumulation of scrap?
125. Has the overall inventory been reconciled? For example,

Beginning inventory (at cost)		xxx
Purchases		xxx
Total available		xxx
Less sales (at cost)	xxx	
Less scrap (at cost)	xxx	(xxx)
Ending inventory		xxx

126. Has the effect of local personal property taxes been considered in the storage of inventory?
127. Does the company know the cost of maintaining inventory records (personnel, space, data processing)? If yes, how much is the cost?
128. If inventories vary substantially over the year, is a reporting form of insurance coverage used?
129. If no, could it be used?
130. Does the company know the cost of maintaining inventory (space, taxes, interest, insurance, personnel, obsolescence)?

MAINTENANCE

1. Does the company have enough facilities and equipment to warrant a formal maintenance program? If no, go to next section.
2. If yes, is there a formalized in-house maintenance program?
3. If no, does it appear that such a program could pay for itself?

4. Is control of the maintenance program in the hands of one person who has it as a prime responsibility?
5. Does the maintenance program provide servicing on a planned basis; that is, is maintenance performed in a timely manner to prevent breakdowns?
6. Are maintenance, labor, and material expenses charged directly to the production departments in which the work is performed to yield a basis of functional accountability for maintenance expenses?
7. Is the production department encouraged to report impending problems and otherwise cooperate with maintenance?
8. Are reports from production of impending problems given high priority and quickly followed up?

Information

9. Can maintenance requisition and receive engineering assistance on any problem in a reasonable period of time?
10. Have the items of equipment in the plant that require scheduled maintenance—including motors, machinery, controls, scales, structures, materials handling equipment, plant services, and lighting—been identified?
11. Have work content and frequency of each maintenance job been determined on an economic basis to avoid overmaintenance?
12. Are frequencies and work content of maintenance jobs encompassed in a comprehensive control system that insures job scheduling as specified?
13. Are equipment maintenance histories kept?
14. If yes, are the costs and elapsed times of maintenance tasks accumulated and used to set up standards by which maintenance productivity can be measured?
15. If yes, are the standards used?
16. Are repair costs for individual machines summarized for periodic review to make possible economic justification for machine replacement?
17. Are maintenance men allowed to keep their own time records without verification by timekeepers or supervisors (thereby making it impossible to discover idle time or job loading)?
18. Do maintenance men complete any checklist or similar device that can be reviewed to assure that all necessary work has been undertaken by the person assigned at the quality level desired?
19. Is expense of maintenance that is performed by company personnel evaluated against the cost of and other factors in having the maintenance done by outside contractors?
20. Is a systematic program to apply the latest and best lubrication technology, methods, and so on to the plant in effect?
21. Is plant lubrication properly controlled by means of periodic checklists, reports, or other control devices?
22. Are potential problems (imminent damage or breakdown) promptly reported as a result of preventive maintenance inspections?

23. Are the frequencies of preventive maintenance inspection or jobs determined by factual, technical, and economic analysis?
24. Are breakdown reports analyzed for the detection of failure patterns that can be corrected by adjustments in the preventive maintenance program?
25. Are backlog records and work load balances accurate enough to be used in the making of priority, contract, and overtime decisions?
26. Are corrosion, fatigue, wear, and erosion rates throughout the plant being completely and effectively studied?
27. Does maintenance—through analysis of preventive maintenance records, repair histories, inspection reports, or other means—routinely contribute information on production capacity for use in production or process planning?
28. Are the various types of preventive maintenance work identified in the cost-reporting system to permit routine analysis of preventive maintenance as a separate category of expense?
29. Is there a daily force report to show the disposition of the maintenance men according to kind of work and area to which the men have been assigned?
30. Is overtime less than 5 percent of the total?
31. Does maintenance management regularly attend and contribute to plant operating and planning meetings?
32. Are labor and material charges accumulated to individual work orders by accounting and are reports made to maintenance and others affected by the comparison of actual cost with estimated cost?
33. Is an up-to-date equipment record file kept in the maintenance department?
34. Are significant details of maintenance and repair work routinely entered in the equipment record to provide a factual basis for decision?
35. Does the maintenance department operate under a budget system based on a projection of workload and productivity objectives?
36. Does accounting, at regular intervals, compare actual maintenance with budgeted cost and show variances?
37. Is maintenance routinely supplied with current and suitably detailed job cost information?
38. Is the percentage of actual hours worked on planned work compared with total hours planned?
39. Is the percentage of plant down time for maintenance reasons less than 10 percent?
40. Have written instructions that cover purchasing, inventory, and stores procedures been prepared and distributed?
41. Are usage records employed to determine stock order points and order quantities?
42. Does the operating department recognize the problems of efficient maintenance performance and cooperate in overcoming them?
43. Does the operating department have to justify, on a review basis, the amount of emergency work incurred?

44. Does the operating department have to justify the need for overtime prior to its use?
45. Is the operating department responsive to suggestions from maintenance that would lead to reductions in maintenance work through changes in operating procedure?
46. If departments other than maintenance are charged with inspection responsibility, does maintenance routinely receive copies of inspection reports?
47. Do all work orders require operating approval before work is done?
48. Are all work orders screened to determine whether engineering attention is required?
49. Does maintenance management contribute to labor contract negotiation planning?
50. Is maintenance management a party to contract negotiations regardless of who actually conducts the negotiations?
51. Are jurisdictional agreements clear, unambiguous, and adjusted to current plant needs?
52. Is the measurement of productive effort a recognized right of management?
53. Are all grievances steered through the maintenance department before industrial relations is involved?
54. Are industrial relations policies and activities directed toward protection of management's position?
55. Who has final say about policy on hires, fires, promotions, and demotions within the maintenance department?
56. Are maintenance supervisors properly trained and instructed in dealing with the bargaining unit?

Planning

57. Has the operating department accepted the necessity for planning and scheduling?
58. Is emergency and No. 1 priority work 25 percent or less of the total?
59. Is 85 to 90 percent of all the maintenance work that is done planned and scheduled?
60. Is every job in progress reviewed against the schedule every day?
61. Are shutdowns or other major projects planned sufficiently far in advance to permit allocating manpower, materials, and tools?
62. Is the concept of planning fully accepted by maintenance supervision?
63. Do maintenance supervisors make every effort to follow the schedules?
64. Once recurring problems are identified, are they turned over to specialists for correction?
65. Are maintenance schedules that involve production equipment agreed upon in advance?
66. Are starting and completion dates, or equivalent priority classification, published in schedules?
67. Are vacation schedules determined in keeping with maintenance planning and known peak loads?

Controls

68. Are more than 25 percent of the mechanics who are assigned to areas or production departments assigned to standing or open labor accounts (which would indicate control of routine repair work at its source)?

69. Are checklists covering lubrication, scheduled overhauls, hydrostatic tests, safety valve inspections, and so on used in guiding preventive maintenance craftsmen?

70. Are preventive maintenance inspections required in separate or blanket form orders, that is, by machine, groups of machines, equipment, or department?

71. Are the selection and application of paints and other industrial coatings under the control of the preventive maintenance engineer (or his equivalent)?

72. Is the performance of preventive maintenance jobs inspected on a random sample basis by maintenance supervisors?

73. Is a work order system that requires written orders for all types of maintenance as well as construction work in effect?

74. Is 80 percent or better of all maintenance and construction work covered by the work order system?

75. Is each job checked for necessity and correctness before the work is scheduled?

76. If yes, is each job, after it is checked, analyzed and broken down into job steps and labor requirements?

77. Does the work order system cover shop and outside fabrication work?

78. Are closed work orders or other maintenance cost reports analyzed to spot recurring maintenance problems?

79. Are causes for deviation from schedules and variance from estimates determined and followed up?

80. Do foremen inspect each job as it is completed?

81. Are there established standards that outline the specifications of jobs that are to be routinely costed as to labor and materials?

82. Are estimates of both labor and material costs actually made for maintenance jobs?

83. Are authorities spelled out for approving work in various cost categories? That is, are maximum cost approval levels set and are approval authorities specified?

84. Are cost estimates submitted to the approving authority before work actually commences?

85. Does the maintenance department operate under a budget system based on projection of workload and productivity objectives?

86. Is there a staff group or other specific assignment of responsibility for cost reduction and methods improvement studies?

87. Are maintenance costs charged to the departments or cost centers that benefit directly from the incurred expense?

88. Is control over the letting of maintenance work contracts vested in the maintenance department?

89. Are maintenance productivity studies periodically or ever made?
90. Have work standards based on time study, work sampling, or methods study been developed?
91. If yes, are the standards employed in the planning and scheduling of maintenance work?
92. Is continuing effort to improve productivity through improvements in maintenance tooling and equipment under way?
93. Have supervisors been given basic training in principles of work simplification and other appropriate industrial engineering techniques?
94. Are order points and order quantities calculated on an economic basis?
95. Does purchasing make material or equipment substitutions without consulting maintenance?
96. Is maintenance allowed to specify individual manufacturers or suppliers as it deems necessary?
97. Is maintenance allowed to specify method of shipment as it deems necessary?
98. Does purchasing routinely follow up and expedite purchase orders?
99. Does purchasing expedite when requested?
100. Does purchasing notify maintenance of any change in original commitments?
101. Is maintenance permitted to make direct purchases locally?
102. Is maintenance permitted to contract work to local shops with purchasing cooperation?
103. Can transfer of repair work to local shops or the employment of maintenance contractors be freely made (without labor contract restriction)?
104. Is parts inventory activity systematically recorded and reported to maintenance and jointly used by purchasing and maintenance in managing inventory?
105. Is maintenance regularly consulted on the setting of minimums and maximums on all stock items?
106. Does stores report to and discuss with maintenance items that show zero activity in 12-month periods?
107. Can stores remove a maintenance item from stock category without maintenance agreement?
108. Does stores accept less than unit quantities for credit?
109. Are reclaimed items returned to stores' custody accepted as equivalent of new?
110. Are tools and maintenance supplies properly located and controlled by authorized personnel?
111. Is a tool check or similar system used to check maintenance tools in or out of the crib?
112. Are substores, under control of stores, located close to point of use for low-value, fast-moving items?
113. Is there an established review procedure to decide on obsolescence, scrap, and excess quantities?

114. Are inventory dollar values readily available and are they routinely used in material management decisions?
115. Is there an established spares program containing review provisions?
116. Are studies periodically made of stock outages to keep tabs on levels and trends?
117. Are personal hand tool requirements (whether personally or company owned) established for craftsmen and are tool boxes periodically inspected?
118. Is the cost of processing a purchase order known?

Personnel and Organization

119. Are the maintenance department's manning charts based on actual or level work loads rather than hypothetical or peak work loads to avoid idle maintenance labor or make-work projects?
120. Is there a continuing effort to train production personnel to operate equipment properly and to avoid unnecessary damage, wear, and repairs?
121. Is the responsibility for auditing, design, and execution of the preventive maintenance program formally delegated?
122. Are consistent and sincere efforts made to employ craftsmen in work that matches their pay grade and skill classification?
123. Are salaries and other rewards sufficient to retain and motivate competent maintenance management?
124. Are appraisals made of supervisory performance?
125. Are provisions for staff functions (planners, engineers, technicians, and so forth) adequate?
126. Is the number of organizational levels at the required minimum?
127. What is the ratio of hourly maintenance workers to maintenance supervisors (including administrative personnel, staff technical, and maintenance superintendent)?
128. What is the ratio of hourly production workers to direct supervisors? (Consider only those supervisors working in direct contact with hourly personnel.)
129. Are the maintenance forces assigned to dark and weekend shifts sized to cover emergency work only?
130. Is there a formal program covering the indoctrination and training of new maintenance employees?
131. Is an effective formal or informal suggestion system for hourly workers, supported by some type of incentive program, in effect?
132. If yes, are the suggestions received acted upon or are reasons for not acting upon them quickly given to the authors?
133. Is maintenance planning and scheduling a formal and disciplined operation with one person in charge?
134. Are capital additions and changes in plant layout and design subject to maintenance review prior to final approval?
135. Are machine and process equipment modification designs subject to maintenance review prior to final approval?
136. Is a materials, equipment, and spare parts standardization program in effect?

137. Are there in the plant long-standing high-cost maintenance situations that indicate unsolved engineering problems?
138. Do foremen have adequate disciplinary authority?
139. Are all disciplinary decisions reviewed at the next higher echelon before they are executed?
140. Does each foreman select men for his crew, and can he get rid of a man who is not pulling his weight?
141. Are there too many hourly labor classifications (such as special job rates, first-, second-, and third-class mechanic rates, and multiple helper rates) that make work assignments rigid and costly?
142. Is maintenance of a high and uniform craft skill level handicapped by contractual or past-practice problems such as job bidding, automatic upgrading, absence of definitive qualification tests, or prohibited hiring of journeymen?
143. Are meetings regularly held by supervisors to focus attention on corporate, departmental, and safety policies and regulations?
144. Are maintenance supervisors brought together for refresher sessions on corporation, departmental, and safety policies and regulations and involvement in general policies for improvement?
145. Are new and substitute materials constantly being sought against plant requirements?

ACCOUNTING

Cash and Currency

Note: If cash receipts are not significant, skip this section.

1. Is the mail opened by someone other than the cashier or accounts receivable bookkeeper?
2. Does the company use a lock-box system?
3. Is the mail distributed by someone other than the person who opens it?
4. Is a record of the money and checks received prepared by anyone?
5. If yes, is the record prepared by someone other than the person who opens the mail?
6. If yes, is the record given to someone other than the cashier for verification of the amounts recorded and deposited?
7. Does the person who prepares the bank deposits also have anything to do with customers' ledgers?
8. Are deposits made by mail?
9. If no, are deposits made by messenger?
10. Is it company policy to have receipts deposited in the bank and recorded in the cash receipts books daily? If no, record in notes the frequency of doing so.

11. If deposits and record of deposit are not made daily, does the frequency of deposits seem reasonable? If no, state in notes the evidence for that conclusion.

12. Are receipts deposited intact (that is, as received) and without delay? If no, describe exceptions to that practice in notes.

13. Does the company obtain duplicate deposit tickets after authentication by the bank? If yes, describe in notes how they are received.

14. Are authenticated deposit tickets received by an employee who is independent of the cashier and of the person who makes the deposits?

15. Are authenticated deposit tickets compared with the record of incoming remittances and the cash book?

16. Are deposits or collection items charged back by the bank (because of insufficient funds and so forth) delivered directly to an employee other than the cashier?

17. If cash registers, counter sales slips, collectors' receipts, and so forth function as proofs of cash receipts, are such proofs checked by someone other than the cashier?

18. Are sales tickets prenumbered and made out in duplicate or triplicate?

19. If cash registers are used, is each sales clerk assigned his own machine, is the machine cleared by a responsible officer, and is access to locking mechanisms of registers withheld from sales clerks? If no, describe exceptions in notes.

20. If a responsible officer clears cash registers, does he do so at least twice a day? If no, what is the frequency? _____

21. Are receipts for sundries such as rents and cash sales clearly accounted for?

22. Are postdated checks recorded on the books as received? If no, describe procedure in notes.

23. Are postdated checks held in safekeeping until deposited?

24. Does the company receive a large volume of remittances daily? If yes, what is the average daily number? _____

25. Is a high percentage of remittances in the form of currency? If yes, what is the approximate percentage? _____

26. Are remittances often in high dollar amounts, such as above $1,000?

27. Is there an established method for handling C.O.D.'s?

28. Are C.O.D. receivable records kept independently of the shipping department?

29. Are collection items charged back by bank paid by cash and not charged back on bank statement?

30. Are negotiable assets other than currency, checks, or drafts in the custody of an employee other than and independent of the cashier?

31. Is the cashier responsible for cash receipts from the time they are received in his office until they are deposited in the bank? If no, state in notes who, if anyone, is responsible.

32. Do company rules require that branch office collections be deposited in a local bank account subject only to home office withdrawal? If no, describe arrangement(s) in notes.

33. If yes, are branch deposit slip duplicates mailed directly by the bank to the home office?

34. If yes, are the duplicate deposit slips compared in detail with advices from the branch office?

35. Is there a formal procedure for handling unsatisfactory remittances—for example, those drawn with excessive discount deductions? If yes, compare in notes the cost of handling exceptions to dollars lost.

36. If there are customers' ledgers, are they and the monthly statements inaccessible to the cashier?

37. Does the cashier have duties in addition to keeping the cash records? If yes, list them in notes.

38. Are the cash receipts book totals footed at least monthly? If no, state in notes at what frequency.

39. Are all bank accounts authorized by the board of directors?

40. If the company uses more than two bank accounts (general and payroll), what is the purpose of the other account or accounts?

41. Have instructions been issued to the bank not to cash checks payable to the company and to accept them for deposit only? List below names of parties authorized to sign checks.

| | | Date of Minutes |
Name	Title	Authorizing Signature

42. Is countersignature on checks required? If yes, list names of parties authorized to countersign checks.

Name	Title

43. Do countersignatures serve a valid purpose?

44. Are there different signatories for different accounts? Comment in notes on the need.

45. Is a check register prepared by a mechanical device simultaneously with the preparation of the check?

46. Is a check protector used?

47. Are authorized signatures limited to employees who have no access to accounting records, cash receipts, or petty cash funds?

48. Is it the company's policy to have vouchers and supporting documents presented simultaneously with checks for signature?
49. If yes, are they approved by responsible officials of the company?
50. If yes, are such vouchers and supporting data effectively canceled after related checks have been signed to preclude duplicate payment?
51. Are signed checks mailed without returning them to the one who prepared them?
52. Are cashiers forbidden to cash checks or to make advances to employees from cash funds?
53. Is the signing or countersigning of checks in advance prohibited?
54. Does the company have instructions relative to cashing of company checks? If yes, attach a copy of the instructions.
55. Are prenumbered checks used?
56. Have you examined some of the checkbook or check sets to ascertain whether spoiled or voided checks are accounted for?
57. Are bank reconciliations made by someone who had nothing to do with the cash procedures, including the signing of checks?
58. If yes, does the same person obtain the bank statements directly from the banks?
59. Is the practice of examining paid checks for date, name, check number, cancellations, and endorsements followed by those who reconcile bank statements?
60. If a mechanical check signer is used, is the signature die under control?
61. If yes, are there other controls to prevent misuse of the check signer? Mention them in notes.
62. Is the practice of drawing checks to "cash" prohibited?
63. Is there adequate control of old outstanding checks?

Cash Management

64. Is size of demand deposits excessive in line with cash needs? Give method of determining answer in notes.
65. Does the company use the float of outstanding checks in determining cash needs?
66. Are cash needs projected annually for shorter periods?
67. Is excess cash used for short-term investments?

Inventories

68. Are cost records tied to the financial accounts?
69. Are perpetual inventory records maintained with respect to raw materials and supplies, work in process, and finished stock?
70. Is inventory on the retail method; that is, are records of goods in stock maintained by cost and also retail prices?
71. Is there a unit control of high-value items?
72. Are all material purchases delivered to central stores as opposed to direct delivery to production units?

73. If yes, are the stores records maintained by employees functionally independent of the storekeepers? (Whenever possible, the physical and accounting controls of an item should be separate.)

74. Are perpetual inventory records checked by physical inventories at least once a year?

75. If yes, are such physical counts taken by employees who are independent of storekeepers and those responsible for maintaining perpetual records?

76. Are discrepancies between stores records and physical inventories promptly investigated, particularly with regard to continued differences in the same items and/or differences of a material nature?

77. Is there written approval by a responsible employee of adjustments made to perpetual records based upon physical inventories?

78. If yes, does the system include provision for periodical reporting to a responsible employee of slow-moving items, obsolete items, and overstocks? Show in notes which are not.

79. Are the following classes of inventories under accounting control: (a) consignments, (b) material in the hands of suppliers, processors, and so on, (c) materials or merchandise in warehouses, (d) merchandise shipped on memorandum? Show which are not in notes.

80. Is merchandise on hand that is not the property of the company, such as customers' merchandise and consignments-in, physically segregated and under accounting control?

81. As to year-end inventories, are written instructions prepared for the guidance of participating employees?

82. Are the following steps double-checked: quantity determinations, summarization of quantities, unit conversions, prices used, extensions, additions, and summarizations of detailed sheets?

83. Is there control over the accumulation and sale of scrap?

84. Is insurance adequate with respect to inventory wherever located?

Petty Cash

85. Is the imprest fund system used?

86. If no, does it appear that such a system could be used advantageously?

87. If yes, supply the following information about each imprest or petty cash fund:

Amount	Name and Title of Custodian	Is All on Hand or Part in Bank?	Who Signs Fund Bank?	Checks on Account?
_____	_____	_____	_____	_____
_____	_____	_____	_____	_____
_____	_____	_____	_____	_____
_____	_____	_____	_____	_____

88. Is responsibility for each fund vested in only one person?
89. Is there a responsible alternate to cover during absences and vacation?
90. Is the custodian independent of the cashier and other employees who handle remittances from customers and other receipts?
91. Are the accounting records inaccessible to the custodian?
92. Does the custodian obtain formal vouchers for all disbursements made from the fund?
93. If yes, are such vouchers executed in ink or in some other manner that would make alterations difficult?
94. Are the amounts of such vouchers spelled out as well as written in numerals?
95. Are the vouchers approved by a department head or some equivalent employee?
96. Is it required that approval be given before payment is made?
97. Are reimbursement vouchers and attachments canceled at or immediately following the signing of the reimbursing check so that they cannot be misused thereafter?
98. Are funds audited by surprise counts by an internal auditor or other independent persons?
99. If yes, how often?
100. If the imprest fund is represented in whole or in part by a bank account, has the bank been notified that no checks from outsiders, payable to the company, should be accepted for deposit?
101. Are petty cash funds restricted as to amount not exceeding requirements for disbursements for a period of two weeks or less?
102. Are petty cash expenditures limited to a specified amount?
103. Is an internal audit of reimbursement voucher and attachments made before reimbursement?
104. Are the petty cash custodians properly bonded?

Notes Receivable

105. Are notes receivable periodically confirmed with customers by company?
106. Are notes and renewals authorized by a responsible executive?
107. Is the custodian of notes independent of the cashier and bookkeepers?
108. Is negotiable collateral, if any, in custody of an employee other than the cashier or the person who maintains applicable accounting records?
109. Is someone charged with responsibility for seeing that the total of notes on hand agrees with the customer accounts? Does the system provide for this being done regularly? If yes, how often?_____

Accounts Receivable

110. Are accounts independently confirmed by company personnel with customers?
111. If yes, are they confirmed in total or sampled?_____

112. Is the management of the credit department completely divorced from the sales department?
113. What is the annual cost of operating the credit department? $_____
114. What is the percentage of sales cost of the credit department compared with industry standards?
115. Are routine audit decisions handled by clerical level personnel?
116. Is there a credit policy?
117. Are bad debts so low as to suggest lost sales because of a restrictive credit policy?
118. Does the person who prepares sales invoices have access to cash?
119. Are the reasons for items being returned examined as a symptom of operational weakness?
120. Are allowances for discounts in violation of regular terms of sale specifically authorized by a responsible official?
121. Does a responsible official approve returns and allowances and other credits, including discounts to customers?
122. Are credit memoranda under numerical control?
123. Are officials approving credits under 120 and 121 denied access to cash?
124. Are disputed items handled by someone other than accounts receivable bookkeepers?
125. Is approval of the credit department a prerequisite to payment of customer credit balances?
126. Are the duties of the accounts receivable bookkeeper separate from any cash functions?
127. Is it the company's policy to have monthly statements sent to all customers?
128. If yes, does that appear to be necessary except as an audit procedure? (Many companies pay by invoice rather than statement.)
129. If yes, are statements independently checked to account balances and kept under control to insure their being mailed by someone other than the accounts receivable bookkeeper?
130. Are customers' accounts balanced with controlling account?
131. If yes, does the system provide for that being done regularly? If yes, how often?_____
132. If customers' accounts are balanced with control accounts, is the balancing done by someone who does not handle the accounts receivable records?
133. Are delinquent accounts periodically reviewed by an officer? If yes, how often?_____
134. Is there a regular policy of converting accounts receivable into notes receivable? If there is more than one accounts receivable bookkeeper, are the account sections for which the bookkeepers are responsible changed from time to time?
135. Are cash postings made simultaneously with the posting of the cash receipts records by means of a machine bookkeeping device?
136. Is the collection department independent of the accounts receivable bookkeepers?

137. If yes, does the collection department constitute a check on accounts receivable bookkeepers?
138. Is it company policy to require approval by responsible officials of accounts written off?
139. Is control exercised over bad debts after they have been written off? If yes, describe the control in notes.
140. If the accounts receivable are factored, is there control over the forwarding of accounts and money?
141. How many days of sales are represented by the receivables? (Divide annual sales by 365 and divide answer into accounts receivable.)
142. What is the trend of days of sales compared with that of the industry and with the company's own history?
143. Is the proportion of accounts receivable due in 30, 60, and 90 days followed for change in aging?

Sales

144. Are customers' orders subjected to review and approval before acceptance by sales, order department, or credit department?
145. Where do instructions for shipment of sales originate?
146. Does the system provide that all shipping records be checked against billing?
147. Are shipping advices prenumbered?
148. Are sales invoices prenumbered?
149. Does the system require accounting for all invoice numbers?
150. Are invoices checked for accuracy of quantities billed, prices used, and extensions and terms?
151. If yes, has the cost of the checking been compared with the error found? (Consider customer audit of errors *against* company as signal.)
152. Are invoices compared with the customers' orders?
153. Are returned items cleared through the receiving department?
154. Are invoices summarized and classified by a department other than the accounting department in a manner to provide a check on recorded sales?
155. Are sales to employees, scrap-and-waste sales, sales of equipment, C.O.D. sales, and cash sales cleared and recorded in the same manner as sales to customers? If the answer to any of the above is no, describe the method of control in notes.
156. Can units of sales be correlated with units of purchases (or production and inventories)?
157. Is there a check on freight allowances?

Investment Securities

158. If securities are kept in the office, who is the custodian?
159. Are securities kept under lock and key?
160. Who has access besides the custodian to securities?
161. Are the securities kept in a safe deposit vault?

162. If yes, is it necessary for more than one person to be present to open the box?
163. If yes, are the persons independent of record keeping?
164. Are securities periodically inspected? If yes, how often?_____
165. Is a record kept by anyone in the accounting department of each security, including certificate numbers? If yes, by whom?_____
166. If securities are held by a bank or broker, are the statements from them regularly checked against accounting records?
167. If yes, how often?_____
168. Are purchases and sales of securities authorized by an officer or the board of directors?
169. Are securities held for others or as collateral recorded and segregated?
170. Are securities that have been written off or for which a full reserve has been provided followed up as to possible realization?
171. If securities are held by a custodian (such as a bank), is a record kept of coupon clipping and receipt of interest and collection of dividends?
172. If securities account is in nominee's name, is the company getting credit for the income to which it is entitled?
173. In connecton with a nominee or custodian account, check to see whether there is a related cash account into which are deposited income and proceeds of the securities.
174. Is the income from securities checked against an independent security list?
175. Are market values checked to determine the unrealized short- and long-term gain-loss position? (The greater the significance of investment securities, the more frequent the check.)
176. Is the yield from investment securities regularly computed and compared with standards such as Dow Jones?

Property, Plant, and Equipment

177. Are plant ledgers maintained?
178. If yes, are they balanced at least annually with general ledger controls?
179. Are capital expenditures over a certain amount preauthorized by the board of directors or some authoritative management group? If yes, over what amount?_____
180. If yes to Question 179, are actual expenditures later compared with the authorized estimates?
181. If capital expenditures are not preauthorized, are actual expenditures approved by the board of directors or one or more officers?
182. Is approval necessary to scrap items?
183. Is a periodic inventory of plant items taken?
184. Have periodic appraisals been made for insurance purposes?
185. Is there adequate security to protect the physical plant?
186. Are retirements reported in a routine manner that provides reasonable assurance that they will be treated properly in the accounts?

Questionnaires

187. Would the company benefit from long-term mortgage financing, using the plant as collateral?
188. In the past two years has the company reviewed the advisability of sale and leaseback of property, plant, and equipment to obtain additional cash?
189. Are physical inventories taken of movable equipment and tools?
190. Is approval necessary to scrap material items?
191. Does the company take periodic inventory of plant items?
192. Are periodic appraisals made of structure and plant items for insurance purposes?
193. Does the company have a well-defined policy to govern accounting for capital additions as opposed to maintenance and repairs? (Example: A company doing $10 million in sales might expense all items under $500.)
194. Is control of scrapped items maintained to insure reporting of sales thereof? (Control is difficult unless plant and equipment items are permanently tagged.)
195. Is a system for the safeguarding of small tools in effect? (Possible approaches are dollar limits per employee or per weight or quantity of material processed and requiring old tools to be turned in to get new.)
196. Are depreciation policies reviewed at least annually?

Notes and Accounts Payable

197. Are borrowings authorized by the board of directors?
198. Are the banks from which funds may be borrowed specifically mentioned in the minutes?
199. Are the officers who are empowered to borrow specifically named in the minutes or bylaws?
200. Are creditors' accounts balanced with the controlling account?
201. If yes, is that done regularly? If yes, how often? _____
202. Are statements from vendors regularly compared with recorded liabilities?
203. Are special adjustments of recorded accounts payable required to be supported by executive approval?
204. Are debit balances handled by the credit department?
205. Does the company independently test-confirm balances of notes and amounts payable?

Capital Stock

206. Does the company employ independent registrar and transfer agents?
207. If no, are unissued certificates and stock certificate stubs in the custody of an officer?
208. Are surrendered certificates effectively canceled?
209. Does the company employ independent dividend-paying agents?
210. If no, is control exercised in preparing, mailing, and accounting for unclaimed dividend checks?

Payroll

211. Is preparation of payroll distributed among a number of employees?
212. Is payroll approved by someone in authority?
213. Are unpaid employees' checks under control?
214. Are clerical operations in preparation of payrolls double-checked before payment? (Need they be? A costly operation if no collusion exists or other controls can be used. Sample-test or use employees as auditors; company will hear if error has been made against employee.)
215. Are the duties of those preparing the payroll rotated?
216. Is it the policy of the company to have the envelopes distributed occasionally by someone other than the personnel who usually do so?
217. Is the original salary rate authorized in writing by someone in authority?
218. Are all changes in rates, additions, and dismissals authorized in writing?
219. Would a service bureau offer efficiency, backup, or cost savings?
220. Is the time record made on time clocks?
221. Are time tickets checked against or compared with production schedules or payroll distribution?
222. Do foremen sign the weekly payroll sheets?
223. Are employees paid by check?
224. If yes, are the checks prenumbered?
225. Are bank checks secured and controlled?
226. Are payroll checks signed by employees who do not participate in the preparation of the payroll, custodianship of cash funds, or maintenance of accounting records?
227. Are payroll disbursements made from an imprest bank account restricted to that purpose? (See end of section.)
228. Are checks written on machines with automatic totals?
229. If checks are used, is the bank payroll account regularly reconciled?
230. If yes, are the duties of the employees who reconcile the account unrelated to the payroll department?
231. If the payroll is in cash, are receipts obtained from employees?
232. Does the company have an independent pay agent—armored car or other service?
233. If no, are paymasters rotated at varying intervals; are paymasters' functions independent of payroll preparation; and is the paymaster accompanied by a person who has nothing to do with the preparation of payroll?
234. Does procedure followed when payroll bank accounts are reconciled include the checking of names on payroll checks against payroll records and the examination of endorsements on checks? (State no if person who prepares payroll has access to cash or if person who disburses payroll has access to cash.)

Questionnaires

235. Are footings in payroll journal checked to pick up excess footings that might conceal fraudulent entries?
236. Consider using two or three imprest bank accounts for payroll. Use account 1 for the first pay period, account 2 for the second, and account 3 for the third. Deposit into each account only the exact amount of the net payroll. Normally, by the end of the third period the first account will be in balance, which will obviate the need to reconcile it.

General

237. Are accounting manuals in use?
238. Is the accounting department function completely divorced from sales, manufacturing, purchasing, cash receipts, and disbursements and insurance?
239. Does the company have a controller and an internal auditor?
240. Does the internal auditor report to the controller?
241. Are employees' duties rotated in sensitive areas?
242. Are all employees required to take vacations?
243. Are known relatives among employees so employed as to make collusion improbable?
244. Are the books of account adequate for the business?
245. If yes, are they kept up to date?
246. If yes, are they balanced at least monthly?
247. Do internal reports to the operating management appear to be prepared in a manner to highlight unusual variations in operating and other figures?
248. Are the major expenses and costs under budgetary control?
249. Does some responsible employee periodically review insurance coverage?
250. Are journal vouchers approved by a responsible employee?
251. Are journal vouchers or entries in the journal adequately explained or supported by substantiating data?
252. Is accounting control exercised over branch operations? (State no if there are any branch officials who also are executives of other business enterprises, other than known affiliates, with which the client does business. State no if there are any bank accounts in the name of the corporation or employees' branch associations that are not recorded on the books.)
253. Are all employees in positions of trust bonded? If yes, by how much? $_____

APPENDIX

HONEYWELL INC.
CORPORATE OPERATIONAL AUDIT
GENERAL QUESTIONNAIRE

Division _____   Date Prepared _____

Location _____   Date Received _____

Auditor Preparing Questionnaire   Received by _____

_____   _____

INDEX

Note: For questions pertaining to other items such as professional activities, accountability, relations with other departments, reference materials,
and special programs and activities, see the specific subject questionnaire.

Initial Issue 2/1/68

MANAGEMENT CONTROL—A CONCEPT

This questionnaire deals with the concept of management control. Our intent is to develop a questionnaire that can be used in an audit of any department (such as Purchasing, Accounts Payable, Production Control, etc.) regardless of its role in the organization.

Since management control is a concept, its definition has been the subject of much thought. Many points of view have emerged. Most authorities agree, however, that it concerns the processes of administration which are:
1. Setting objectives
2. Planning
3. Organizing
4. Controlling
Each of these processes can be defined.

Setting Objectives
Objectives are precise end results to be accomplished. They should describe the goal precisely and locate it in time, place, and number. They must be classified according to importance (i.e., "musts" and "wants") and must conform with overall company and divisional objectives.

Planning
Planning is an outline, a draft, a map, a scheme, etc. for making, doing, or arranging something. It is the key to getting results. Without planning such things as good concepts, good procedures, good instructions, etc. have no lasting effect. Any results are almost accidental.

Organizing
Organizing is arranging, establishing, instituting, bringing into being—it is the classification of activities of a group of individuals united in working towards a common goal. Its purpose is to achieve the most effective utilization of available resources. It involves structuring the organization to reflect the flow of work and the need for cooperative effort between individuals, groups, departments, functions, etc. It involves staffing the positions with qualified people. It involves establishing clear lines of authority and responsibility.

Controlling
Controlling is verifying whether everything occurs in conformity with the plan adopted, the instructions issued, and principles established. Its purpose is to point out weaknesses and errors in order to correct them and prevent recurrence. It includes the establishment of standards, the measurement of performance, and the correction of deviations. To be effective controlling requires as a minimum, the following:
1. Identifying key factors to be controlled to achieve results.
2. Specifying the basis for establishing standards of performance.
3. Defining the information that must be accumulated to measure performance.
4. Establishing a reporting structure that identifies performance, relates causes and effects, signals trends, and identifies results by responsibility.

In using this questionnaire, bear in mind that it is simply a guide and *not* a detailed program.

Obviously, there is no clear-cut pattern to be followed in any audit, and in fact, there should not be. This questionnaire has been developed to document key questions that form the basis of the audit. You are encouraged to add questions and modify existing ones.

The questionnaire is divided into two main sections. Section I contains questions directed to the General Manager. It should be used in situations where the audit involves departments reporting directly to him. These same questions can also be directed to a department head when the audit involves, for example, a disbursements audit function.

Section II contains questions directed to the person responsible for the department, function, system, under review and the people reporting to him.

By comparing answers received from several levels of management and by evaluating the various answers received, the audit should get a good and relatively fast insight into how well the department is managed. The verification and final evaluation processes should come much easier if this questionnaire is used properly. *Use it!*

One final word: This questionnaire is to be used along with a *specific* questionnaire, i.e., one that pertains exclusively to the department function under review. Together, the two questionnaires, this one on management controls and the specific one—should serve as the basis for determining the path the auditor will follow during his review.

Be sure to answer all questions!

SECTION I QUESTIONS FOR THE GENERAL MANAGER

	Yes No N/A	Brief Comments and/or W/P Reference
1. Has the role of the department under review been defined in writing?	___	_____
2. Has the role been communicated to other departments?	___	_____
3. Is there mutual agreement between the department manager and yourself concerning the role?	___	_____
4. Has authority been delegated to carry out the role?	___	_____

5. Have you specified how the department's performance is to be measured:

    1—Staying within budget? _____ _____

    2—Recovery of operating costs? _____ _____

    3—Number of people? _____ _____

    4—Feedback from other departments? _____ _____

    5—Personal judgment? _____ _____

    6—Cost savings? _____ _____

    7—Customer complaints? _____ _____

    8—Schedule performance? _____ _____

    9—Accomplishment of objectives? _____ _____

    10— _____ _____

    11— _____ _____

    12— _____ _____

    13— _____ _____

    14— _____ _____

6. Have standards or levels of acceptable performance been established in these areas you have selected in question #5? _____ _____

7. Have department objectives been established in writing? _____ _____

8. Are they classified according to importance (i.e. musts and wants)? _____ _____

9. Are they located in time, place, and number? _____ _____

10. Is accomplishment of objectives reported regularly? _____ _____

11. Is nonaccomplishment reviewed with the department manager (or supervisor):

    Orally? _____ _____

    In Writing? _____ _____

12. Are you satisfied with the department's overall performance? _____ _____

13. Are there any particular areas or problems in the department where you would like us to concentrate our efforts?

14. Have you reviewed and approved the department's annual operating plan? _____ _____

15. Are you receiving regular reports which show accomplishments against that operating plan? _____ _____

16. Have you ever had an audit, survey, or appraisal made of the department's activities? _____ _____

SECTION II QUESTIONS FOR THE DEPARTMENT MANAGER AND SUPERVISION UNDER HIM

	Yes *No* *N/A*	*Brief Comments* *and/or* *W/P Reference*

A. ROLE OF DEPARTMENT (OR FUNCTION)

1. Has the role of the department been defined in writing? _____ _____

2. Does the role specify:
   —function in broad terms? _____ _____

   —major limitations? _____ _____
   —general responsibilities and authority? _____ _____

   —relationships with other units? _____ _____

3. Has the role been communicated to other departments? _____ _____

4. Is there general agreement on the assigned role:
   —between you and your boss? _____ _____
   —between you and your subordinates? _____ _____
   —between you and other managers? _____ _____

B. OBJECTIVES OF THE DEPARTMENT

1. Have departmental objectives been established? _____ _____

    2. Are they in writing?

    3. Are they classified according to importance (i.e., musts and wants)?

    4. Are they located in time, place, and in number?

    5. Is accomplishment reported regularly?

    6. Is nonaccomplishment reviewed with management:

                                     Orally?

                                   In Writing?

C. PLANNING

    1. Does the department have an annual operating plan?
       (a) Does it also have a long-range operating plan?

    2. Are the plans broken down into definable projects?

    3. Do these projects have detailed schedules?

    4. Do all levels of supervision participate in planning?

    5. Is management aware of the plan?

    6. Has management approved the plan?

    7. Are all employees in the department aware of the plan?

    8. Have responsibilities been assigned to carry out the plan?

    9. Is performance against the plan measured?

   10. Are changes in the plan communicated up and down the line?

   11. Are changes in the plan frequent?

      (a) Infrequent?

   12. Does the plan contain units of measure such as costs, number of employees, dates, etc.?

   13. Are reports of progress against the plan ever issued?

D. ORGANIZING

1. Have you or are you having any staffing problems?

2. Are you satisfied with the quality of personnel in the department?

3. Does the department have any formal on-the-job training program?

4. Are outside training courses taken by employees?

5. How is an individual's performance measured:
   —objectives?

   —work measurement?

   —other standards?

6. Do employees know how they are measured?

7. Is performance measured regularly?

8. Is it reviewed with the employee?

9. Are job descriptions written for each position?

10. Are they distributed to employees?

11. Are there adequate advancement opportunities?
    (a) Are they in the department?
    (b) Outside the department? (Determine where)

12. Are employees aware of these opportunities?

13. Has turnover been a problem? (Determine the turnover rate)

14. Have any personnel been promoted out of the department in the last two or three years? (Determine number and percentage)

15. Does the department have formal organization charts?

16. Are they distributed?

17. Do you feel you have an excessive number of people and/or functions reporting to you? (Determine number)

18. Have you changed your organization in the last:
    (a) year? _____ _____

    (b) two years? _____ _____

    (c) three years? _____ _____
19. Has every supervisor or person reporting directly to you been rotated at least once in the past three years? _____ _____

E. CONTROLLING
  1. Policies
     A policy is a guide for carrying out action in order to achieve objectives. It is effective today and thereafter, until it is either replaced or declared invalid. _____ _____
     a. Does the department have written policies? _____ _____
     b. Are they organized in a manual? _____ _____

     c. Are they up-to-date? _____ _____

     d. Are they enforced? _____ _____
     e. Are they distributed to personnel in the department? _____ _____
     f. Are they distributed to other departments? _____ _____

     g. Are they clearly written? _____ _____

     h. Is the format standardized? _____ _____
  2. Procedures
     A procedure is a document that explains the way to proceed and to work and carry out the policies. Procedures minimize the chance for irregularities or improper practices and act as a reference in determining that policies are carried out.
     a. Does the department have written procedures? _____ _____
     b. Are they organized in a manual? _____ _____

     c. Are they up-to-date? _____ _____

d. Are they monitored for compliance?

e. Is a procedure written for all policy statements?

f. Are procedures distributed to department personnel?

g. Is the format standardized?

3. Forms And Files

"Forms" is a general term and it refers to the information and the media used in the formal communication system of the department (with the exception of the reporting structure). It would include such items as purchase orders, invoices, labor tickets, move orders, etc.

"Files" constitute the formal storage of information in a department. It would include filing cabinets, tub files, notebooks, etc., for the purpose of reference.

Forms

(a) Does the department have a forms control program?

(b) Is it consistent with the divisional program?

(c) Does it utilize a system of stock control and replenishment?

(d) Is forms design handled within the department?

Files

(a) Is access to departmental files unrestricted?

(b) Do files document accurately entire transactions in one place?

(c) Are files purged according to a planned records retention program?

(d) Is there a procedure covering records retention?

(e) Does it comply with Company policy?

Appendix

4. Standards of Performance
Control is impaired unless steps are taken to measure results against anticipated standards of performance. These indicators point up situations requiring attention by management and would include forecasts, budgets, standard costs, lead times, inventory levels, etc.
   (a) Has management specified how the department's performance is to be measured?
   (b) Has the information (operating data and statistics) been defined that must be accumulated to measure performance?
   (c) Has a reporting structure been established that identifies performance?
   (d) Are reports:
      —prompt?

      —accurate?

      —concise?

      —impartial?

      —are they *used*?
5. Budgets
   (a) Does the department prepare an annual budget?
   (b) Is it approved by the next level of management?
   (c) Do supervisors participate in budget preparation?
   (d) Are budgets modified when conditions change?
   (e) Are regular reports, showing actual costs and variance, received in the department?
   (f) Are large variances explained?
   (g) Does the budget provide for such things as:
      1) Books and Periodicals?

      2) Reference Materials?

3) Travel? ____ _____

4) Training and Education? ____ _____

5) Membership and Dues? ____ _____

6) Business Meeting Expenses? ____ _____

6. Protective Controls

Protective controls are the various techniques used to safeguard the physical assets of the company. These assets include inventory, furniture and fixtures, cash, machinery and equipment, buildings, accounts receivable, etc.

(a) Are strategic control points identified? ____ _____

(b) Have controls been established for these points? ____ _____

(c) Has work been subdivided so that no employee has complete control over any record or transaction? ____ _____

(d) Are employees rotated from jobs in sensitive positions? ____ _____

(e) Are frequent, unannounced spot checks made of all employee operations in sensitive positions? ____ _____

(f) Is the security system adequate? ____ _____

(g) Has any audit or appraisal ever been made of your department or portions of your activity? ____ _____

(h) If so:
—By the Public Accountants? ____ _____

—By Government auditors? ____ _____

—By survey teams? ____ _____

—By Management? ____ _____

—Other? ____ _____

7. Reporting
   a. Does the department pre-
      pare and issue any written
      reports that are:
      (1) Statistical only?

      (2) Narrative only?
      (3) Statistical and narrative
          combined?
   b. Are these reports issued
      regularly?
   c. Are any of these reports
      "exception-type" only?
   d. On statistical reports, do the
      dollar figures "tie-in" to the
      books?
   e. Are any reports issued on
      unusual items such as over-
      time, overload help, long
      distance phone use, travel,
      etc.?
   f. Are any of the department's
      reports directed specifically
      to:
      (1) Top Management?

      (2) Sales Manager?

      (3) Purchasing Director?

      (4) Advertising Manager?

      (5) Controller

      (6) Production Manager(s)?
      (7) Director of Engineer-
          ing?

      (8) Other (Specify)
   g. Are these reports action-
      type reports?
   h. Are these reports issued for
      information only?
   i. Is there evidence of any
      action being taken as a re-
      sult of issuing these reports?
   j. Does the department pre-
      pare most of its report ma-
      terial by hand, or is it ob-
      tained as a by-product of
      accounting or by an auto-
      mated process?

   k. Does the Controller help you in any way in getting the data for your reports? ____ _____

   l. Does the department receive any reports other than the budget report? ____ _____

   m. Are these reports mostly action-oriented? ____ _____

   n. Do they pertain directly to the operations you are responsible for? ____ _____

   o. Are these reports mostly for information? ____ _____

   p. Could you honestly do without most or all of them? (Determine which ones.) ____ _____

F. FACILITIES, EQUIPMENT, LAYOUT, AND LOCATION

   a. Is the department located near the people it serves and near the people it comes in constant contact with? ____ _____

      (1) Accounting? ____ _____

      (2) Sales? ____ _____

      (3) Purchasing? ____ _____

      (4) Management? ____ _____

      (5) Shipping?
      (6) Order and Customer Service? ____ _____

      (7) Production? ____ _____

      (8) Engineering? ____ _____

      (9) Other (Specify)

   b. Are quarters adequate in terms of:

      (1) Space? ____ _____

      (2) Noise level? ____ _____

      (3) Lighting? ____ _____

      (4) Other (Specify) _____ ____ _____

_____ ____ _____

c. Does layout of department seem
   logical? _____ _____

d. Are the employees in good view
   of supervision? _____ _____

e. Is equipment up-to-date and
   adequate to do the work efficiently and accurately? _____ _____

Index